W9-DIW-584

"I'm not sure that even Ross Dawson realizes how radical—and how likely—his vision of the future is. Ideas that spread win, and organizations that spawn them will be in charge."
- **Seth Godin,** author, *Unleashing the Ideavirus*, the #1 selling e-book in history

"Dawson is exactly right—pervasive networking profoundly changes the business models and strategies required for success. *Living Networks* provides invaluable insights for decision makers wanting to prosper in an increasingly complex and demanding business environment."
- **Don Tapscott**, author, *Wikinomics*

"Ross Dawson argues persuasively that leading economies are driven by the flow of information and ideas. The ideas in his own book can position any individual or company at the center of that flow. It's a fast read, fun and full of examples."
- **Thomas H. Davenport,** Professor and Director of Research, Babson College, and author, *Competing on Analytics*

"*Living Networks* is a fast-paced tour of today's business frontier. Rich with examples drawn from a myriad of settings, every page forces the reader to ask "How can I use that?" Beware! This book will make you think!"
- **David Maister**, author, *Managing the Professional Service Firm*

"This is the most accessible introduction to the role of networks and networking I have yet seen. Ross Dawson speaks from his own experience in a language which will make it clear to managers what steps to take next. Networking with own staff, customers and professional peers is here to stay."
- **Napier Collyns,** co-founder, Global Business Network

"This is one of the most exciting books I've read in several years. Ross Dawson deftly examines the evolution of networks, organizations and strategy. He has more than succeeded in his intent, which is to produce a practical business book that shows business people how to leverage networks."
- **Melissie Rumizen,** author, *The Complete Idiot's Guide to Knowledge Management*

"The author has demonstrated that the success of his first book was no mere flash in the pan. His book is the one I would choose as a guide to understanding and action for the practical business person."
- **Bill Godfrey,** Editor, Change Management Monitor

"This is a great standalone book about businesses, organisations and networks. *Living Networks* links relationship of network technologies and people networks in a readable, useful way."
- **Patti Anklam,** author, *Net Work*

"Integration is the catalyst many companies are using today as their competitive strength. *Living Networks* shows how to make integration strategies work to deliver competitive long-term advantage."
- **Louis Columbus,** Senior Analyst, AMR Research

"Ross Dawson has loaded *Living Networks* with good illustrations and even better insights. The book lays out dozens of principles for thriving in an increasingly networked world. *Living Networks* will challenge you. And if you're going to win, then you must respond to the challenges Dawson puts forth."
- **Douglas K. Smith,** author, *Make Success Measurable!*

LIVING NETWORKS

Leading Your Company, Customers, and Partners

in the Hyper-Connected Economy

For Napier, who has done more than anyone else to bring the networks to life!

Ross Dawson

Ross Dawson
27 March 2008

Living Networks was originally published by
Financial Times Prentice Hall in November 2002.

Living Networks: Anniversary edition is published by Lulu in January 2008.

Living Networks is licensed by Ross Dawson under a Creative Commons Attribution-
NonCommercial-ShareAlike 2.0 License. For use of any excerpts of this book, attribution
to Ross Dawson and www.rossdawsonblog.com (with a link to this site for any online use)
is required.

Company and product names mentioned herein are the trademarks or registered
trademarks of their respective owners.

For discounts on corporate or government bulk purchases of this book, please contact
Advanced Human Technologies Inc. on (415) 439 4890 or aht@ahtgroup.com.

ISBN: 978-1-84799-560-5
Printed in the United States of America

To everyone in my social and business networks,

and all those wonderful people around the world who are

bringing the networks to life with their energy and passion.

About Ross Dawson

Ross Dawson is globally recognized as a leading authority on business strategy. He is CEO of international consulting firm Advanced Human Technologies, and Chairman of Future Exploration Network, a global strategy and events company. Ross is author of the Amazon.com bestseller Developing Knowledge-Based Client Relationships, and over 100 articles and white papers. Strong demand for Ross's expertise has seen him deliver keynote speeches on six continents and consult to leading organizations worldwide such as Ernst & Young, Microsoft, Macquarie Bank, Morgan Stanley, News Corporation, and Procter & Gamble. Ross's frequent media appearances include CNN, Bloomberg TV, SkyNews, ABC TV, Washington Post and many others.

Services to leverage the Living Networks

Keynote speaking and executive workshops
Ross Dawson speaks at conferences and corporate meetings worldwide and works with senior executives as a strategy leader and facilitator.
www.rossdawson.com

Advanced Human Technologies

www.ahtgroup.com

Organizational network analysis
Use of sophisticated network approaches to enhance performance within organizations and in key business relationships.

Relationship leadership
Support in building high-value client, supplier, and partner relationships, including implementing key relationship management structures.

Influence network analysis
Original techniques to analyze influence networks in B2B and consumer decision-making and to identify effective marketing and sales strategies.

Future Exploration Network

www.futureexploration.net

Strategy consulting and scenario planning
Helping clients to develop clear, actionable strategies in highly uncertain environments, using a variety of future and strategy techniques.

Research
Deep research into technological, social, and business trends to support clients' strategic thinking and decisions.

Thought leadership content
Compelling print and online content to engage attention-poor senior client executives and to support key messages on technology and business trends.

LIVING NETWORKS

Leading Your Company, Customers, and Partners
in the Hyper-Connected Economy

Table of Contents

Preface to the Anniversary Edition

It is fascinating to reflect on the five years that have passed since *Living Networks* was first published in November 2002. In many ways that was the dawning of the age of networks, though by then it hadn't yet been widely recognized. In those days the idea that the networks were coming to life was a pretty radical idea. Today many people simply nod in immediate understanding at the concept of the living networks.

Soon after the publication of *Living Networks*, the emergence of Friendster, MySpace, LinkedIn, and Facebook—to name just a few among a vast proliferation of social networks—provided literally hundreds of millions of people across the planet with a direct, personal experience of the rise of a networked world.

The first words of *Living Networks* are about how companies were using blogs. Since I first came across blogs I have believed they were a transformative tool. Certainly the intervening years have borne that out, with now over 100 million blogs existing worldwide, and blogs now comprising over 20% of the 100 most popular online media sites. My own blog Trends in the *Living Networks* (rossdawsonblog.com), launched five years ago to accompany this book, has been central to the extremely pleasing growth of my companies.

Organizational network analysis, which I described in Chapter 6, has since become a mainstream business tool. The success of the University of Virginia's Network Roundtable, a consortium of 100 leading organizations where I am now a research leader, has demonstrated the power of network approaches to improving performance across business and government.

Living Networks is founded on extensive examples and case studies of actual corporate practice. It's interesting to see that many of the stories I used are still very current. Some of the most prominent business books out in the last year, including *Wikinomics*, *The Starfish and the Spider*, and *Open Business Models*, have used many of the same case studies that I did five years earlier. Stories such as Canadian miner Goldcorp's use of open source approaches, Collabnet, Innocentive, Procter & Gamble's Connect & Develop program, and many others described in *Living Networks* are still viewed as cutting-edge examples years later. "We the Media," a section title in Chapter 1 of *Living Networks*, was later used as the title for a book.

So why am I relaunching *Living Networks* now? In hindsight, the book came out before most people were ready for the message, and in the depths of the dot-com bust. As such, the book probably didn't get the attention it might have if it were released a year or two later.

Five years after it was first published, certainly some of the value of relaunching *Living Networks* is as an historical document, in seeing where things stood as the networks were being born.

In some ways the world has moved on substantially over the last five years. The rise of what is now called Web 2.0, assisted by new technologies including AJAX, has changed the nature of the Internet. The landscape of digital rights management has changed dramatically from the playing field of 2002. Software-based services have progressed substantially over the last five years. Word of mouth marketing has become an entire industry with its own association.

However much of what was covered in *Living Networks* is still at least as relevant today as five years ago. Standards strategy is shaping industry structure more than ever. The power of distributed innovation is even more compelling today, and still barely tapped by most corporations. In our hyper-connected economy, trust, relationships, and personalization only increase in importance. Participative strategy development is finally becoming a common approach to strategy and leadership. The free agent economy is becoming ever-more enabled by the living networks as years go by.

The flow economy framework for business strategy I proposed in Chapter 7 is if anything even more relevant and useful today than five years ago, as many of my clients have discovered. Most importantly, collaboration across boundaries is becoming increasingly critical to the future of business, making executives' attitudes to this issue absolutely central to their success.

Two years ago I founded Future Exploration Network, what is now a global strategy and events company that helps organizations understand – and create – the long-term future of business. Much of my speaking and consulting work today is about the future of business.

Journalists love to find out what 'futurists' have predicted in the past so they can see how right – or wrong! – they were. In Chapter 11 of *Living Networks* I made 10 predictions for the future of business. Many of the predictions were long-term, so we can't expect them all to have fully come to fruition five years later, but it is a good time to take stock and see how well I did. Have a read and judge for yourself.

Every single day I find myself staggered by the enormity of what is happening as the networks come to life. The accelerating pace of developments illustrates the power of the shift to a world dominated by networks.

Over the last five years we have truly experienced what I described in 2002 as "participating in the birth of a new higher order life form" – that of the networks. The living networks are just out of the crib. We are privileged to be part of the early, rapid growth and evolution of an extraordinarily networked economy and society. It's an amazing journey which has just begun.

My original dedication to the book - to those who are bringing the networks to life - still stands. I hope that you too will continue to bring the networks to life in the exciting years ahead.

Ross Dawson
Sydney and San Francisco
November 2007

Preface to the First Edition

When I was a child I had a powerful vision of the immense web created by the world's telephone lines. Anyone, anywhere, who had this little plastic box with a cord going into the wall could repeatedly spin a dial, create a connection with any other similar plastic box you chose on the globe, and have a conversation with whoever picked up the receiver. In those days a long international telephone call could easily cost $100 or more, so it hardly created fluid connections between people, but the sheer scope and potential of this pervasive global network inspired in me a deep sense of awe.

Today, the networks that connect us have progressed several stages beyond this. Close to one billion people and businesses comprise a global community that can exchange information and ideas in almost any form, easily, cheaply, and instantaneously. New emerging technologies such as peer-to-peer and web services are now building on the fundamental transformational power of the Internet to unleash the true power of this connectivity. Together, the planet's population and the technologies that connect them create a vast, vibrant network. The networks are literally coming to life, demonstrating all of the complexity and unpredictable behaviors of a living system. This is the most exciting time in the history of humanity to be alive, as we witness and participate in the birth of a new higher-order lifeform.

This book is designed to be a practical business book, providing useful guidance in these swiftly changing times. It examines how the current surge in connectivity is transforming the flow of information and ideas that underpins the economy. It goes on to present the full scope of the implications for business, and provides clear recommendations for businesspeople on what they must do to prosper as the networks come alive. Whether you are a company executive, an entrepreneur, or a free agent, the core message is the same. The world is rapidly evolving, and new ways of working, new business models, and new attitudes are required. You must provide effective leadership on how to shift into this new world both within your firm, and to your customers and partners. Those that do this well will reap the richest rewards. Throughout this book you will find straightforward advice and practical prescriptions on how to achieve this.

The primary audience for this book is those who are already actively engaged in leading their organizations and business partners in this rapidly changing world. This includes not just senior executives, independent workers, and innovators, but everyone in the workforce. You have the personal responsibility of leadership, and this book is intended to give you the tools to lead more effectively in our connected economy. I believe that business students will also find the book valuable, in gaining insight into the impact of technology on business, and linking that to successful management practices. I also think that people who are interested in the broader social implications of connectivity will find the book relevant and useful.

This book is divided into four parts: Evolving Networks, Evolving Organizations, Evolving Strategy, and Future Networks. Part 1 examines the Evolving Networks. Chapter 1 covers how connectivity is changing society and business, while Chapter 2 looks at the emerging technologies taking the networks to the next phase. Part 2 is about Evolving Organizations. Chapter 3 looks at leadership in a world of blurring boundaries, while Chapter 4 goes on to examine how relationships are changing. Chapter 5 discusses how intellectual property changes as innovation increasingly takes place across organizational boundaries. In Chapter 6 we cover how firms can build their presence in the networks. Part 3 goes on to look at Evolving Strategy. An overview of the "flow economy" and new approaches to strategy are presented in Chapter 7. Chapter 8 goes into more detail on the world of content, while Chapter 9 discusses digital and professional services. Chapter 10 wraps up by looking at the free agent's perspective on the issues presented through the book. Part 4, on Future Networks, offers a glimpse into what lies ahead for us, providing 10 predictions for how business will evolve in the networks.

Many people are due thanks for their valuable input to this book, ranging from stimulating and informative conversations to useful feedback on draft chapters. I would like to express my heartfelt thanks to Fred Abbey, Verna Allee, Eric Best, Stewart Clegg, Ed Flynn, Sharon Goldie, Ann Graham, Rodney Gray, David Hardidge, Jean-Marc Hauducoeur, David Kelly, Elynn Lorimer, David Maister, Iain McGregor, Paul McKeon, Peter D. Moore, Rody Moore, Tony Morriss, Martin North, Jim Papageorgiou, John Peetz, Rob Pye, Greg Rippon, Samantha Ritchie, Melissie Rumizen, Mark Runnalls, Kim Sbarcea, Stephen Scheeler, John Scott, Fred Seibel, David Shannon, Tom Stewart, Bob Sutor, Karl-Erik Sveiby, Michael Terrell, Cris Townley, and Michael Vitale. There have been many others who have provided valuable thoughts and ideas along the way, so forgive me any oversights!

It has been a real pleasure to work with Tim Moore as a publisher. His unwavering support throughout the process, and his knowledge of what makes a successful business book, have helped shape what's best about this book. The invaluable input of development editor Russ Hall has unquestionably made this a far better book than it would be otherwise. Louis Columbus' extremely useful comments based on his deep understanding of the field helped me to refine many key ideas. Corinne Gregory also provided very useful input. Everyone on the Financial Times/Prentice Hall team has been outstanding—thank you to Gail Cocker, Bryan Gambrel, Anthony Gemmellaro, Allyson Kloss, and the rest of the team.

My agent Henning Gutman was instrumental in bringing this book from conception to reality. It's great to work with someone who really understands the ideas as well as the market for them. Of course special thanks to Napier Collyns for the introduction to Henning—as always acting as a connector! Thank you and much love to Mum, Dad, Janet, Amy, and Graham for their love and support now and always—it matters deeply to me. Not least, I want to express my gratitude to everyone in my social and business networks, for providing inspiration and learning.

LIVING NETWORKS

PART 1: Evolving Networks

We are connected. Information and ideas are the currency of today, and they now flow freely, changing how we relate, and how we do business in the hyper-connected economy.

In Part 1 of *Living Networks*, I will examine how the networks that underlie this new world are evolving. In Chapter 1 you will discover how our world is shrinking, and how the rich flow of information and ideas is bringing the networks to life. Chapter 2 will cover the emerging technologies that are taking the networks to the next stage, and the foundations of strategy as business becomes based on standards.

In Part 2 I will go on to examine how organizations are evolving. Companies must lead their customers and partners into new types of relationships and ways of working, and participate in the collaborative development of intellectual property. In Part 3 you will discover how to develop and implement strategy in an economy dominated by the flow of information and ideas, while Part 4 will look briefly at the future of the networks.

CHAPTER 1
The Networks Come Alive

What The Changing Flow Of Information And Ideas Means For Business

Connectivity is shrinking our world, and in the process transforming business. As communication between people becomes more fluid and pervasive, it is creating what looks like a global brain, in which ideas procreate freely and we collaborate to filter an ever-expanding universe of information. But just a small proportion of the planet's population is connected. It is critical that we extend participation as broadly as we can.

Macromedia, the company best-known for selling Flash software, is blogging. Weblogs—usually fondly abbreviated by their devotees to "blogs"—are essentially online publications of people's stream of consciousness, available to anyone who cares to drop in to their websites. Opinions and personal perspectives are offered freely and informally, almost always in the context of breaking developments and others' views. This means that blogs are liberally filled with links to whatever is most interesting in the ever-shifting landscape of information on the Internet.

Usually, when Macromedia releases new versions of its software, it provides detailed documentation to its community of software developers, and if it has announcements, posts the news on every related Internet forum it can find. When in May 2002 it brought out updates to four of its main packages, it asked five of its most switched-on staff to each create their own weblogs to discuss the intricacies of the new releases. In addition to offering their own insights and personal perspectives on the software, they provide links to all the other interesting online discussion happening worldwide, and independent developers link to their sites when they post something worthwhile. The rich network of links between these ongoing, informal discussions means that what is most interesting to the community is swiftly known to all, and less valuable information leaves barely a ripple in the flow.[1]

Instant messaging was not long ago seen as the domain of teenage girls, who compulsively sit at their computers and chat in cryptic abbreviations about music, boys, and hairstyles with their girlfriends in the next street or the other side of the world. It didn't take long for instant messaging to be appropriated by Wall Street. Eight of the top investment banks have implemented an instant messaging system that links their bond traders and salespeople with 2,000 institutional investors. Information about market conditions and trade execution flows far more swiftly and easily than ever before.[2]

Macromedia's foray into what it calls "the blog strategy,"[3] and the bond market's use of instant messaging, provide simple illustrations of how business is being transformed. Already, relatively recent technologies like e-mail, mobile telephony, and text messaging, are changing the way people communicate, and the way companies work. Now, a new phase of emerging technologies such as XML, web services, and peer-to-peer, are taking us a stage further. The networks that are the foundation of all society and business are literally coming to life. Our economy is now dominated by the flow of information and ideas, and that changes the rules of success. In this book we will take a journey together to understand how the foundations of the economy are shifting, the profound implications for business, and how we can be extraordinarily successful as organizations and individuals in this new world.

The coming of hyper-connectivity and the living networks has implications for almost every aspects of business. There are five key issues that we will examine through this book.

- **How companies create value with their customers, suppliers, and partners.** The rapidly increasing ease and speed of information flow is blurring the boundaries of organizations. To survive and thrive, companies must create new kinds of relationships with their customers, suppliers, and partners, based on transparency, collaboration and sharing value. This requires new ways of working. Nabisco and the grocery chains that distribute its products share information and collaborate to result in higher sales and lower inventory costs for all partners.[4] Corporate Executive Board is a membership-only consulting firm that gathers vital information and best practices from its members… and sells it back to them.

- **How people work within organizations.** Work today is based on people's networks within and across organizations. Knowledge needs to flow by connecting the right people, and diverse groups working in different locations and often different companies need to collaborate effectively to do their work. The lawyers at New York virtual law firm Axiom Legal work from home or their own offices, but are connected to shared legal resources and each other to perform their work. Eli Lilly's Research and Development group uses an internal collaboration system based on the principles of how insect swarms function, to allow the best ideas of a distributed research team to emerge.

- **Innovation and intellectual property.** Our sophisticated economy is increasingly dominated by innovation and intellectual property. However the increasing complexity of technology means that collaboration is becoming essential to develop valuable ideas. This results in a need for new models to share in the value of intellectual property. At the same time, an ever-larger proportion of intellectual property can be captured in digital form, and thus flow freely between consumers, requiring a shift to new business models for content. Investment bank Dresdner Kleinwort Wasserstein uses an open source model to develop its systems integration software, which makes it freely available for anyone to use. Capitol Records promotes the rock group *Radiohead* with a suite of digital marketing tools, including providing the more than 900 fan sites for the group with the entire album *Kid A* before its release. The album hit #1.[5]

- **Strategy and positioning:** Almost all economic activity is converging into a single space based on the flow of information and ideas. This emerging *flow economy* comprises a vast array of industries, including telecoms, technology, media, entertainment, publishing, financial services, and professional services. Every company in this convergent space is facing new competitive threats, and seeing massive new opportunities open up. Budget travel guide publisher Lonely Planet has used its powerful position with its customer base to sell telecommunications services, television programs, music, and interactive handheld city guides. JP Morgan Chase is leveraging its strength in payments to help its clients present and process invoices, allowing it to become central to the flow of business information inside and between corporations.

- **How individuals provide leadership and create personal success.** In this world of connectivity, collaboration, and blurring, executives no longer have control over most things that matter, sometimes even including their own business processes. They must provide true leadership inside and outside the organization to successfully implement new ways of working, while skirting the associated risks. Free agents also need to develop new approaches to create success in a networked world, both by positioning themselves effectively within networks, and fully exploiting the intellectual property they create. Bob and Steve Buckman of Buckman Laboratories have helped create a firm that builds trusting, highly collaborative relationships with its customers. Successful science fiction writer Eric Flint not only chooses to provide his books online for free to help him sell books in bookstores, but has also supplied the facilities and encouragement for other authors to do the same.

In order to fully understand the implications for business, and what we must do to be successful in this new world, we must first examine the foundations of the living networks. These are connectivity, the rapidly changing flow of information and ideas, and the creation of what looks very like a global brain.

How connectivity shrinks our world

In trawling through one of the private online discussion forums in which I participate, I came across a question on shifting high-value customers to online services, so I put in my two cents worth. It turned out that Chris, who had posted the original question, worked in London for one of the global professional services firms that I know well, so we exchanged a few e-mails directly, and arranged to meet the next time I was in London. We went from his office in the early evening rain to a cozy local pub for a pint, where we met up with someone he thought I should meet—one of his former colleagues who has established a network of specialist consultants. After a couple of pints we adjourned from the pub for a curry—as you do in London—and discovered further common interests, values, and beliefs as we hoed into the vindaloo, washed down with Indian lager beer.

Fortunately I escaped before I was too damaged to do justice to the workshop I was running the following day, but we had shifted from an exchange of brief e-mails to friendships and the foundation of future business collaboration.

This illustrates how communication technologies allow like-minded people from different sides of the planet to find each other and share ideas (and in this instance, also beers). The impact of the new forms of communication available to us is far broader than that. The whole way people meet and communicate is changing. E-mail, SMS, instant messaging, cell phones, online forums, chat, video-conferencing… Each of these allows and even encourages ways of communicating and relating with others that are fundamentally different from what has come before. Together, they dramatically change the *structure* of society and how people interact.

When did you last say or hear someone say "what a small world"? People have an unquenchable fascination with how richly we are connected, never ceasing to be amazed by the seeming coincidences of how one friend knows another through a completely different route. Yes, it is a small world, and growing smaller all the time. The well-known phrase "six degrees of separation" suggests that we are connected to every person on the planet by no more than six steps.

The concept of six degrees of separation originally emerged from experiments performed in the 1960s by Harvard sociologist Stanley Milgram. He gave letters to randomly chosen residents of Kansas and Nebraska, and asked each one to try to get the letter to a specified person in Massachusetts by forming a chain, starting by sending it to the person they knew that they thought would be most likely to be able to pass the letter on to the nominated target. It turned out that a median of six steps were required for the letters to get to their destination.

Recently, a new branch of mathematics known as "small world theory" has emerged to study and explain this phenomenon.[6] The heart of the matter is the diversity of our connections. In the past, most social circles were relatively closed—people tended to know the same people as the others within their social group or local community. Let's say Joe knows 50 people. If all those 50 people know only each other, then it's a closed group. However if any one of the group has more diverse social connections and knows people outside, that provides a link through which everyone is connected to the rest of the world.

Small world theory—in its simplest form—studies a circle of people, as shown in Figure 1-1. If each person only has contact with the four people closest to them, then it can take as many as five steps to reach everyone in a world of just 20 people. If we add just a handful of more distant connections across this "world," as shown in Figure 1-2, then it takes far fewer hops to reach others. It is the connections that bridge distinct and distant groups that create the small world.

Figure 1-1: It is a big world when you only know your immediate neighbors

Figure 1-2: Adding just a few more diverse connections can create a small world for everyone

The formation of these diverse bridges between people describes what is happening in our hyper-connected world. Increased mobility and migration mean that even in a small community you are likely to know people born in many different countries. You can easily keep in touch or reconnect with people you've gone to school or worked with by e-mail or alumni web sites. You can communicate and form friendships with people you meet online, as I did with Chris in London. Children and teenagers consider it commonplace to chat or play games online with people from all around the world. It is no longer unusual for people to have met their life partners online. From six degrees, we are moving closer to four degrees of separation from anyone on in the world, with the possible exception of a few isolated tribespeople. We live embedded in an intensely connected world.

New forms of communication are giving us new ways to interact socially. In the past, when we met someone we could only give him or her our address or telephone number. E-mail gives us more choices. It's easier to give people your e-mail address than your telephone number, and it's easier to contact someone that way. Mobile telephony allows us to lead far less structured social lives. Instead of making firm arrangements to meet, people go out and then use cell phones to meet on the move. Social events are becoming far easier to organize and more diverse, because all it takes is a quick e-mail or text message to get a large group together. I run the Party Alert Network e-mail list, which can in an instant let several hundred people know of social events. A friend sends out text messages to let people know of art exhibition openings and social events. In this way, digital communication is resulting in a substantial broadening of people's social connections. Similarly, employees can connect far more widely within their organizations, and those who would be afraid to walk into their chief executive's office with an idea are often happy to send an e-mail.

Micro-messages make communication fluid

Sit in a central café in any European city early on a Friday evening, and you will see troupes of teenagers and young adults sporting that essential accessory: mobile phones. They're speaking into them, swinging them around casually as mating displays, and as often as not, using two thumbs to type brief messages with a practised ease. The global Short Messaging Service (SMS) protocol allows 160 character text messages to be sent to or from any mobile phone.

In 2001, around 40 billion text messages were sent on mobile phones, with a forecast of close to 50% annual growth in the subsequent years.[7] For over 100 million people, mainly in Europe, Asia, and Australia, this new style of communication is becoming a core part of their daily lives. The uptake in America has been stymied by the inability of US telecoms companies to agree on standards, meaning subscribers usually can send messages only to other customers of the same network. In the meantime, the rest of the world is busy exploring a whole new mode of connecting with others.

The spectacular take-off of instant messaging has paralleled the SMS boom. Instant messaging enables people who are connected to the Internet to compile "buddy lists" of their friends around the world, see when they are online and sitting at their computer, and send text messages to them. The major differences with e-mail are that not only can you interact in real-time in what is closer to a live conversation than sending letters, but also the "presence" function means you know whether your buddies are there to chat with. From its roots as a social tool, instant messaging is shifting to become extensively used in organizations. Salespeople in the RE/MAX real estate franchise network, covering over 4000 offices worldwide, use instant messaging both internally for sharing referrals, and externally to converse with prospects and clients. The US Navy is rolling out instant messaging across the whole fleet, to streamline technical conversations. Communication within IBM is dominated by the technology, with over two million instant messages sent daily by employees even in early 2001.

Instant messaging and SMS are examples of what I call *micro-messages*. They are short, informal, and unintrusive—you can see the message and choose how to respond, unlike a telephone call. In practice, these new forms of communication rarely replace existing communication, but add to it. People still meet and call each other, but for other exchanges they may use SMS or instant messaging. Most importantly, the informality of these micro-messages lowers the barriers to communication—while something may not have been worth a phone call, it's easy and unobtrusive to send instant text. This results in a far greater *fluidity* of communication. When the only way you can communicate with distant people is in large bulky chunks—letters, e-mail, telephone calls and the like—it means there has to be a good reason to do so. Micro-messages allow smaller things to be communicated, and for many teenagers—and increasingly adults—they have become a means of sharing their daily experience and thoughts. SMS and instant messaging can be powerful marketing tools, if treated appropriately, as you will discover in Chapter 6.

The making of the global brain

There are curious parallels between the human brain and human society. The 100 billion or so neurons that make up the brain are deeply connected—each neuron can trigger approximately 1000 other neurons. By firing other neurons in turn, any two neurons in the brain are separated by no more than four or five steps. All of our thought and behavior emerges from the interactions between these billions of neurons. Human society looks increasingly similar. The world's population is around six billion. The average person in the developed world knows around 300 other people. And the vast majority of people in the world are now connected by less than six steps.

Soaring connectivity is giving rise to what increasingly resembles a global brain. The idea is hardly new. Early proponents include the nineteenth century evolutionary biologist Herbert Spencer, who coined the phrase "survival of the fittest," and science fiction writer H.G. Wells, who wrote a book *World Brain* outlining his vision for human minds coming together as one.[8] The revolutionary mystic Pierre Teilhard de Chardin introduced the term *noösphere*, meaning the global domain of mind.[9] Yet communication technology—the domain of hard-nosed engineers—is now allowing the incredibly rich flow of information and ideas that creates this single mind, that can integrate all of our intelligence and insight.

This is far more about many people who are connected, rather than the connections themselves. Ideas are the still the sole domain of people, despite the latest advances in artificial intelligence. There are two key aspects to this thinking process of the global brain—and the individual minds that comprise it. The first is generating and developing ideas. The second is filtering the universe of information, paying attention only to what is important and useful.

The sexual life of ideas

Ideas don't like being alone. In fact they like copulating promiscuously with any other idea in sight. There is no such thing as a virgin birth in the world of ideas. Ideas are always born from other ideas: interacting, mating, and procreating. This often orgiastic coupling takes **There is no such thing as a virgin birth in the world of ideas.** place in the fertile substrate which is the human mind. Our minds are hotbeds of unspeakable activities—ideas have a life of their own, but they need somewhere to carry on their flirtations and breeding.

In her book *The Meme Machine*, Susan Blackmore suggested that humans are purely and simply carriers for *memes*, which means ideas or behaviors that can be passed on to others.[10] Our species has evolved to become a more refined vehicle for propagating ideas. One result is the desire to produce and consume mass media that seems so intrinsic to our race. Another is our drive to implement communication technologies, to engage more richly with others, and to publish on the Internet.

Using these new technologies, the ideas in our minds can participate in online discussions, starting from the voyeurism of watching other ideas interacting and playing, to the flirtation of engaging with others, however still fairly safe in the limited self-exposure afforded by a text-only discussion. At the other end of the spectrum, when people get together with the explicit intention of creating intellectual property, ideas are essentially procreating. In the free-flowing sexual life of ideas, one of the key dangers is losing your seminal creativity, bearing offspring without sharing in the rewards. There is no child support due in the world of ideas; rather your children may support you. The most fecund propagators of ideas can choose to intermingle freely with others, or guard their worth carefully, like the expensive semen of a prize racehorse.

Idea-X is an online idea exchange established by consultancy Cap Gemini Ernst & Young. Participants can either propose ideas or ask for ideas to address a specific problem. A suite of tools allow people to see how other members rate each of the ideas and the people proposing them, and to keep track of the best ideas on the site. The problem with Idea-X and similar forums is that everyone can see the ideas and use them as they will. At the other end of the spectrum is PLX.com, an online market for intellectual property. Participants can buy and sell intellectual property they have generated, though in order to do so it must first be legally registered, for example by patent, copyright, or trademark. We will examine strategies for those who propagate ideas and generate wealth from them in Chapters 5, 8, and 10.

Collaborative filtering saves humanity!
Effectively filtering the information that assails us is essential for our survival. We would be completely overwhelmed if we were not able to reduce the millions of sensory impressions we receive to something our logical brain can cope with. Schizophrenics can be understood as lacking the usual filters that protect them from being swamped by their sensory input. Instead of perceiving only the outstanding features of their environment, everything stands out for them. LSD works by temporarily disabling our brain's sensory filtering mechanisms.

In the information age, this ability to filter effectively has moved from an essential of survival to one of the primary determinants of success. Information overload is the defining feature of our times. Those who are most effective at making sense of the flood of incoming information and turning it to action lead our world. You can read about them in the *Forbes* rich list.

Filtering performed at the group level is called *collaborative filtering*. Instead of everyone individually attempting to make sense of the universe of information we swim in, we can work together. This is not new. Whenever you share a recommendation for a book, movie, or restaurant with a friend, you are collaborating to narrow down the wealth of choices you have available. You don't need to try every book or restaurant yourself in order to find those that you like the most. When people talk about word-of-mouth—usually in the context of marketing—they are referring primarily to the way people share information with friends about what they like... or don't like.

Technology now enables this process of collaborative filtering to happen globally rather than simply between friends. A simple but well-known example is the recommendation service of Amazon.com. If you liked a particular book, you can see what others who liked that book are also reading. You can read the comments of people who have read those books. You can far more easily discover new books that are likely to interest you.

Many websites—simply by providing links to selected resources—are acting as filters. The search engine Google was a late entrant to a crowded field. When it started business there were literally dozens of search engines that people used regularly. Google has come from behind to become the top pure search engine. The heart of Google's search algorithm is identifying the sites that have the most links from other sites. Rather than simply identifying websites that contain the keywords you are looking for, it shows you those that have proved to be most popular with others. You are benefiting from the exploration and judgments of all other web surfers, by following what others find useful. More recently, Google is looking at getting users to rate the websites they visit, in a more overt implementation of collaborative filtering.

Corporations are using collaborative filtering software to make sure their employees only spend time reading the information that is most relevant and interesting to them. The Sun ONE ebusiness platform incorporates software that takes users' ratings of the value of documents they read, together with their work profiles, to provide people with accurate predictions of how useful will find any given information. The system's foundation of people's considered opinions of value provides far more accurate ratings than purely technology-based approaches. Throughout this book we will explore some of the vital business implications of collaborative filtering, notably in Chapter 4 on relationships, and in Chapter 8 on content distribution. We will also look at the role of collaborative filtering in the future of the networks in this book's Postscript.

We, the media

The brilliant visionary Marshall McLuhan accurately described the media as an extension of our senses. Your eyes can see what's happening in your immediate vicinity, your ears can hear what people are saying in the same room as you, but with television and radio as an adjunct to your senses, you can see and hear anywhere around the world. All of the cameras and microphones of the world's media are an extension of your eyes and ears, and journalists are your personal emissaries to report on their findings and impressions.

Now connectivity is extending your senses to all the connected people on their planet. Media is becoming a participatory sport. You can tap into what any of a vast army of people are seeing and thinking, or contribute yourself to the global flow. This certainly doesn't mean the end of mass media. Most people will always choose to access a common frame on the world, that gives views of politics, society, and entertainment that provide a basis for interaction and discussion. However the new world of media is at the heart of how the networks are coming to life.

Go to the Slashdot news website for the technology community, and it looks much the same as many other news services for that audience.[11] The difference is that the stories are all submitted by readers, reflecting what they believe to be most important news to their peers. At least as important as the actual news is the commentary from the highly sophisticated community. All participants can rate how interesting and useful each comment is, so readers can choose to view comments with whatever rating level they choose, from everything to only the very best. An elaborate system gives temporary special privileges to those whose contributions are judged most valuable by the community. Since the software behind the system is openly available, over 100 other websites, each with a different focus and community, are using the same system.

As you saw at the opening of this chapter, weblogs are the stream of consciousness of the networks. Now over half a million bloggers—as weblog writers call themselves—regularly post their thoughts and links to interesting material. Some of the best-known bloggers, such as Dave Winer of Scripting News, can attract tens of thousands of readers **The highly interlinked nature of weblogs means that they are in themselves a powerful form of collaborative filtering. What is most interesting and worthwhile quickly becomes most visible,** every day. Sometimes bloggers report news directly. It's increasingly common for conference organizers to provide wireless connectivity in conference rooms, which means you can sometimes almost feel like you're there just with Internet access. Dan Gillmor, who is both a reporter for the *San Jose Mercury* and a weblog devotee, was writing directly into his blog during a presentation at PC Forum. Before the question session, the speaker had time to look at his laptop, and corrected something Gillmor had written. Other mainstream journalists are doing weblogs, blurring the boundary between established media and this burgeoning new medium.

The highly interlinked nature of weblogs means that they are in themselves a powerful form of collaborative filtering. What is most interesting and worthwhile quickly becomes most visible, as we saw at the beginning of this chapter. This effect is enhanced further by specialist search engines. MIT's Media Lab provides a "top hits" site that searches all the weblogs each day to identify the most common links.[12] Every day you can discover what this large and diverse community of often quirky people consider the most interesting news and websites, and if you wish you can include your own weblog in the daily tally. Not surprisingly, the results are usually rather different from the newspaper or TV news headlines.

The limits of the networks

El-Ghar is a town of around 100,000 people, situated in the Nile basin about 50 miles from Cairo. Most of the inhabitants work on farms surrounding the town, with the burgeoning market providing an outlet for their produce. Despite the basic day-to-day life of its inhabitants, there are many poorer areas in Egypt, and certainly through Africa. Between the 100,000 denizens of El-Ghar, there is precisely one telephone line.

This solitary telephone line is not a shared commodity, but the proud possession of one of the town's wealthiest people. The United Nations Development Programme has sponsored over 80 access points to the Internet for poor people in Egypt, and provided Arabic-language content that is specifically useful for farmers and other rural poor. The program's volunteers came to El-Ghar, intending to show people the resources they could access, but at the last minute the telephone line owner changed his mind about allowing them to use his precious status symbol. As a substitute, the volunteers downloaded some of the system's pages onto their laptop, and used them to show the villagers what they could access if they went to the Internet center in the nearby city. One of farmers later happily reported that he'd discovered improved fertilization methods on the system.[13]

Sitting comfortably in the USA or other highly-developed countries, calling colleagues on cell phones, picking up our e-mail on mobile devices, and downloading music files on the Internet, it's easy to forget quite how starkly different life is for the majority of the world's population. Our lovely planet Earth is packed with well over six billion people. Of those, half have never made a telephone call, and less than one in ten has access to the Internet.

The global networks that are the focus of this book link not everyone on the planet, but for the moment just those one billion people or so people who are "wired" to varying degrees. The implications of this gap are central to the future of our world. Today, connection to the global networks is the primary means of production and wealth. In economies based on scarce resources such as land, if someone else gains, then you lose. In an economy based on networks, not only you don't lose if someone else connects, but you and everyone else benefit as the networks grow in scope and diversity.

I hope that the evocation of the living networks in this book underlines how critical it is that we bring as many people as possible in to participate, to join us in this exciting adventure. Endeavors such as the Internet access centers in Egypt described above are small but essential steps to help bridge the divide. In Bangladesh, just 3% of homes have a telephone. Grameen Bank, set up to lend small amounts to the poor to help them become self-sufficient, enables villagers to buy mobile phones, which they pay for by charging others for usage.[14] In one step the whole village becomes connected. As with much of the developed world, mobile telephones are enabling connections where installing a fixed telephone line would be prohibitively expensive.

For most of the more than one billion people who earn less than $1 a day, food and clean water are probably higher priorities than Internet access. However beyond the absolute basics, access to the networks will be critical in helping them to improve their lives, and to participate in the potential ahead.

Shock! Horror! Globalization!

The battle raged for five days in the streets of Seattle, as the World Trade Organization met in late 1999 to discuss lowering barriers to trade. Over 40,000 anti-globalization demonstrators were met by riot police lobbing tear gas and spraying pepper-spray pellets and rubber bullets. A state of emergency was declared as shops were looted and vandalized, buses smashed, and the city center closed down. As the trade delegates and protestors left the city and the tear gas slowly drifted away, the world had gained a new symbol of globalization.

Globalization seems have become something not to mention at a dinner party. People are sharply polarized over whether it's a good or bad thing, though in doing so they are usually attributing quite different meanings to the same word. Of the multiplicity of themes encompassed by the term "globalization," two are especially relevant to the emergence of the living networks. The first is the increasingly borderless nature of the global economy, especially when the majority of economic activity is comprised of information-based services. The second is the apparent cultural integration of the world.

An executive from an animation company told me that he was choosing between Chinese and Hungarian animators for a particular project. The Chinese were excellent at depicting action scenes, but the Hungarians were especially skilled at rendering subtle facial expressions, he said. What was clear and remained unsaid was that for such labour-intensive work he wouldn't dream of hiring expensive American or Western European artists. It didn't matter a jot to him that the animators would be on the other side of the world; he could see their work daily and communicate closely with them at all stages of the project.

For a very large and increasing proportion of work, it doesn't matter where in the world it's done. This creates many opportunities for developing countries. The Phillipines is a major call-centre location for the Asia-Pacific region. India's software engineers do work for companies globally. Ugandan companies provide data-entry services for US clients. At the same time this puts pressure on developed world workers. The solution is absolutely not to stop these services being done overseas; among other issues this would hold developing nations back in an agricultural economy. The simple and inevitable result is that developed world workers must upskill themselves, do the higher-level work that differentiates them. We can give thanks that over the last half-century the economy has shifted to virtually eliminate production-line jobs, allowing people to shift to more meaningful work. A similar process is at play now.

Vietnam is a delightful country, with warm, friendly people and beautiful scenery ranging from the ethereal floating world of the Mekong Delta through alpine vistas to spectacular craggy islands. However, it took someone else to point out to me one of the things that makes it so different from everywhere else I've been: there is no McDonald's or Coca-Cola. Almost anywhere else in the world there is no escaping the golden arches or familiar curlicued white-on-red logo.

Certainly brands are becoming increasingly global. Entertainment is transnational—Hollywood films can be seen almost wherever you go. People from around the globe chat in English on Internet sites. Of the more than 5,000 living languages today, as many as 80% are expected to become extinct over the next century. So are we moving towards a single uniform culture worldwide?

If so, then that's something we must guard against. The value of the connections that bring the global networks to life is not in producing homogeneity. If everyone's the same, why would we need to collaborate? The true value is in bringing together the greatest diversity—that is the source of higher intelligence. Multiple perspectives lead to richer, more complex mental models and ways of thinking about the world. It is critical that we encourage and nurture diversity and different approaches.

Vital Connections: Chapter 1

This chapter has introduced you to the living networks. Connectivity is dramatically changing the way people are connected. That in turn is transforming the flow of information and ideas. As this flow becomes immensely deeper and richer, the age-old dream of a global brain is coming to reality. Ideas copulate promiscuously, we collaborate to filter staggering information overload, and a new form of participative media is extending our senses far more broadly than ever before. However we must be wary of the impact of only part of humanity accessing the invaluable fruits of connectivity.

In the next chapter, we will examine the key emerging technologies that are combining with connectivity to transform business. All networks are founded on people sharing a common standard. This results in a business environment in which companies require new approaches to strategy. In Part 2 of the book, we will explore the implications for organizations, including how to lead your customers and partners into new ways of working. Part 3 will examine how to develop and implement strategy in this hyper-connected economy

CHAPTER 2

Emerging Technologies

How Standards And Integration Are Driving Business Strategy

Standards are the foundation of communication, and of all networks. Building on the existing foundation of powerful standards and connectivity, there are three sets of emerging technologies that are driving the next stage of the networks: XML and web services; peer-to-peer; and network interfaces. In the connected economy, standards and network strategy are at the heart of all business.

The first digital augmentation of human capabilities dates back over five millenia. The invention of cuneiform allowed the Sumerians to record information using a set of defined characters that could be copied exactly any number of times. Reeds were used to inscribe patterns of wedge shapes into clay tablets, which were sometimes baked hard and still exist today, probably showing far better longevity than most digital systems of our age. To create the world's first written language, the Sumerians had to agree on what each cuneiform mark meant. They had to establish standards.

The result of establishing a standard for digital storage and communication transformed Sumerian society. It enabled laws to be written down and standardized for the first time, rather than relying on memory or a judge's foibles. It also gave rise to the first accountants. The government of the day required all business transactions to be recorded, and many of the Sumerian cuneiform tablets still in existence are sales receipts or other transaction records. Platoons of scribes were kept busy learning to read and write the complex script, and then recording sales for tax purposes. Perhaps things weren't really that different from today.

Standards provide the foundation for all communication. Only when a group of people agree that certain sounds or inscriptions denote specific concepts, can they communicate. Just as the standard of language allows people to understand each other, technology standards allow devices or systems to connect, and for information to flow between them. As such, all networks exist only by virtue of standards.

The Internet is not a communications infrastructure. It is a set of standards that allows any computer to be connected and to exchange information. Only once a set of standards is universally agreed can anyone tap into the "cloud" of the Internet at any point, and access or transfer information to anyone else. The World Wide Web Consortium (W3C) proposed standards, and only because everyone has accepted these has a truly global network been born.

In economic and strategic terms, a network is formed wherever there is a common standard that allows connection and communication, whether or not that capability is actually used. Users of Apple Macintosh computers form a network, irrespective of whether they actually communicate directly with each other. Their systems are based on the same standards, which gives them common interests. Everyone benefits from a larger network. The more Mac users there are, the easier it is to share information, the more high-quality software will be written, the lower the costs of hardware and software, and the more valuable their skills will be.

These are examples of *network effects*, the benefits that members gain through a larger network. The most important single characteristic of networks is positive feedback. In any true network, the greater the number of participants, the more the benefits to those who are connected. In addition, this draws in providers of associated services, further increasing the benefits, and attracting yet more users, as illustrated in Figure 2-1.

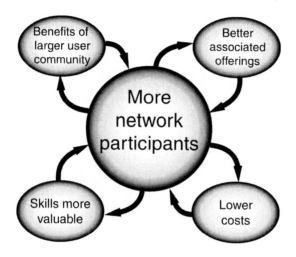

Figure 2-1: Positive feedback means network growth feeds on itself

These simple dynamics mean that you rarely get an information-based industry that is evenly balanced between competitors. Positive feedback can help your network grow, as in the diagram, or it can accelerate your misfortunes as you lose users and their benefits wane. As soon as there is a clear winner, users will defect to the other network. As such, network-based markets tend to result in winner-takes-all battles (or often winner-takes-most, in which the second-ranked player survives with a sliver of the market). Beta vs. VHS in video, Lotus 1-2-3 vs. Microsoft Excel in spreadsheets, Netscape Navigator vs. Internet Explorer in web browsers, Windows vs. Apple in computer platforms, are all classic examples of network battles. Any not-so-young music lover will have experienced the standards transitions from LP and cassette to CD and onto DVD, or may even remember back as far as the 8-track standard!

In the second half of this chapter we will examine in more detail the world of standards, and the core strategies that businesses need to adopt. But first, we will cover the most powerful emerging technologies today, that are truly bringing the networks to life.

I am sure you are already well familiar with the primary driving forces that have created today's networked world: powerful computing for individuals;

rapidly increasing bandwidth; and mobile communications. We are very rapidly shifting into a world in which we are always richly connected—if we choose.

The next wave of critical technologies are those that enable far greater connection and integration. The history of computing is fraught with incompatible operating systems, competing standards, diverse communication protocols, and different languages. Probably as much has been spent by large corporations on "systems integration" as on hardware and software. We have already seen that standards are the foundation of networks. However if we can find ways to connect and integrate different systems more easily, then smaller pools of connectivity can be combined to rapidly form far larger networks. The reality is that today there are still many constraints on the free flow of information, and the ability for business processes to be linked and integrated. Once systems can be integrated far more easily, business has the potential to shift to become part of a single, truly global network.

There are three vital sets of emerging technologies contributing to this integration:

- XML and web services
- Peer-to-peer networks
- Network interfaces

The language of the networks: XML and web services

On September 23, 1999, the Mars Climate Orbiter—NASA's first interplanetary weather satellite—approached the red planet. At 2:01am Pacific Daylight Time, right on schedule, it fired its main engine in order to slow itself and enter orbit. Five minutes later NASA lost contact as the Orbiter passed behind Mars. It was never heard from again. Subsequent investigations showed that the problem had been caused by one part of the satellite's internal systems using measurements in meters, while another part worked in feet.

This is a fairly common type of communication problem. It's just that in this case it led to the loss of a $327 million satellite. Businesses may not usually lose quite as much due to one information mismatch, but the accumulated costs of miscommunication between companies are massive. We may be connected, but we're not always communicating. This is the world in which XML (eXtensible Markup Language) is emerging as the foundation for the next level of interconnectivity.

XML is basically a standard for formatting and describing information. If information is sent in an XML format, this can allow any two computers to understand and use it in the same way. HTML is the language used to write web pages—it presents information so that people can understand it when they see it. XML performs the same function for machines.

The essence of how XML works is very simple. Each piece of information in a transmission between computers is given a "tag" that describes it. The XML standard defines the format of those descriptions. For example, if a company's computer were sending information about the length of a steel bar it is delivering, it might use XML conventions to label the data as follows:

<LENGTH_IN_METERS>2.3</ LENGTH_IN_METERS >

If the computers of the company's business partners have been provided with the same list of descriptions, then it will always know how to deal with information when it arrives as part of any communication. In the case of the steel bar it could either store this figure as the length of the bar in meters, or convert it to feet if that's what its systems use. It doesn't matter if the two companies use different types of computers, different software, different processes, or even whether the computer's users speak English.

The wonderful part about XML is that you can use it to transmit any type of information you like. If suddenly you agree with your partners that it's essential your systems can communicate about the color of the delivery box, you can define a new XML tag:

<BOX_COLOR>green</BOX_COLOR>

It is this power that earns XML its moniker "extensible". Once you have defined its basic rules, you can extend it however you like. But what happens if another partner has decided to use a tag that says <COLOR_OF_BOX>? It could very soon become a Babel of different versions of the language. Clearly it's critical for industries to collaborate to produce common descriptions of information, so all firms can use these with confidence that all their partners can readily use them in their systems.

This standard is built on XML

Every industry you can think of—and more—has spawned multiple bodies developing XML-based standards for exchanging information. In this thick alphabet soup of acronyms, the health industry has ASTM E31.25 and the slightly more evocatively-titled CISTERN (Clinical Infosystems Interoperability Network) among its standards under development; real estate has RETML (Real Estate Transaction Standard Markup Language) and CRTML (Comprehensive Real Estate Transaction Markup Language);

while the financial services industry proudly sports dozens of XML organizations. Stirring the pot further reveals a mind-numbing total of well over four hundred acronymed standards bodies. Even chess has rival XML standards, including the imaginatively-named ChessML (Chess Markup Language) and ChessGML (Chess Game Markup Language).

As you have seen, XML is a standardized way to attach descriptions to information. However if every organization implements it differently, it will be useless for exchanging information. The value comes when all participants in an industry agree on specifically what information they want to communicate, and in what format. Once there is that intent, XML provides a powerful common foundation to do this easily and effectively. Implementing industry information standards is in almost everyone's interest, as it makes communicating and integrating with partners substantially cheaper and more effective. In Chapter 3 we will examine how standards for exchanging information within industries are being developed, and the role companies should play in this.

Implementing industry information standards is in almost everyone's interest, as it makes communicating and integrating with partners substantially cheaper and more effective.

While XML-based standards are being applied to highly specific issues of information exchange within industries, they also provide a foundation for general communication issues such as how firms exchange messages and documents, and integrate them into their respective business processes. The emerging dominant standard for these general business applications is ebXML (short for e-business XML), boasting primary sponsors including a United Nations body. Released in May 2001 after 18 months of development, ebXML is now acknowledged as a true global standard, and is being incorporated into many higher-level and industry-specific initiatives. At a lower level still, XML is allowing the development of standards for how computer programs themselves can connect and integrate. As you will see, there are vitally important implications for business.

The promise of web services

"One degree of separation," was the slogan for Microsoft's initial $200 million advertising campaign for its .NET suite of services, implying companies can now be connected directly with their customers, partners, and employees. That is indeed the promise of the emerging technologies called *web services*. However the whole reason that web services enable this direct connectivity is that they are based on open standards, in turn built upon XML. Microsoft is just one of many leading players keen to sell the software that enables these powerful technologies.

Web services are essentially a set of standards that allow computer applications to interconnect. As a result, any programs can link together seamlessly, irrespective of the computers they run on, the operating systems they use, or the programming languages in which they are written. One of the key web services standards allows software to search a global directory of available programs, identify the best fit, and integrate it into its own functionality. There are three key implications of web services.

- **Easier integration inside and outside the organization.** Integrating systems is often the largest IT expense for a big company. The way that programs designed using web services can interface directly helps make it far easier to integrate applications. This saves costs internally, and smoothes the way for integrating systems with customers and partners. General Motors, Merrill Lynch, and Dell are among the companies that have placed web services at the heart of their information technology initiatives.

- **Modular organizations.** Web services allow what used to be monolithic software packages and business processes to be broken into a set of modules. These modules can now integrate perfectly with each other, requesting information or tasks to be performed as if they were part of the one program, whether they are running on the same computer or on systems on opposite sides of the world. Costs are saved because each of the modules can be easily adapted or reused directly in other applications. Ford Credit estimates it has saved $15 million by applying these approaches.[1]

- **New business models and structures.** Business processes are increasingly implemented as software. The general acceptance of web services means that it suddenly becomes far easier to share your business processes with your customers, suppliers, and partners. You can now define far more easily exactly what your company is best at, and what others can do better. This not only changes the nature of the company, it also means new models must be found to charge for the services you offer. Google is offering software developers the ability to use web services to access search results and use them in their programs. At the time of writing, this is available for free, but only for a limited number of queries per day. However Google is likely to charge for this service in the future, based on usage.

We will examine these implications of web services in more detail in Chapter 9.

Peer-to-Peer Pressure

The year 2000 was marked by the explosion of the music file-sharing system Napster. It was pretty hard to miss the news as the company's then 19-year old founder Shawn Fanning hit the covers of *Fortune, Forbes, Business Week*, and *Time* in rapid succession. Napster's users had created the fastest-growing network in history, in less than one year gathering over 70 million registered participants who shared music files with their peers around the globe.

As history tells, the legal eagles of the music industry swiftly swooped in and began relentlessly pounding away at Napster. They eventually succeeding in shutting it down as a file-sharing system in mid-2001, only to see a host of similar systems such as Kazaa and Morpheus leap in to take its place. By then file-sharing had slipped from the forefront of popular consciousness, but the concepts were already being applied to new domains. The awesome—albeit brief—success of Napster set an inspiring example for others to emulate.

Napster was perhaps most important for how it changed the way people think about the Internet and connectivity. Traditional computer networks are based on a "client-server" structure, in which a large central "server" provides resources to many "client" computers. *Peer-to-peer systems* like Napster allow people or computers to connect directly with each other.[2]

The peer-to-peer structure itself is not revolutionary. The telephone network is, in fact, a peer-to-peer system. Any telephone can be linked directly to any other telephone in the world—all you need to do is to dial the correct number. However the impact of both individuals and software developers changing how they think about the networks is creating a whole new set of tools and behaviors. The shift is towards distributed systems, where resources are spread through the networks rather than centralized. There are five key domains in which peer-to-peer technologies are being applied. Each has the potential to have a major impact on how business is done.

> • **Distributed content.** What was revolutionary about Napster was that it meant that everyone who was connected effectively shared parts of his or her hard disks. Instead of being limited to your own storage, you can now have many millions of people's hard disks appear to be part of your own system. Deloitte & Touche UK uses the peer-to-peer software system NextPage to allow easy access to a wide range of information held in different computers and locations both inside and outside the firm. This can substantially improve the productivity of its auditing staff who need to access disparate documents in the course of their work.

• **Distributed computation.** Do you believe that there is intelligent life in the universe beyond our planet Earth? If there is, you can help to find it. The Search for Extraterrestrial Intelligence (SETI) initiative takes an immense amount of data from the world's largest radio telescope as it scans the sky, and submits it to intensive analysis in order to detect possible signs of intelligent life. Since most people use only a fraction of their PCs' processing power, and then for only a small part of the day, the SETI@home initiative taps that unused processing power. Less than 18 months after the system's launch, well over two million PCs in 226 countries were at work, effectively creating a global supercomputer from donated computing power.[3] The same principle is now being applied to a range of scientific endeavors, including cancer research and gene design, which are now competing for people's spare computing power. Companies are also using similar approches. First Union Bank has implemented distributed processing systems for its financial risk management, a notoriously computing-intensive task.

• **Collaboration.** Ray Ozzie, the creator of Lotus Notes, left the company for some thinking space after it was bought by IBM. In an interview, Ozzie described how he watched his daughter using instant messaging to collaborate with her friends on her homework, and his son playing with his online friends the multi-user blast-and-destroy game *Quake*. He was struck by how *Quake* provided competing teams with an extremely effective collaborative space, and the stark contrast to the very simple tools such as e-mail that office workers have to work together.[4] Ozzie didn't dally, swiftly launching a new company, Groove Networks, that sells peer-to-peer collaboration software. The firm's product, *Groove*, allows any group of people to share and annotate files, draw on the same whiteboard, chat, have voice conversations, browse together, and create a space that enables them to work effectively together. Companies that have already implemented *Groove* include pharmaceutical firm GlaxoSmithKline, which uses the software to enable its researchers to work closely with outside organizations, such as universities and clinical research firms, and Raytheon, which is applying it to help develop collaboration between teams at companies it has acquired.[5]

• **Distributed processes.** Business processes are increasingly distributed across organizations, crossing boundaries and involving disparate teams, as we will explore further in Chapter 3. Peer-to-peer systems can directly connect any group of individuals involved in a process, irrespective whether they're in the same organization or location, or the systems they use. Many of the examples of peer-to-peer systems being used in distributed processes are in supply chain management, but they are also relevant to many other processes. United Technologies, a conglomerate that includes Pratt & Whitney and Otis Elevator, is deploying peer-to-peer software from Oculus Technologies. The system allows engineers to share information about the products they are developing directly from PC to PC. United Technologies expects use of the system to substantially accelerate the design process.[6]

• **Markets.** A marketplace matches buyers and sellers. For large transactions, a peer-to-peer system can be ideal. Rather than funneling all interaction through a single exchange, it can put buyers and sellers in touch with each other to negotiate terms directly. Liquidnet is an institutional share trading system launched in April 2001, that within 6 months had racked up transactions of over 300 million shares. Institutional investors are anonymously linked to the firms that are on the other side of the trades they want to execute, allowing them to negotiate prices directly. The result is that the vast majority of trades are executed at prices better than could be achieved on an exchange. The investors on both sides of the trade are happy, and neither the stock exchanges nor stockbrokers see any part of the business.

The interfaces that merge people and technology

The characters in the 1999 cult science-fiction movie *The Matrix* had a small socket built into the base of their skull. To enter the illusion of the matrix they simply plugged themselves into the machine, accompanied by the frisson of a long steel jack sliding deep inside their brain. It will probably be another few years before we can plug ourselves directly into the networks. For now we have to make do with our existing interfaces: computer displays, keyboards, and that ubiquitous symbol of computing, the mouse.

The networks are ultimately about people connecting with other people. The easy bit is connecting the technology that sits in the middle. The difficult part is allowing people to interface more effectively with the technology, to blend into the vast networks comprised of both machines and people. This is critical to move us towards the formation of a true global entity.

Can you touch-type? If so, you're in a small minority. The productivity of two-thirds of the US workforce depends on how well they can use a keyboard to write and enter information, yet only 20% of those people can touch-type. The rest pick their way at varying speeds across the keyboards. What an incredibly artificial and clunky way to have to communicate!

This is the world that is beginning to be revolutionized by the next generation of voice recognition and synthesis. Human communication began with the spoken word and gestures, and that is still most people's preferred way of expressing their ideas to others. There is certainly a role for written documents, but it is generally far more effective to get the words into computers by speaking rather than tapping at an awkwardly-designed layout of small buttons at our fingertips. It will be a vast liberation for the human race when we transcend the keyboard.

Networks bringing people together

Every conference organizer will tell you that people mainly go to conferences to meet and interact with interesting and useful people. For some strange reason the very same organizer usually designs a conference in which delegates file in and out of darkened rooms to listen to a dizzying succession of speakers, leaving coffee breaks and lunches to strike up random conversations in the hope of fortuitously meeting someone interesting and useful.

To address this problem, researchers at the famed MIT Media Labs have developed a device they call a cricket. Delegates at a conference or other event are each given a cricket, and asked to attach it to their lapel, having programmed it with their profile and interests. When someone who has similar interests walks within range, the crickets "chirp," suggesting the two people should speak. The technology alerts you to who you are likely to want to speak to, in a natural and unforced way, as part of the natural flow of people in a large group.

In mobile-mad Japan, "proximity dating" has had a big success. As in Internet dating, you complete a profile of both yourself and your desired partner. Instead of suggesting people to exchange e-mails with, the service rings you on your cell phone to let you know that someone with a matching profile is within a few hundred yards of you, and allows you to arrange to meet them. Since high bandwidth mobile technology is now available in Japan, the system can also allow you to see each other on your mobile videophone before you meet.

Video-conferencing is rapidly becoming a standard business tool. For example, investment bank UBS Warburg has set up its major clients so any phone call to them also uses high-quality desktop video. However it's the next generation of technologies that will really bring people around the world together in powerful ways. Talk of teleportation may evoke Star Trek, but the products of start-up company Teleportec allow people to appear anywhere in the world as a 3-dimensional image, to see the room, and hold eye contact with their counterparts. In addition to the obvious applications of meetings and conference presentations, a British bank has experimented with offering financial advice using the system. Virtual reality pioneer Jaron Lanier is working on what he calls "teleimmersion", which uses multiple cameras and extremely high bandwidth connections to simulate sitting in front of your distant counterpart, also allowing direct eye contact.

Together, the key emerging technologies of XML, peer-to-peer, and the next phase of network interfaces, are integrating the networks and bringing them to life. This makes it essential for companies to understand and apply the strategies relevant to an intensely networked world.

Standards and network strategy

Whenever you go to a website and are presented with a snazzy animated introduction, you are seeing Macromedia Flash at work. The free Flash Player software that enables people to view these animations is now running on around 97% of PCs that are connected to the Internet. At the outset, Macromedia had a clear-cut challenge. Web surfers would only download Flash Player if there were interesting websites using Flash, while website designers would only use Flash if a sufficient proportion of their target audience had installed the software. Macromedia makes its money by selling the software for developers to create Flash files, but to make it a viable market it had to give away the Flash Player software.

The basis of any network is *interoperability*. Only if systems can share information and work together do they form a network.

Along the way, Macromedia made a bold decision. It published the specifications for the SWF files used by the Flash Player software, and committed to keeping these open. This meant that any other company could take advantage of the large installed base of Flash Player software, and sell software to compete directly with Macromedia's Flash software, which was its only source of revenue from the exercise. Indeed, arch-rival Adobe rushed to market with a directly competitive product, based on the specifications made available by Macromedia. The reason Macromedia made Flash open is that it provided an immense impetus to make it a de facto standard for Internet multimedia. If it hadn't released it, others would have come out with competitive formats, and Flash may never have broken through to become dominant. Macromedia may not have all the market for Internet multimedia design software, but having established the standard format clearly gives it a big headstart on all its competitors, and it has guaranteed a total market size almost as big as the Internet.

As you saw at the beginning of this chapter, the basis of any network is *interoperability*. Only if systems can share information and work together do they form a network. Every mobile phone in Europe uses the same standard, GSM, so you can go to any country and make calls and send and receive text messages as if you were at home. In the US, there are multiple mobile communications standards, resulting in several distinct networks of users that can't always link directly.

So who owns these standards? The value of doing so is immense. Just ask Bill Gates. However it takes immense market clout to be able to set an effective standard, to beat out all other competition. Windows is a proprietary technology that dominates the market, but still has significant competitors in some fields, such as Apple and Linux. In order to establish its leading position, it had to publish programming interfaces, so that other companies could create software, in turn making the Windows platform more valuable to users.

In the case of Macromedia, it recognized it may not have the clout to establish Flash as a standard on its own, so opened the way for competitors, enabling it to become an accepted standard. In the games console market, Microsoft's Xbox has joined the Sony Playstation 2 and Nintendo to result in a three-cornered battle. Each is building its own network of users and game developers, and struggling to take market share from the other aspiring standards. Any wins or losses are amplified through network effects.

When a company can't realistically hope to control a market on its own, it will seek to establish alliances, gaining critical mass by getting enough large players together. The DVD format was agreed in 1995 by ten of the largest consumer electronics firms, making it a virtually guaranteed slamdunk success. Sony and Phillips had been promoting their own standard since 1993, with Toshiba working on its own incompatible version. Eventually other industry players brought the two sides together and made them see the benefits to all in establishing a common standard. The patent holders behind the format charge licensing royalties, but have kept these low enough so that they were not an obstacle to DVD being broadly adopted.

The real drive today, however, is towards "open standards". Essentially this means they are controlled by unaligned bodies, that publish specifications so anyone can adopt them and create interoperable systems, and are driven by the interests of the entire community of users rather than any group of vendors. Standards bodies like the World Wide Web Consortium (W3C), the International Standards Organization, and any number of industry organizations fit this bill. However just because a standard is open, doesn't mean it is accepted by everyone. Standards bodies themselves can have competitors. For example Linux is a truly open standard in that it is entirely known and no group controls its development, but it has many competitors as an operating system. The basic standards on which the Internet is based, such as TCP/IP and HTTP, are both open and broadly accepted. That alone is what has enabled the networks to emerge.

Figure 2-2 illustrates how standards can be controlled by single companies, alliances, or standards bodies, and in each case be either in a competitive situation, or have moved towards or achieved broad market acceptance.

There are powerful trends towards both open and accepted standards. Customers understand the value of the larger networks enabled by

Since the trend to open, accepted standards is clear, it is far better to go with it rather than fight it. Long-term success must be based on aligning yourself with these shifts.

standards, and the reality is that each industry as a whole benefits from standards. This doesn't mean that Microsoft will suddenly crumble, or the games console manufacturers will open their systems tomorrow. There will

always be domains of emerging standards that will see bitter battles to establish dominance.

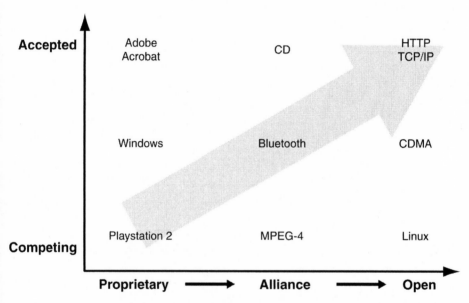

Figure 2-2: The (very) gradual shift to open, accepted standards

Since the trend to open, accepted standards is clear, it is far better to go with it rather than fight it. Long-term success must be based on aligning yourself with these shifts. Over time, the greatest rewards will go to those who provide effective leadership towards standards, while implementing clear strategies on how they are positioned and create value within the unfolding landscape. We will explore this theme of standards leadership throughout this book.

The essentials of standards and network strategy

American Express launched its Blue card in 1999, within 18 months accounting for 10% of all Amex cards, and expecting to hit 10 million cards issued in 2002. The Blue card is a smart card, meaning it is embedded with a microprocessor that can store and process information, and run multiple applications. The initial function was to provide additional security for Internet purchases. This requires a special smart card reader to be attached to users' PCs, however Amex gave this away for free for subscribers during the initial launch period. Since then Amex has added further functions, and teamed up with retailers to promote the card.

A partnership with Virgin Megastores has put point-of-sale terminals that can be used with the Blue card in all its US stores, and provided discounts to card holders on featured CDs. Another deal with concert promoter SFX Entertainment allows cardholders to order tickets online, and then pick them up at special windows fitted with smart card readers. The Blue card uses open standards technology at its core, but for the meantime American Express is intent on building a network of card holders using its platform, which can gradually be broadened into other applications and markets.

Business strategy changes in a world increasingly based on standards and networks. Executives need to understand and consider positive feedback in networks, how networks compete, and the role of standards in their business model. Increasingly, alliances are no longer a tool for specific situations, but an essential part of doing business. Amex is endeavoring to use its market power to more or less go it alone in building its Blue card network, but it still needs to bring in partners, and has to align its technology with industry standards.

Carl Shapiro and Hal Varian of the University of California at Berkeley have been among the leaders in exploring in depth the new economics and business strategies of networks, notably in their excellent book *Information Rules*.[7] Here we offer four essential steps for managers to develop network strategies. These provide a foundation for what we will cover through the rest of this book.

DEVELOPING NETWORK STRATEGIES

1. Decide where you want open standards and where you want to own the standard.
2. Participate strategically in alliances and standards bodies.
3. Align your strategies with the evolving standards landscape.
4. Adopt new pricing and business models.

Table 2-1: Action steps to developing network strategies.

1. Decide where you want open standards, and where you want to own the standard

When AOL and Time Warner were seeking regulatory approval to merge, key competitors, notably Microsoft and Yahoo!, publicly attacked AOL for keeping its instant messaging service closed. They argued that AOL, in not allowing other instant messaging systems to interoperate with its market dominating offerings such as ICQ, was blocking innovation and consumer benefits, and they demanded that AOL be forced to open its systems. Then Microsoft began to successfully build its MSN Messenger network, helped by including it in its Windows operating system, and Yahoo! Messenger grew through being integrated into some of the firm's other services. Gradually the strident tone changed as the two pretenders started to benefit from having their own significant proprietary networks.[8] All three major players now adopt the rhetoric of open standards, but none seem to be in any special hurry to integrate their systems. Providing instant messaging software is creating powerful networks, that help them to keep their customers in the fold.

Undoubtedly the instant messaging networks will eventually merge, through a combination of other firms providing systems that link them, and the three major players grudgingly accepting the push to open standards from their customers. Users' demand for the benefits of standards are too strong to resist indefinitely. Imagine if you could only make telephone calls to people who used the same phone company. However before we get to interoperability between all instant messaging systems, each key player is going to try to extract the greatest benefits for itself. How they go about it will affect how long it takes to get to open standards.

Do you want a level playing field? A simple question, it would seem. Yet the answer depends on the specific domain, and can change over time, as you've seen in the case of instant messaging. In essence, you will want open standards in every field except where you think you can gain a competitive advantage and dominate the market. Selecting precisely where you choose to compete is now one of most fundamental strategic decisions for every company.

One of the situations in which the decisions are most challenging is when you have a competitive advantage, yet open standards will help to grow the industry and the market. This was the context for Macromedia's decision to open up the Flash standard. The industry leadership role of Ingram Micro, discussed in Chapter 3, illustrates how building standards can strongly benefit a company by making the industry as a whole—including its competitors—more profitable.

2. Participate strategically in alliances and standards bodies

In 1994 mobile telephone manufacturer Ericsson started developing a communications protocol to link mobile phones with their accessories. Ericsson then recognized that the protocol would be of limited use unless it was adopted by manufacturers of all kinds of devices. In 1997 it started to talk to other firms about joining with them to create a standard. The Bluetooth Special Interest Group was formed by an initial core group of Ericsson, IBM, Intel, Nokia, and Toshiba, to develop and promote a wireless standard to link devices within 10 meters at speeds of up to 1 Mbps. Part of the promise of the technology is dispensing with cables inside offices, and allowing mobile devices to communicate with local systems wherever they go.

Ericsson stated to its partners it wanted to make the standard open, and committed to providing the supporting intellectual property to Bluetooth free of any royalties. This necessary foundation for the initiative helped to bring in other key players who both could see the benefit of having an industry standard for short-distance wireless networking, and the potential for benefiting from sharing in the licensing of the technology if it took off. Each firm was watching to see who else would join. Toshiba only signed up after IBM had made the move.[9] The evident clout of the founders quickly convinced other key players like Microsoft and Motorola to join at top-tier status in the group, with over 2,000 firms then joining to gain access to inside information on the system.

The jury is still out on whether Bluetooth will gain market traction before its competitors, however the way the alliance has been developed shows some of the key drivers for those who initiate and participate in standards alliances. Each of the participants in Bluetooth has different objectives. In any alliance or standards body, it's important to understand the motivations of the participants. Sometimes it's quite genuinely simply to create a standard that will create benefits for consumers and the industry, but there are usually vested interests. One of the central issues is how each participating firm's intellectual property will be affected. Careful positioning is required, as we will discuss in Chapter 5. Certainly participating in an alliance or standards body at very least gives you an inside seat on how standards may evolve, and insight into the resulting business opportunities.

3. Align your strategies with the evolving standards landscape

Sometimes business is like a day at the races. You can study the form guide and try to pick the winner, but you know that the unexpected happens more often than not. Do you put all your money on the horse with the lowest odds, or do you place multiple bets so you have a chance of doing OK even if there is an upset? This is the kind of decision that companies have to make when they need to adopt standards to develop or market their offerings, but there are several contenders in the field.

In May 2000, seven major banks joined to form FXall, an online foreign exchange trading system. It allows its large clients to link directly to all of its member banks so they can access research, compare prices, execute transactions, and process trades. The founding banks had tried hard to get the three banks with the largest FX volume—Citibank, Chase Manhattan, and Deutsche Bank—to join them, but they all declined. The following year, by which time FXall had around 30 banks providing prices, the three leaders, together with Reuters, made their move. They formed a direct competitor to FXall, called Atriax, involving some 50 banks around the world. Between the two online systems, the vast majority of global FX liquidity was covered. But clients weren't happy. They didn't want to have to log on to two different systems, and so they either chose the one they thought was better or more likely to win, or just as often decided to wait until a winner emerged. For smaller banks, the costs involved meant they had to choose the one they thought their clients would use, otherwise they could lose business. A couple of banks opted to participate in both. The industry watched to see what would happen—would there be a winner, could they coexist, would they merge? Eventually in April 2002, Atriax closed down. It had been behind FXall on the technology front, simply hadn't gained sufficient momentum, and merger talks had failed. The three founding banks of Atriax joined FXall.

In this case, the competition was to form the leading network of service providers and clients in the industry. Clients ultimately wanted a single network, rather than having the market split in two. Along the way, both banks and clients had to develop strategies to align with the winners. It's a similar situation for content providers, who need to deal with a plethora of standards for music, ebooks, Internet broadcasting and so on, as we will discuss in more detail in Chapter 8. In the case of both standards and customer networks, companies need to develop clear strategies, including contingency plans, of how to align with the evolving landscape.

4. Adopt new pricing and business models

When Microsoft launched its Xbox games console in November 2001, it was priced at $299. This was generally estimated to be between $20 and $100 below its manufacturing cost, which would result in direct losses of up to $2 billion.[10] The simple logic was that the money in the business is made by selling games, so it can be worth losing a hefty whack to establish a wide network which then reaps the dough. However the price proved to be not low enough. Within six months the price of the Xbox had been substantially cut in most countries in the world, and then finally in the US, despite achieving reasonable sales. Microsoft was considering profitability for the entire product lifecycle in forcing itself into yet larger short-term losses.

It was easier for Adobe to distribute its Acrobat Reader software for free as a way of building the pdf document format as a standard. Because it's an information-based product, there are almost no costs in distributing as many copies as it wishes. Yet it still needed to make decisions about how to price the full-featured Acrobat software from which it made its revenue.

Presenting a business case for investment has become far harder in a business environment based on standards and networks. The rewards are potentially enormous, but often a very large upfront investment is required for a very uncertain and usually long-term payoff. Pricing strategies must be based on revenue and other benefits over the entire life of the product, but this usually means offering incentives early, and thus starting with sometimes substantial losses.

Vital Connections: Chapter 2

In this chapter you have seen how all networks are founded on standards, that allow people and systems to connect. Three sets of emerging technologies—XML and web services, peer-to-peer, and closer network interfaces—are helping to integrate the networks far more deeply, and bring them to life. As a result, every company needs to develop business strategies that are relevant in a highly networked world.

If truly open standards are in place, then the playing field becomes perhaps not quite level, but certainly a lot flatter. This is precisely when business relationships become the primary source of value. Not just the relationships with your customers, but also those with your suppliers, partners, and industry peers. Throughout Part 2 of this book we will examine how these relationships are changing, and how to lead your customers and partners into new ways of working together.

Part 3 of the book builds further on the foundations of standards and networks strategy presented in this chapter. It examines the emerging flow economy, which is based on the flow of information and ideas, and now encompasses most business activities. We will use a new framework for developing powerful strategies, based on how the central issues of standards and relationships can be combined with connectivity, interfaces, content, and services to create business success.

PART 2: Evolving Organizations

Organizations are not what they were. Their boundaries are blurring, and every aspect of business and value-creation is becoming ambiguous. In this world, leadership is needed. You will fail if you take counsel from the risks of uncertainty. Those that lead their company, customers, and partners into new ways of working will reap ample rewards.

In Part 2 of *Living Networks* I will cover how organizations are evolving in the hyper-connected economy. Chapter 3 examines how companies can lead their industries to models based on transparency, collaboration, and sharing value. In Chapter 4 you will find how to develop trusting relationships in a transparent world, and capture the scarce attention of your customers and partners. Chapter 5 covers the world of distributed innovation, in which intellectual property increasingly must be created by working collaboratively. Chapter 6 explores how companies can boost their presence in the networks, in marketing, building customer feedback loops, and nurturing the flow of knowledge within the firm.

Part 3 goes on to explore in detail how to develop strategy in the emerging "flow economy". Companies must position themselves effectively, develop new approaches to distributing content, and reframe how they provide digital and professional services. Individuals are at the heart of the networked world, and they too need to develop effective strategies. Part 4 examines the future of the networks, and the implications for business.

CHAPTER 3
The New Organization

Leadership Across Blurring Boundaries

The boundaries between organizations are blurring as technology reduces the costs of transactions. It is becoming essential for companies to work closely with their customers, suppliers, and partners, however this involves very real risks. In this world leadership is required to take whole industries and supply chains into new ways of working based on transparency, collaboration, and sharing value. Those that embrace the networks and lead the way forward will reap the greatest rewards.

At 6:53pm on November 9, 1989, an official of the East German government stated in a press conference that a new policy had been instituted to allow its citizens to travel to the West. Within minutes mobs formed outside the Berlin Wall. Before long the first bold few scrambled over the Wall unscathed, unlike the 61 people shot dead trying to escape during its grim 28-year history, while others grabbed hammers and anything else they could find to begin destruction of the hated barrier to freedom. An artificial, rigid, and guarded boundary dividing a country and millions of families had succumbed to the fluidity of the times. The same sense of rigidity and boundaries were also evident in the Eastern Germany economy. The East Berlin post office, before the fall, incorporated not just a restaurant and kindergarten for its employees, but also an auto repair shop and fishery.[1] The difficulties in getting anything done meant that managers put boundaries around their organizations and tried to do everything possible inside them, resulting in immense duplication within the economy.

In the West too, it's not so long now since an organization's boundaries were crystal clear. The organization was where the organization man went to work a steady job and get a regular salary. It bought raw materials, made things from them, and then sold the final product to consumers. The salespeople did their rounds, took orders, and tidy rows of delivery trucks streamed out from the warehouses to deliver the products. It was totally clear what was inside and outside the organization, and if you dealt with a company you were almost certainly either a buyer of their products or selling something to them in a straightforward relationship. The world has changed dramatically since then. Blurred relationships and ambiguity are the order of the day.

Take a look at Convergys, the world's largest operator of outsourced call centers. Some outsourcing initiatives, like fleet management or running corporate cafeterias, simply take functions that are peripheral to a company's mission, and place them in the hands of outsiders. In the case of call centers, it's a completely different ball game. For many firms, the only direct contact they have with their end-customers is through call centers. Don't they feel they are losing control and valuable information if they outsource customer contact? The deep integration and alignment of processes between Convergys and its clients means that they can often get even better information flows than if they run customer contact internally.

Sometimes Convergys' clients—which include AT&T, Compaq, Microsoft, Sony and other corporate leaders—outsource all of their call centers, but more often they already run their own call centers, and choose outsourcing to cope with growth and expansion. In this case—just as when a single firm runs multiple call centers—the key issue is utterly seamless consistency across the operations. When a customer calls Sony's 1-800 number, she should get exactly the same experience whether it's routed to a Sony call center, or one of the Convergys call centers that service Sony. To achieve this, Convergys and its clients create almost perfect mirror images of their technologies, processes, training, and work environment. Almost every Convergys call center employee works on a single client account, immersed every day in that company's products and issues, some even work at the client's premises, and understandably they can sometimes feel a greater affiliation to the client than the company that pays their wages.

In order not only to make itself transparent but to actually enhance the free flow of information from the end-customers back to its clients, Convergys uses a variety of technologies and processes. Many firms are attracted to Convergys because it provides detailed recording and reporting systems. A company may run its own call center, but unless it has the right systems, processes, and culture in place, management may still not learn much about its clients. In addition to monitoring calls on call center visits or remotely as they choose, clients are encouraged to run focus groups with the Convergys agents that answer their customers' calls. After all, these are the people who have the richest, most detailed interaction with their customers. One Convergys client invites the call center staff to man its booths at industry fairs, so they can get and share different perspectives on their customers. These feedback channels can flow into all sorts of problem-solving and product development processes. One large European sports drink manufacturer redesigned its distinctive bottles on the basis of customer feedback reaped through Convergys.

Convergys creates value together with its clients, with their joint processes so deeply integrated that it's next to impossible to say where one company ends and the next begins. Information flows richly on myriad levels between the firms, as it has to, since otherwise Convergys' clients would be working in a vacuum, totally isolated from their customer community. The whole economy is shifting to one built entirely on these rich flows of information across as well as within firms, in which success is based largely on how well you can integrate your operations with others.

The boundaries are blurring

In 1932 a young Englishman used a scholarship to sail over the Atlantic and study American industry. The mild-mannered 22-year old gave a lecture on his findings, and a few years later published a paper titled "The Nature of the Firm". Worldly recognition sometimes comes slowly, but in 1991 Ronald Coase was awarded the Nobel prize for economics, and his work is now proving invaluable in understanding the tectonic shifts in today's economy. Coase pointed out that any transaction incurs a variety of costs. Among other costs, we have to search for a supplier, compare between competitors, negotiate a deal, monitor the quality of supplies, and seek redress if our chosen supplier is not performing.[2]

Any organization will seek to minimize these costs. One obvious way is to implement centralized purchasing. If every individual staff member who required pencils, business cards, a chair, or any of the other paraphernalia of day-to-day business went out to search for, compare, and negotiate with suppliers, the total cost in time and effort would be immense. On the other hand a centralized purchasing function is itself a cost, essentially being a bureaucracy for organizing external transactions. Coase proposed that a firm exists whenever the costs of maintaining that bureaucracy is lower than the transaction costs. If transactions cost nothing, there is no need for any bureaucracy, or arguably for any firm of more than one person.

Perhaps the single best way of understanding the impact of technology on the economy today is that it has dramatically reduced transactions costs. The Internet allows cheap and easy information search, and the ability to compare prices, functions, and quality globally. The vast growth in outsourcing over the last decade is due to the far greater ease and reduced costs for firms to locate business functions outside the organization's boundaries.

Now that workflow—comprised primarily of the movement of messages and documents—is becoming almost entirely digital, it is increasingly irrelevant where work is performed. It matters little whether a colleague in a business process is located in the same company and building, or working in another company on the other side of the planet. Technology is making the boundaries invisible.

Creating the new organization

Corporate Executive Board is a membership organization. Rather a curious one. Over 1700 corporations pay an annual fee of $30,000 to be members of the Washington D.C.-based firm. Their membership fee gives them access to reports and conferences on specific industry issues and common management challenges, such as employee retention and minimizing regulatory costs. The first interesting feature is that almost all of the content for the reports and briefings comes from the members themselves. Corporate Executive Board specifically positions itself to draw out the solutions that member firms have successfully developed for themselves, and make them available to other members, frequently their competitors.

A second intriguing feature: this membership organization that is based on firms sharing their strategic resources is a public company. In the 2001 fiscal year it earned over $16 million on revenues of $103 million, and *Business Week* placed it in fifth spot on its list of Hot Growth companies. At a time when big-name consultants were smarting from clients tightening their budgets, it was profiting from exactly the same trend. In addition, the vast global membership network it has grown—including firms such as IBM, General Electric, and Alcoa—means that it would be enormously difficult for another firm to break into its market and compete with the same business model. What's intriguing about Corporate Executive Board's model is that the value is largely contributed—and then bought back—by the firm's customers. And external investors share in the value created.

In today's world of blurring boundaries and increasing ambiguity, organizations are nothing more than vehicles for creating and appropriating value. In a capitalist world, shareholders own the legal entity called the company. The managers of the company apply its financial and other resources—in combination with other organizations—to create value that end-customers are prepared to pay for. They also must negotiate terms of engagement with other companies so that they can extract a fair share of the value created by the firms **The art of management is now about positioning the firm to extract value from its participation in a broad economic network.** working together. The key difference in thinking from previous conceptions of the organization is that value is created by the network, not by the organization. The art of management is now about positioning the firm to extract value from its participation in a broad economic network.

Corporate Executive Board provides a fine illustration of this. Arguably the member organizations provide the bulk of the value, at least in terms of the inputs. Yet the firm has carved out an economic niche in which it brings together a network, and plays a central role in having that network create substantial value for participants, by synthesizing and communicating ideas so they can be applied effectively. As such, the shareholders in this amorphous entity profit not only from how it creates value for its clients and partners, but even more from how it has positioned itself to extract value from a network encompassing over 1700 major firms. We will explore the fine art of strategic positioning in more detail in Chapter 7.

The idea of the core competence of the firm dates back to 1990—hardly new stuff.[3] What is new is the extraordinary fineness of resolution with which managers can decide what is and isn't core to the company, and implement that. As you saw in Chapter 2, emerging technologies are giving rise to the modular organization. We used to be able to think of a company as a set of business processes. Now that processes exist primarily as information flows, they are often distributed across a number of companies. A company may contribute just one part or module within an overall business process. Some of the issues in implementing the modular organization will be covered in Chapter 9.

In this world in which value is increasingly created across organizational boundaries, by working closely with customers, suppliers, and partners, you no longer have a choice. You must integrate your processes with other companies. You have to share valuable information with your customers, partners, and sometimes even competitors. It is essential to collaborate outside the organization in every aspect of your business, from product development through to marketing. Those who try to keep their companies as self-sufficient islands will see them waste away, simply unable to compete effectively. Consulting firm The Yankee Group estimates that in the next five years companies can save $223 billion through digital collaboration.[4] But that is just the beginning. Even greater benefits are available to those who transform how their companies work and collaborate in the new connected world.

Boldly showing the way forward

Just because it's essential for companies to work in new ways, doesn't mean that it's easy. A whole new set of challenges arise for the companies that take on the challenge of working closely with their customers and partners in the hyper-connected economy. There are four key risks that increase substantially in a world of collaboration and integration.

• **Information loss.** In 1999, online exchange Priceline.com discussed a marketing alliance with Internet travel agent Expedia, disclosing information about its business model in the process. After talks broke down, Expedia started offering very similar services to Priceline.com, sparking a suit from Priceline.com which Expedia eventually settled by agreeing to pay royalties.[5] Working closely with others means that valuable information and intellectual property can be exposed.

• **Systems security.** Security is near the top of the priority list for every CIO. It's not quite as hard to protect your systems if you can isolate them entirely. But that's not an option. Companies have to closely connect and integrate their systems with their customers and partners to be competitive, making the job of protecting them a lot harder. We will examine this issue in Chapter 4.

• **Reputation.** Any company that was proudly associated with the dynamic, innovative company that was Enron suddenly found its own name besmirched when the house of cards collapsed. Your corporate reputation can be impacted—both positively and negatively—by the fortunes of your business partners.

• **Ability to extract value**. When you work closely with other firms to create value, it's not always obvious how to share the rewards. This ambiguity can create opportunities for those that hold the balance of power in relationships, or that help create new approaches to collaboration, but some firms may find themselves with a lesser share of the fruits than they feel they deserve.

This daunting set of risks is enough to make most executives quail. However those that shrink back into their shell to avoid the risks of engaging in the networked economy will soon enough find that this is riskier still.

The reality is that virtually every company is in the same situation, understanding the necessity of shifting into new ways of working, but hesitant in the face of these risks and challenges. This provides an immense opportunity for those companies that are willing and able to demonstrate leadership to their customers and partners, to show how to implement new kinds of relationships based on transparency, collaboration, and sharing value. Things don't happen by themselves. If business is to benefit from connectivity, some will have to boldly show the way forward for everyone. What defines the new business environment is that companies no longer have control over much of what matters. This requires a shift from management to leadership. A manager is someone who makes decisions within a defined sphere of control. A leader influences and creates beyond what he or she can directly control. Today, you must be a leader across a domain that often extends far beyond the borders of your company. In order for your company to succeed, the whole value network within which you work must succeed as well. Unless you provide the leadership for that to happen, you become the subject of industry forces rather than creating them. Industries will inevitably shift dramatically as the network economy comes to life, and those that will take best advantage of those changes are those that lead them.

Leadership in a collaborative world

Walk into the office of a senior technology executive, and there's a good chance he or she will be sitting on an Aeron executive chair, a sleek and comfortable expression of power. Furniture manufacturer Herman Miller has built itself a solid place in the network economy, through both its range of creative designs that appeal to the full spectrum of establishment figures, funky entrepreneurs, and home office workers, and the way it connects digitally with its customers and suppliers.

In 1995 Herman Miller launched a new line of furniture called SQA, for "simple, quick, affordable," intent on reducing the time taken to manufacture and deliver a customer order from months to ultimately just one week. It realized that to achieve this it needed to revamp its entire sales and manufacturing process. Sales representatives were provided with a laptop application that allowed them to sit with their customers to design and specify complete office systems on the spot. Customers were delighted to participate in the streamlined process and get faster delivery. But to make the whole system work, the firm's suppliers also needed to get more timely and accurate information, as the materials required to construct the furniture were only shipped to the manufacturer once an order was placed. Herman Miller is now able to provide its suppliers with access to real-time information from its systems. Orders, invoices, engineering data, delivery schedules, and lead times, are all displayed on one screen. Suppliers save time and money in their operations, and Herman Miller has lifted on-time fulfilment from 75% to over 95% despite the vastly accelerated deliveries.[6]

Herman Miller began by making sure it understood not only the information requirements of its partners, but also their technological capacities. It designed an easy-to-use system accessible on the web rather than requiring more sophisticated technology, shifted internal processes to make the information on the systems reflect the latest updates available within the firm, and provided training for its suppliers to use the system effectively. Herman Miller acted as a true leader in changing the ways of working of an entire collaborative business network, providing benefits to itself, its customers, and its suppliers.

Digital connectivity and the ability to share information with partners is not new, but technologies like the Internet and XML have made it vastly easier. EDI (Electronic Data Interchange) from the late 1970s promised to allow corporations to link digitally and collaborate effectively with their major suppliers and clients. Despite the many potential benefits, the impact has been limited. The heart of the problem was that every implementation of EDI was specific to the two organizations being linked, requiring a large and expensive one-off project to integrate their systems, and thus limiting its application to large corporations. Herman Miller had tried earlier to implement EDI with its suppliers, but as they were mainly smaller firms they lacked the expertise and resources to adopt the systems.[7]

Connectivity alone doesn't transform business. Firms and industries must agree on information standards in order to integrate their systems, apply new technologies to implement collaborative processes, and work together closely to run supply chains more efficiently.

Implementing information standards

In early 1998 Charles Hoffman, a CPA with a small accounting firm based in Washington state, began to look at the possibilities of using XML for financial reporting. He convinced the American Institute of Certified Public Accountants (AICPA) and his own firm to fund further studies, with a committee formed soon after by interested companies, including all five of the largest global accounting firms, and several computer companies, notably Microsoft. The result was XBRL (eXtensible Business Reporting Language), which provides a global, agreed format to present companies' financial reports. This standard enables organizations to easily consolidate information from many divisions, get extremely timely management information, and report to regulatory authorities and shareholders. What's more, analysts can far more easily sift through comparative financial information to identify investment opportunities, and external auditors can integrate their processes with those of their clients.

The interests of the financial reporting community are highly aligned. It's in everyone's interest to have common standards adopted, simply because that's the only way that major efficiencies can be gained. Each of the key participants have their own motivations for getting involved and demonstrating leadership.

Bank of America has embarked on an ambitious and broad-ranging initiative to promote XBRL. The bank needs to perform credit analysis of the financial reports of all of the companies to which it lends, so it has begun a pilot to get its national client base of 20,000 companies with revenues between $10 million and $500 million to adopt XBRL. This will streamline the loan approval process for all parties, and if it means better information on its clients for the bank, could ultimately result in lower lending rates. Initially Bank of America will accept standard electronic data forms from its clients, that can be converted internally for use in its credit systems. It is hoping the initiative will demonstrate to its clients the benefits of using XBRL, so they adopt it in their own systems. Bank of America ultimately intends to roll out the program to over 100,000 commercial clients.[8]

Morgan Stanley, Reuters, and Microsoft were among the first companies to present their financial reports using XBRL. Each will benefit in different ways from the standard being broadly adopted, and they are promoting the cause by providing a lead to others. In the government domain, the Australian Prudential Regulatory Authority was the first regulatory body in the world to adopt XBRL, announcing that it will use the standard to collect data from 11,000 financial institutions, saving substantial costs for these companies and itself. Each of these leaders is helping to take the entire business community forward.

In Chapter 2 you saw how every industry has its own XML-based initiatives to enable easy information sharing and system integration between companies. This only ever happens because of a few leaders. They help to create benefits for everyone in the network, but their leadership also keeps them at the forefront of the resulting opportunities. Later in this chapter we will look at how Ingram Micro drove the birth of RosettaNet, a consortium that is developing information and process standards for the computer manufacturing industry.

Creating collaborative processes

In early 2000, at the height of the B2B frenzy, the top three US automakers—Ford, Chrysler-Daimler, and General Motors—announced the launch their own industry exchange, Covisint. Its initial conception—in line with thinking at the time—was primarily as a procurement gateway that would increase efficiencies, and enable the auto manufacturers to get more competitive pricing for their supplies.

The reality has been that Covisint has struggled.[9] The main problem with the B2B movement was that it in essence tried to reduce supplier relationships to information flows of product data and prices. Covisint—and most of the other B2B exchanges that are still alive today—have by now realized that a large and increasing proportion of the value of supplier relationships stems from close collaboration. You want to get closer to, not further from, your best suppliers. Now one of Covisint's most important components is its Virtual Project Workspace, that allows automakers to work with their suppliers on product design.

Auto design is a highly collaborative effort, and suppliers are swiftly taking increasing responsibility. While automakers still drive the design process, it depends on what the component suppliers can provide, the impact of design specifications on cost, the way in which components from different suppliers will fit together, and many other variables. Being able to exchange and modify engineering diagrams and documents as well as discuss issues in real-time changes the design process to one that is shared between the manufacturers and their suppliers. General Motors, by using these kinds of collaborative systems, has reduced car development time from 42 months to less than 18 months.[10]

Perhaps the greatest focus in information technology today is building more effective tools for collaboration. Lockheed Martin, to fulfil its $200 billion Joint Strike Fighter contract for the US Defense Deparment, is working with 80 suppliers, and using 90 different software tools to link them all seamlessly together. The technologies allow the 40,000 or so researchers, designers, and engineers that are working together on the project to act as a single, tightly-integrated organization.[11]

As you saw in Chapter 2, peer-to-peer technologies are about directly connecting computers to computers and people to people. There are no central servers, no intermediaries, and no boundaries. When you connect with others it's utterly irrelevant whether you sit next to each other within the same company, work in different companies, or are located on opposite sides of the globe. The concept of a sequential "chain" of information flow falls to pieces—there's no reason why any two people cannot connect directly. If a supplier to a food manufacturer wants to forecast demand better, it can easily communicate directly with the retailers who sell the manufacturer's products.

Pharmaceutical development is a great example of large numbers of researchers spread around the world needing to collaborate closely. GlaxoSmithKline, one of the world's largest pharmaceutical companies, is using peer-to-peer technologies to link both its researchers and its external collaborators that are working on drug development projects.[12] This illustrates the type of ad-hoc collaboration that is so suited to peer-to-peer approaches. Form groups with whoever you want, define the rules of how you'll work together and who you'll invite to join, share information as it's available, and bounce ideas around in real-time. Tools that scientists from the past would have given their right arms for are now at work speeding the development of new life-enhancing drugs.

These kinds of technologies can help distributed teams to work seamlessly. However in order to make these tools valuable, it's also necessary to implement new processes. Companies need to redesign how they work within collaborative processes, and implement the necessary new steps and skills. In addition, it is essential to develop the attitudes and culture of collaborative work through the company, as we'll discuss later in this chapter.

From linear chains to living networks

I challenge you to find a person who has never bought or used a Procter & Gamble product. The search could take you far from the beaten track, as the corporation's wares reach almost 5 billion consumers in 140 countries. One of the single most important issues for the consumer goods giant is the efficient distribution of $40 billion worth of products annually through an immensely complex global supply chain.

The essence of managing supply chains is a very simple dynamic. How do you reduce inventory (since that costs money to keep) while at the same time ensuring your products are always on the shelves to buy (since you lose sales and goodwill if they aren't)? Until recently one of the key issues in supply chain management has been trying to get other participants to hold inventory, with the relative power of companies along the supply chain, from manufacturers through distributors to retailers, largely determining the allocation of inventory and costs between them. Two drivers are now shifting the whole nature of the business.

The first driver is the ease with which detailed information can be gathered internally and transferred between companies. Visibility is everything. The more information that all players in a supply chain have about demand, manufacturing, shipments, and everything else that makes the flow of products to end-customers transparent, the better they can manage their operations. The current state of information technology now makes it possible in theory to make the entire supply chain visible to all. The reality is that this is very difficult to implement, because it's far more an issue of processes and people than the relatively straightforward technology component. In addition, having the technology to share information does not mean that it happens. Trust remains a major limiting factor that we will explore in detail in Chapter 4.

The second driver of change is the vastly increasing complexity of product distribution. The term "supply chain" evokes images of products or their components moving along a series of links until they reach the end-consumer. This dated model may still apply in parts of some industries, but the majority of the economy now functions very differently. The phrase "value network" is far more relevant to business today, reflecting both that the creation of economic value consists of far more than shuffling products around, and that this value is brought together by complex networks, and not a series of links in a chain. Moving from linear chains to complex multi-player networks creates real challenges. Each participant makes decisions and acts on the basis of the information it has available, and what it sees as its own best interest. So far, so good. The problem is that if each individual network member acts in what it believes is an optimal fashion, these behaviors combined across these massively complex networks will usually result in lower profitability for the network taken as a whole, and indeed for most if not all participants.

In many ways, these richly connected value networks themselves can be considered to be alive—the complexity of their interactions is leading to unpredictable behaviors. The linear models that have been used for decades to help plan supplies are falling flat on their faces. So, how can firms within a value network work effectively in this world? As a very first step this requires some way of sharing information across the entire network. This information needs to be applied so that all companies benefit, for example by reducing total inventory for the network as a whole, and sharing the resulting benefits between participants. These objectives are by no means easy to achieve, yet there are immense potential rewards. Industry leadership is essential.

So what has Procter & Gamble done to address these vital issues in its supply chain? One of its key projects has been to work with some of its major retailers such Wal-Mart, Target, and Tesco to implement Collaborative Planning, Forecasting, and Replenishment (CPFR), an inter-industry standards initiative to enable transparency and collaboration in the supply chain. If Procter & Gamble, together with its partners, can improve the information flows that allow effective forecasting and stock replenishment, this will in turn reduce inventory and increase retail availability. The first step was to work with its partners to map the current processes and flow of information and goods, before developing a joint plan to enhance effective collaboration. Even the early stages of the pilots yielded

10-20% improvements in replenishment time, representing substantial savings for all participants.[13]

Procter & Gamble believed that it was a doing a good job at implementing existing supply-chain management techniques, but wanted to try new things to see if it could improve further. So it chartered BiosGroup, a joint venture between Cap Gemini Ernst & Young and Nobel Prize winner Stuart Kaufmann, to apply complexity science to optimizing its supply network. BiosGroup developed a series of agent-based studies, which use models of the behavior of the many elements of the supply chain, and examine what happens when key variables or policies are changed. One of the studies looked at Procter & Gamble's policy of trying to wait until trucks were fully loaded before sending them to their clients. The models suggested that sending partially full trucks and pallets would reduce safety stock levels, and field experiments confirmed the results, providing immediate efficiency gains.

BiosGroup is also developing supply network software in conjunction with enterprise software vendor SAP. This allows multiple players in a supply network to gain a far better view of forthcoming deliveries. SAP software already has a feature "available to promise", that can be used to allow clients to see both what is currently in stock, and expected to be available. If clients can also see how that stock depends in turn on that company's suppliers, and gain insight into their production situations, they are able to make far better management decisions. Getting both the systems and the cooperation to share information within a supply chain can result in far greater efficiencies for all participants.

Embracing the networks

Ingram Micro is one of the largest computer product distributors worldwide. It has consistently played a leadership role in its industry, first by founding the Global Technology Distribution Council, which brought together 14 of the largest firms in the business, with a combined revenue of almost $100 billion, and then driving the formation and development of RosettaNet, the standards body for the computer manufacturing industry.

In the mid-1990s Ingram found that it—along with its major customers, suppliers, and competitors—was suffering from high and escalating costs due to massive inefficiencies in the industry. Less than one third of computer parts had the same product code across all distributors—the rest needed to be ordered in different ways depending on who you bought them from. Lack of detailed information on products resulted in frequent and costly returns. Distributors had to work with different system interfaces for every supplier and client they worked with. As a result, up to half of the resources of resellers were absorbed by their back-office operations, much of it consisting of learning the different interfaces and procedures for each partner with which they dealt.[14] In addition, Ingram was manually adding 120,000 new products to its databases annually, soaking up significant resources that each of its competitors duplicated.

Ingram responded to these problems by implementing an extranet that connected thousands of suppliers and resellers to its information systems, but it quickly realized that this was inadequate. In order to get the cost savings and process improvements it sought, an industry-wide initiative was needed. To get it off the ground, Ingram first had to build a consensus among both the manufacturers and other distributors that this kind of industry collaboration was worthwhile and merited a significant investment of time and resources. Together with a few other key industry participants, it worked on defining the planned scope of RosettaNet, and convened the first board meeting in early 1998. The only two full-time executives at RosettaNet for the first two years were both loaned from Ingram.[15]

While Ingram provided the initial push to establish RosettaNet, it is now an industry initiative, and because it must progress by consensus among the participants, the pace necessarily becomes slower than if it were driven by a single company. Ingram still plays a leadership role within RosettaNet, which is positive in helping move the initiative forward, but must be balanced with allowing other members to feel a full sense of participation and ownership. Despite the major distributors being fierce competitors in the marketplace, they have all been very open, reports Michael Terrell, senior vice-president of Ingram Micro Logistics and a former RosettaNet board member. Hamilton—another major technology distributor—shared freely with other RosettaNet members the detailed results of an extensive study on return on investment, showing fabulous paybacks.

Establishing standards for data formats and processes is certainly resulting in substantial cost savings for everyone in the technology supply chain, however at the same time it dramatically changes industry dynamics. The distributors are essentially "middlemen," so making the flow of information far easier can jeopardize their traditional role, creating the possibility of manufacturers selling directly to end-customers. The advent of Dell's direct-to-customer business model has been just one of the major shifts in the industry. In addition to its work on RosettaNet, Ingram is now endeavoring to shape the future of technology distribution, and its role within it.

Ingram regularly brings together product manufacturers and other key industry players in structured conferences to discuss the industry as a whole, Ingram's current initiatives, and the changing role of the distributor. It knows it won't be able to survive indefinitely by continuing to provide the same services, so it engages the manufacturers in open and honest conversations about the value created by different participants in the supply chain, what new business models are emerging, and their relative roles in these. Part of these initiatives is in effect education for its partners that are seeking their own path through a rapidly-changing world, and part is sparking the conversations out of which the new shape of the industry will emerge. Ingram's approach is to be proactive in initiating industry change rather than having to respond to it.

You have seen that the economy is all about connecting and integrating with others. It is not simply a question of linking more closely with customers and suppliers just when it is necessary, but of shifting to a new mode of embracing the networks, of participating fully by actively integrating with other firms. Those who lead within their networks will create value for all participants, but for themselves more than others. Ingram's top management has understood this, and by positioning the firm as an industry leader they are maximizing shareholder value in a challenging environment, at the same time as having a broader economic impact. There are four key steps that companies must take to embrace the networks and play a true industry leadership role, as shown in Table 3-1.

PROVIDING INDUSTRY LEADERSHIP

1. Lead your industry towards information standards
2. Enable information flows
3. Establish policies on information sharing
4. Build a culture of transparency

Table 3-1: Action steps to providing industry leadership

1. Lead your industry towards information standards

Ingram Micro's realization that it needed to establish an industry-wide initiative to address the problems it was facing is reflected in almost every industry. As you saw in Chapter 2, companies must distinguish between where they want standards, and where they want to compete. In almost every case it's a no-brainer to seek to make it easier for information to flow within your industry. The industry as a whole will be more efficient and profitable (unless you let clients take all the benefits). Whoever leads initiatives to standardize information exchange and processes has the chance to shape them, understand them better, and quickly exploit emerging opportunities in the new industry configuration. This means firms can create advantage for themselves even as the playing field becomes more level.

> **Whoever leads initiatives to standardize information exchange and processes has the chance to shape them, understand them better, and quickly exploit emerging opportunities in the new industry configuration.**

Trying to build consensus in an industry group including fierce competitors can be a slow and painful task. The first step is to establish who will benefit in what ways, and convince them of the opportunity. Clients and suppliers may often benefit as much or more than direct industry participants, so their support can help to drive the process. You need to examine not only where costs can be saved, but what the potential impact on industry structure might be. The case for establishing an industry initiative needs to be built, and critical mass gained through the participation of leading players by marketshare or reputation.

Any standards body must be seen as independent, and working in all members' interests. However there is the constant danger of getting bogged down in technicalities and minor disagreements, and someone has to continually reinforce the vision of what's possible. RosettaNet has progressed considerably more slowly than initially envisaged. The immense complexities of the $1 trillion industry, as well as the reluctance of some members to be fully open, have made progress sometimes painstaking, despite real successes such as a broadly implemented standardized order management process. The potential cost savings of between 2% and 10% of each company's revenue make the initiative enormously worthwhile, but to make that happen will require vigorous ongoing support from key participants.[16]

2. Enable information flows

Engaging fully in the network economy is based on the ability to allow information to flow where it needs. This is largely a technology issue, but at the same time often requires process changes in the organization. Extranets can provide external partners with access to a full range of information about their relationship, however this requires not only linking the relevant internal systems to web publishing software, but also ensuring that the information is kept up-to-date. For example many professional services firms provide clients with websites so they can track current billings. This only works if timesheets are completed and posted regularly. Getting lawyers and consultants to shift from monthly reporting on their time usage to daily or even weekly can be a major challenge. However it may be worthwhile, both in providing better service to clients, as well as in streamlining processes. Often, developing better information systems in order to service clients better results in significantly improved information for internal management purposes.

Collaborative technologies, including online workspaces such as eRoom and peer-to-peer systems like Groove, can streamline an immense range of work taking place within and across organizations. Implementing these systems and getting staff familiar with them will allow them to be applied whenever they prove useful. Establishing effective systems security is critical; this will be discussed in more detail in Chapter 4.

As you saw in the case of Herman Miller earlier in this chapter, companies must think through all of the realities of establishing information sharing systems and processes. You need to be aware of what types of systems your partners use, and what their capabilities are for implementing new approaches. In most situations you should be prepared to design processes to integrate well with those of your partners. If you try to force others to do business your way, it is less likely to happen, and far less likely to happen effectively. Training both of your own staff and those of your partners is often an important part of enabling external information flows.

3. Establish policies on information sharing

Former Intel chairman Andy Grove loudly proclaims that "only the paranoid survive," yet Intel has always actively shared sensitive information with its favored business partners—it's the only way it could bring products to market ahead of its competitors. While it is absolutely essential to share information in order to participate in the network economy, that's not to say you should publish your client list and product development pipeline on the Internet. The issue is establishing boundaries for what you share with whom, what remains proprietary, and how you attempt to manage the flow of valuable information.

Companies usually implicitly have "most-favored" partners with which they share information more openly. One approach is to formally classify partners—be they clients, suppliers, or others—by the degree of access they are provided to information. Many of the decisions on specific issues will need to be ad-hoc, but providing guidelines on what level of information is available to different groups of partners can be very valuable. Ultimately it comes down to trust, as we will explore further in the next chapter. Do you trust partners to use your information with discretion, and not pass it on to third parties? That trust will depend on many factors, but largely your previous experience with them. The reality is there is often a Mexican stand-off between companies—each waits for the other to disclose valuable information first. Industry leaders will tend to open up first as a gesture of goodwill, having calculated the risks, and will often see trust in the relationship accelerate. Silicon Valley executives joke that they can never go to a meeting with first signing an NDA—a Non-Disclosure Agreement—but it is certainly an important tool in helping contain the flow of sensitive information in both new and existing relationships.

The very fact of establishing information policies, however informally, helps employees to be aware of the issues in sharing information. It is a fine balancing act between opening the firm to engage in the network economy, and protecting its valuable intellectual assets. Boundaries do need to be put in place, however those firms that tend towards more open information flow will have a major competitive advantage. It enables them to become deeply entrenched in creating value with partners, rather than vainly attempting to work alone.

4. Build a culture of transparency

The technology and processes may be in place to share information with clients and partners, but unless the internal culture is one of being willing to share outside the organization, it will never happen. Often this requires a significant shift. Building collaboration within organizations is a challenge many firms are facing. It's even harder outside the organization. As in any culture change initiative, clear, consistent, repeated messages from leadership are essential. Top management needs to say what they expect, behave in line with that, and support those messages with appropriate recognition and rewards. Any new ways of working need to be encouraged through allowing staff to try systems in a non-threatening way, hearing success stories from their peers, and getting internal evangelists to promote new approaches.

Ketchum PR is one the top ten public relations firm worldwide. While it is wholly owned by communications conglomerate Omnicon, its 29 offices worldwide employing 1500 people comprise a mixed bag of wholly owned, minority owned, and exclusive affiliate firms. After implementing an award-winning intranet portal for knowledge sharing and collaboration, Ketchum sought to take the benefits to its clients. Just by selectively opening parts of its intranet to clients, it immediately gave access to collaborative spaces and parts of Ketchum's global knowledge base, customized for the user. Billings and other ongoing project information helped to increase the transparency for clients.

Clearly Ketchum is well ahead of the curve in providing these valuable facilities to its clients. However it found it was encountering the same issue as almost every firm that is implementing technology to provide transparency to its clients: professionals were frequently reluctant to share information and have their work exposed to the client throughout the process. Paul McKeon, Ketchum's chief ebusiness officer during the system's development, describes the issue as letting the client watch how they "make sausage", opening up the kitchen and allowing them to see that the process can be sloppy along the way. Getting professionals to first use the online applications for internal collaboration allowed them to become comfortable with the systems, and discover the benefits for themselves. As they gradually become more familiar with the new ways of working, hear about success stories throughout the global network, and are provided with incentives to participate, Ketchum teams are becoming far more willing to share work-in-progress with clients, get their input, and immerse them far deeper in the entire process of developing campaigns. For example even simple tools that allow executives at Ketchum's client to vote on their preferred names or logos during the development process can make them feel far more involved, and result in better project outcomes, faster.

Vital Connections: Chapter 3

In this chapter, you have seen how digital connectivity is resulting in a massive blurring of organizational boundaries. To be successful in this world, companies must lead their customers and partners into new kinds of relationships, based on transparency, collaboration, and sharing value.

One of the vital success factors for this is trust, which in the hyper-connected economy is actually increasing in importance. Chapter 4 describes how trust is changing, and how to be more effective in developing trusting relationships with your customers and partners. As information overload swamps us all, businesspeople must learn how to earn their customers' and partners' attention.

Building Trust and Attention in the Tangled Web

Connectivity allows companies to integrate their systems more deeply and form many more business ties, but these opportunities are often neglected. In an increasingly transparent world, trust is becoming more rather than less important, and organizations must take steps to develop trusting relationships with their partners. The one scarce resource today is attention, so you must earn it from your clients and partners in order to create and maintain profitable relationships.

The bitterly cold winds coming off Lake Erie can make winter in Cleveland, Ohio an ordeal. Besides the more prosaic problems of living in a frigid climate, sports fields can become almost unusable due to grass dying and the ground freezing, creating slippery, dangerous playing conditions. So the Cleveland Browns professional football team, for their new stadium completed in 1999, incorporated an underground heating system. Ten inches below the ground, nearly 40 miles of tubing carries 7,000 gallons of a heat transfer fluid created by Dow Chemical. Dow's products touch the lives of almost everyone, but are largely invisible to consumers, as they are mainly used in our infrastructure and to manufacture goods with which we are more familiar.

Dow Chemical has been regarded as an e-business leader in its industry since it established one of the first commercial websites in 1994. It has placed a high priority on enhancing relationships with its clients and suppliers. MyAccount@Dow is an online service provided for Dow clients, that includes order entry and payment, full account information, and detailed product information. In addition, it allows collaboration with Dow staff, with the ability not only to exchange documents in a common workspace, but also to share PC desktops, including simultaneous viewing of applications and Internet browsers. With its larger clients, Dow seeks to link its information systems even more closely, providing direct links and integration. For example, since 1993 it has applied telemetry—making measures at a distance—to gauge how much of its products remain in clients' tanks, and automatically reorder when they need replenishment.

At the same time as Dow has enabled deep information links with its clients, it has also been very active in establishing and joining online exchanges. Just two of these are Omnexus and Elemica, covering the plastics and chemicals industries respectively. Both bring together the major suppliers in its industry, provide a neutral marketplace for buyers to compare offerings, and unlike many other online exchanges, are geared to long-term contracts rather than one-off transactions.. Omnexus—whose other founders include BASF, Bayer, and DuPont—has created common specifications for products, making it easy for clients to find and select alternative suppliers, and provides full order tracking through to payment. Elemica enables multiple suppliers to integrate their enterprise information systems with those of their clients, using a single XML-based interface. For clients, this means they only need to enable information sharing with one external partner—the exchange—rather than implementing it separately with each of their suppliers.

The global networks are in essence an ever-expanding set of relationships. Relationships between people; relationships between companies; relationships between individuals, companies, and governments. Dow's initiatives illustrate two of the most powerful shifts in business relationships that go with the awakening of the network economy. The first is that there is the potential for far *deeper* relationships. As you saw in Chapter 3, companies are now routinely integrating and sharing their processes with other companies, rather than simply buying or selling goods and services. Relationships are most valuable when they deeply enmesh firms together rather than when they are limited to flows of goods and money. The second key shift is that technology now readily enables

> **More than ever, true relationships are not founded simply on digital connectivity, but on two very human drivers. These are *trust* and *attention*.**

a *broader* set of relationships, encompassing ties with a greater number and diversity of partners. Companies can easily deal with many more clients or suppliers without stretching their resources.[1]

The hyper-connected economy is emerging precisely from this powerful shift to both deeper and broader relationships. At the same time, the standards that underlie the networks mean that it is increasingly easy for individuals and companies to switch their allegiances. Connectivity certainly enables deeper and broader relationships, but it also can make them briefer and more tenuous. More than ever, true relationships are not founded simply on digital connectivity, but on two very human drivers. These are *trust* and *attention*. In this chapter we will examine their important role, and how to develop them in a networked world.

Unlike information and digital connectivity, trust and attention are scarce resources. The time and effort required to develop a high degree of mutual trust, together with the reality of the bounds of human attention, result in limitations to companies' and people's ability to form ever-deeper and broader relationships. In fact, the value of closer relationships increases all the time. Every company has a relatively small group of customers and critical suppliers that contribute the most to its profitability. These are the ones with which they must develop a high degree of mutual trust, and earn a substantial proportion of their limited attention. The lion's share of the rewards will go to the companies that can achieve this, regardless of how well their competitors can provide technology-based tools and integration.

Companies like Pfizer, MCI, and KLM Royal Dutch Airlines have realized that relationships rule inside as well as outside organizations. It is now standard practice to run internal service functions exactly the same as if their clients were outside the organization. Information technology, human resources, strategic planning, and many other corporate functions now have to sell their services internally, manage the relationships, and charge market rates for their offerings. Increasingly, their clients—other divisions or departments within the same company—are being given the choice as to whether they buy internally or find better alternatives outside the firm.

Easy integration and lower transaction costs make this perfectly feasible. Clearly internal service departments have an immense head start in building trust and understanding their internal clients well enough to capture their attention, but they must approach relationship development in just the same way as their external competitors.

Developing trust in the living networks

Paper has far from disappeared in the digital age. Every day over 800,000 tons of paper is made around the world, with every man, woman, and child in the USA accounting for 320 kilograms of paper production each year. The machines that produce all the paper our economy consumes— newsprint, fine paper, paperboard, and more—are extremely complex. There is no such thing as a standard paper machine—every single one of these massive installations is different, with its own parameters and peculiarities. Running the machines requires highly specialized engineers that understand the complex interplay of machinery, wood pulp, and chemicals that together yield quality paper.

Specialty chemicals firm Buckman Laboratories is headquartered in Memphis, Tennessee, yet two-thirds of its 1,300 employees work outside the corporate headquarters, servicing the paper, leather, utilities, and chemical processing industries around the world. While it is a chemicals manufacturer, the provision of products is a relatively small part of the value it offers. For its paper and pulp clients, its process treatment programs assist with paper pitch control, deinking, drainage, and a host of other issues faced by papermakers. Rather than simply selling the necessary chemicals to its clients, its sales engineers seek to make Buckman part of their operations. Buckman's job becomes one of understanding the system and production requirements, selecting the chemicals and amounts needed, and advising on their use within the production process.

Tumut, a picturesque town set in the foothills of Australia's Snowy Mountains, was the site chosen by paper manufacturer Visy Industries for a new paper mill constructed in 2001. The mill was designed to rely only on sustainable inputs, and is claimed to use the least amount of water per tonne of pulp produced of any facility worldwide. Buckman was selected to deliver "Total Chemical Management" to the plant, providing the chemicals, managing and optimizing processes, and performing quality control. Its role covered what would normally require dozens of suppliers, and substantial in-house resources from Visy to select chemicals and manage sophisticated processes. Visy is paying Buckman on the basis of selected key performance indicators such as production levels and quality measures, with potential penalties as well as rewards depending on mill performance.

The kinds of relationships that Buckman has with its clients clearly require a high degree of mutual trust. Any trust-based relationship is built on the basis of reputation and consistent experience. Buckman has also recognized the importance of deliberately aligning its clients' processes and ways of working with its own, and when it wins a new client, it runs a clearly defined one-week process it calls a "transition workshop," to streamline the shift from the existing suppliers to Buckman. An initial 45-minute workshop for all key personnel at the client facilities goes through the week's agenda and raises initial concerns. The Buckman team then conducts personal interviews with every participant, identifying specific projects, requirements, measurements, and concerns. These are compiled into an implementation plan, jointly owned by Buckman and the client, that identifies tasks and responsibilities across the two companies, using the terminology of plant staff. Through the week, Buckman staff work in the evenings to develop the implementation plan, and there are always cold drinks and snacks available for any plant staff who wish to observe or participate. Personal relationships are built with all key staff during the exercise, and all issues and concerns are brought out and addressed.

Buckman works by integrating its processes deeply with those of its client, however it understands that this is largely an issue of people forming relationships with other people. It has developed the technologies that enable it to bring its global resources to bear on its clients' issues, and used them to earn their attention. All of this requires trust, and Buckman is effective at developing and maintaining trust with its clients through applying clear processes, as well as having a culture that encourages its clients' faith. In Chapter 6 we will look in more detail at how Buckman has developed its knowledge-sharing culture.

Trust is a business perennial—from the days when chickens were traded for cowrie shells until we start trading with extraterrestrial races, trust has been and always will be the central factor in business relationships. However in the networked world there are three vital shifts in the nature and role of trust.

- **Trustworthiness is swiftly becoming more transparent.** We are now all naked—there is no hiding in the network economy. Your reputation will increasingly precede you as the flow of information through the networks rapidly increases. In the old days someone might have made a few phone calls to try to sound out others' experience with a potential supplier or partner. Now consumers and businesspeople can quickly and easily gather a broad spectrum of experiences and impressions about almost any company in the world.

• **The pace of trust development is being outstripped by technology.** We are entering a "plug-and-play" world, in which businesses can readily integrate their information, processes, and systems. In the past, the pace of developing trust between organizations was accompanied by the practical issues of bringing the firms' operations together. The development of trust often happened as a natural side-effect of working together closely on these kinds of issues. Now companies can integrate their systems and share information far more easily, but that is useless unless solid mutual trust is in place.

• **It has become a key competitive factor to be fast and effective at developing trust with partners.** As the technology landscape becomes more of a level playing field, trust becomes the key differentiating factor. Your products and services can be outstanding, and your processes for sharing information with partners excellent, but unless you can command a high level of trust, you are unlikely to be successful. In the network economy relationships are formed ever-faster, and unless you can build a high level of trust quickly, you will never be considered a top-tier supplier or partner.

Trust in a transparent world

eBay one of those rarities: a highly profitable pure ebusiness. At the heart of its success are its feedback ratings, that compile ratings and comments from all auction participants on the people they have dealt with. The simple principle of eBay is a global marketplace that can link anyone, anywhere. That's enormously valuable, but the problem is you know nothing about the people you're dealing with. Who's to say they won't deliver faulty goods or try to defraud you? eBay's feedback ratings allow you to benefit from the accumulated experience of others.

Collaborative rating systems are being applied to every kind of product and service. Customer ratings were pioneered by Amazon.com and others, and are now standard on e-commerce sites. Zagat has provided restaurant guides based on the feedback of customers instead of professional reviewers since 1979. Now that they have released Internet and Palm Pilot versions of the service, the usability and ease of contributing reviews brings in more comments, makes the feedback cycle far faster, and improves the overall quality of the reviews.

Clearly there are potential problems with simple ratings systems, which can easily be abused by enlisting friends, or by people who hold a grudge. Increasingly sophisticated systems are being evolved that provide more balanced feedback, for example by rating the quality of the raters themselves. Now these types of systems are being applied in the corporate world.

MIT professor Pattie Maes is famous both for developing the first generation of collaborative rating systems, initially focused on music opinions, and for being nominated as one of the world's 50 most beautiful people by People magazine. Maes and her colleagues recognized that bringing together many companies' experience of their suppliers would be a valuable resource for other firms trying to select trustworthy partners. Thus was born Open Ratings. The company offers "predictive supplier performance" systems, working in conjunction with Dun & Bradstreet to provide reports on prospective suppliers. Key concerns, such as suppliers' delivery timelineness, customer support, and responsiveness, are rated by recent customers, covering all the issues that contribute to the total cost of purchase. Highly evolved systems provide a balanced view of this feedback, and how to apply it in purchasing decisions.

> **The genie is out of the bottle. Your strategies for building trust in your customers and partners must be based on the reality of working in a transparent world.**

It's increasingly difficult to hide problems and issues from your customers. Some companies choose to provide discussion forums about their products and services on their own websites. For those that don't—and even many that do—independent discussion sites spring up. Many potential customers routinely look for comments from their peers about products and services they are considering purchasing, or even post specific questions to get feedback from people they would never have met otherwise.

The genie is out of the bottle. Your strategies for building trust in your customers and partners must be based on the reality of working in a transparent world. You can try to control the messages people receive about your company, but if you do you will fail. You can no longer hide. More than ever, honesty is the best policy. At the same time, you can easily research potential suppliers or partners before you start to deal with them. You can expect firms to be more trustworthy, simply because they will find it very hard to survive if they aren't. Those that have bad experiences can easily let other potential customers know. In Chapter 6 you will learn how to approach marketing and branding when information flows freely in the networks.

Accelerating trust development

Participating in the network economy requires very actively developing new and existing relationships with customers, suppliers, and partners. As you saw earlier in this chapter, companies' external relationships are becoming both deeper and broader. Some firms do whatever seems right each time they take on a new customer, supplier, or alliance partner. Others have careful and detailed processes for building closer relationships that benefit both parties. IBM spends almost $1 billion on its alliance program for software developers, getting its return through the generation of over $4 billion in additional sales. It has a formal 40-step process that executives must go through with potential partners before signing an alliance agreement, including examining the fit with IBM, and getting a senior IBM executive to agree to act as an internal sponsor for the alliance.[2]

On the other hand, in high-value professional services such as accounting or investment banking, many firms celebrate winning an account or major client transaction with a boozy dinner, but have no clear processes for actively developing trust and deepening relationships with these accounts. Each industry and situation will call for a different approach to trust development. However since the ability to develop trust faster and deeper with new clients and partners is becoming a key competitive differentiator, it is not something that can be left to chance. There are four key steps in accelerating the development of deep trust in relationships, as shown in Table 4-1.

ACCELERATING TRUST DEVELOPMENT

1. Establish an overt trust development program
2. Create transparency
3. Treat security as a business enabler
4. Streamline legal issues
5. Work to align objectives, culture, and technology

Table 4-1: Action steps to accelerating trust development

1. Establish an overt trust development program

One of the most powerful actions to develop strong trust quickly with partners is simply to openly discuss the issue. Frank conversations can vastly accelerate the process. The first step is to raise trust as a key issue, and together talk about the potential benefits of developing strong mutual trust. You and your clients, suppliers, and partners can together certainly gain far greater value from higher levels of trust, but you need to define the specific activities and ventures that will be made possible by this. Once you start to identify clear opportunities that will depend on mutual trust, this creates a stronger drive towards accelerating trust development, and helps to clearly establish the risks and concerns that prevent these happening immediately. Once you and your partner understand where you want to go with your relationship, and the perceived risks in doing so, you can agree on a staged program for both parties to gain the necessary confidence to build a truly collaborative relationship. This kind of process is very useful across every kind of high-value relationship, however it should be approached slightly differently depending on the situation. For suppliers seeking to develop a relationship with a powerful client, the initial emphasis may be a more one-sided effort to demonstrate the potential value of higher trust levels, and getting clients to precisely articulate their concerns so these can be addressed.

Ultimately, deep trust comes from the repeated experience of positive expectations being met. As such, a trust development program must set a sequence of expectations for both sides. An initial workshop will not only establish where the program is going, but also a series of highly specific commitments from each side. Fulfilling these—or sometimes even the frank communication of reasons why they weren't met—will deepen trust that future commitments will also be met. Trust is all about taking risks. In building trust you need to take a series of steps that each stretch the willingness of your partner to take a risk with you. Every time a risk is taken and trust is shown to be merited, it allows you to move a step further. Expecting too much trust initially can break the relationship—the process must be staged. Depending on the nature of the relationship, regular workshops can be run to review whether the commitments have been achieved, make adjustments to the program, and recognize the activities have been enabled by higher trust levels. Often discussion of the trust development program will be incorporated into the agenda of other regular meetings.

In one case, the European operations of a multinational chemical company worked through a series of workshops with its major client, helping to bring out unspoken concerns, and eventually establish an information sharing initiative with strong mutual benefits. One of the issues that became clear to the chemical firm through the process was the importance of addressing the internal politics of its client.[3] The involvement and interaction of key stakeholders in your partner organizations can enable or derail the trust development process.

2. Create transparency
In today's economy, trust increasingly depends on transparency. Clients or partners may choose not to become closely familiar with every aspect of their external relationships, but the knowledge that they can access and become involved in details provides a solid foundation for trust. This is not just about information systems, but the ability to walk into partner firms, see what is being done, and have frank discussions.

Call center operator Convergys expects executives from its clients to drop in at any time to observe its day-to-day workings and gather information and insights on its work for them. As described in Chapter 9, contract electronics manufacturer Flextronics provides complete transparency on every aspect of its operations to its clients. They have access to the same information systems as Flextronics, and can become involved to any level of detail that they choose in the outsourced operations.

3. Treat security as a business enabler

Systems security should be treated as a business enabler, not as a problem. Security is an absolutely vital issue in a connected world, because so much can go wrong. As companies become increasingly dependent on their information system, and confidentiality and privacy become their legal responsibilities, they will tend to avoid unknown risks. Potential customers or partners will only be prepared to deal with you if they trust that your systems are secure, and that their information and computers are not exposed in any way as a result of doing business with you. Similarly, you won't choose to establish deep relationships involving systems integration or confidential information flows unless you are fully confident in your partners' security. Security issues must be dealt with as a starting point to all trusting, collaborative relationships. However if security is demonstrably sound, it allows a higher level of trust with partners, deeper integration of systems, and in turn real competitive advantage.

Whenever companies exchange information directly, other than through e-mail or website access, they need to engage in a frank discussion about security issues. This is essentially a form of "due diligence," which may include exchanging written security policies, and identifying precisely what technology and policies are in place to safeguard information and systems. Firewalls should be designed to let through only specific traffic, and monitor even trusted clients' communication, in case their systems have been successfully breached by a hacker. Encryption of sensitive information should be standard practice.

Virtual Private Networks (VPNs) are specifically designed to provide privileged access to trusted third parties, making the public Internet safe by creating an encrypted "tunnel" for information flow. These types of systems should be actively implemented for all significant relationships, as they make information flow both easier and more secure, enhancing the ability to create value together, and creating an advantage over competitors. Physical tokens, such as smart cards, can be used along with passwords to make both you and your customers more confident in information security.

4. Streamline legal issues

Trust always trumps legal agreements. You can try to pin down details in long contracts, but without trust there are major limitations to how much mutual value you can create in relationships. However in most cases legal contracts provide a useful foundation to build strong, trusting relationships, especially in the early stages. Perkin-Elmer and MDS Sciex, in establishing their alliance entity Perkin-Elmer Sciex in 1986, set up a basic legal agreement at the outset, but the two firms have never drawn on the documents in resolving issues along the way.[4] Baird Textile learned the value of legal contracts when British retailer Marks & Spencer, which accounted for 30-40% of its sales, suddenly terminated its relationship after

30 years without a legal agreement, despite the retailer openly describing the relationship as a partnership. Baird took Marks & Spencer to court, but lost.[5]

Another approach that can sometimes have value in the early stages of a relationship is bonding, in which one or more parties deposits a bond with a trustee. If any of a specified list of conditions is breached, the bond is forfeited. The problems are in designing an effective bonding contract, and being able to prove that it has been broken. Clearly bonding does not build trust in itself, but it can help to create the conditions for faster initial trust development.

5. Work to align objectives, culture, and technology

Companies need to ensure that they are working in the same direction and communicating effectively. It is very hard to engage deeply unless each party clearly understands the other's objectives from the relationship. Aligning objectives requires designing a partnership so that the same activities contribute to each participant's desired outcomes. Procter & Gamble, when it sets up collaborative supply chain initiatives with retailers Wal-mart, Tesco, and others, begins by establishing and documenting high-level agreements on each party's objectives for the projects.

Often different cultures and ways of communicating can result in unnecessary misunderstandings. Interactive media firm Giant Step hires staff from its major clients' industries, and publishes a glossary of terms for its staff and clients to use. It gives this to its clients, and encourages them as well as its relationship managers to keep it on hand during conversations. Since the Internet world generates an immense amount of jargon, with often different meanings ascribed to the same words, this helps ensure that confusion is minimized. In the following section we will look in more detail at the issue of aligning technology with your clients and partners.

The power of aligning technology

FMC Corporation is a diversified manufacturer of chemicals and machinery that employs over 15,000 people. It operates 90 manufacturing plants and mines in 25 countries; its 10 business units deal with an immense array of customers, suppliers, and partners. According to chief information officer Ed Flynn, FMC is finding that its proactive approach to integrating its information systems with those of its clients is helping them view FMC as a partner rather than a supplier of commodity products.

In one early initiative, FMC has fully integrated its enterprise resource planning systems with a key client, PQ Corporation, that purchases soda ash from FMC. Both firms use SAP software, which assisted in linking the functionality of the two companies' systems over the Internet, partly through the software's ability to convert documents into an XML format. Once the secure flow of information over the Internet between the systems was in place, they were able to directly link PQ's purchase order module with FMC's order process. When PQ's manufacturing system generates a purchase order for soda ash or other products, it links to FMC's system to check that inventory is available, and automatically initiates shipping. Once the goods are received payment is made by automatic funds transfer. The integration of the firms' systems makes it easier, faster, and less costly to do business for both parties.[6] This pilot program was then duplicated across other FMC clients.

FMC is leveraging its leadership in information systems and providing external links to gain new clients and generate more business. Many of its clients in the food and pharmaceutical industries are studying ways of applying information technologies to increase efficiency. On numerous occasions FMC's chief information officer or members of his technology team have accompanied FMC salespeople to discuss with potential clients not only the benefits of integrating their information systems into those of FMC, but also broader strategic technology issues. This creates value for clients, and clearly establishes FMC's intent of being a true partner rather than simply a supplier of chemicals.

Relationships today largely consist of information flows. This means that aligning technology with customers, suppliers, and partners is vitally important. For the relatively simple requirements of consumer markets, the Internet provides a standard platform that makes technology integration usually fairly straightforward. However the diversity of hardware and software used in the market can still result in challenges. Banks that require their customers to load software on their computer to access online banking have to decide whether to provide a version for Apple computers. California's Wells Fargo has chosen to do so, but BankDirect.com has decided not to offer connectivity to Quicken financial software for Apple Macintosh.

In almost all corporate relationships, technology alignment now plays a central role in business development and relationship management. The issue is ensuring that information can readily flow between different firms's systems, and processes can be integrated. The trading arm of investment bank Credit Suisse First Boston (CSFB) buys and sells securities on behalf of its institutional and corporate clients. Its PrimeTrade trading platform was the first Internet-based system to allow clients to trade US Treasury bonds; it now provides access to a range of financial instruments, including foreign exchange and derivatives. It's easy for a CSFB salesperson to set up a client to use PrimeTrade, simply by putting the appropriate agreements in place and providing a password for access. What is harder is to get information about transactions to flow automatically into the client's systems. Straight Through Processing (STP) describes financial market transactions and the related payments being executed and processed without human intervention. Even in the information age, this is the exception rather than the norm, because it still usually requires a one-off effort to integrate two or more firms' information systems. CSFB's technical staff work closely with the firm's clients to establish straight-through processing between the companies' systems, making it more attractive to use PrimeTrade to trade securities than other alternatives. The core of the work performed is a technical integration project. However part of the exercise is discussing technology strategies with the client, and ensuring that as both companies continue to implement new systems, they will be aligned rather than incompatible.

> **For better or for worse, the whole world is becoming like Las Vegas. The one scarce resource in the economy today is attention.**

It used to be possible to lock clients in with proprietary technology. Once they had bought your systems, they had to either continue the relationship, or throw everything out and start again from scratch. As standards increasingly dominate the technology landscape, very few clients are prepared to accept proprietary solutions. In theory this means that clients can readily switch providers, but there are still usually real costs in moving. The firms that have helped them to establish effective systems integration have a real advantage. More important is the ongoing discussion of technology strategy. Once you get involved in your clients' technology directions, you can ensure that your systems—and your relationship—are effectively aligned.

Sticky relationships in the attention economy

Viva Las Vegas! In this happy town, you can be fabulously entertained without a dollar in your pocket. In the space of a short stroll down the famed Strip, you can see the statue at Caesar's Palace come to life, a live re-enactment of a pirate attack on a ship outside Treasure Island, a volcano exploding in front of Mirage, live circus acts all around at Circus Circus, while the highest rollercoaster in the world, over 100 stories above the ground, screams by on the top of the Stratosphere tower. The casinos offer free food and drinks, with sometimes free entertainment thrown in. While the patrons at Excalibur dig into their dinners, sparks fly from the live jousting on stage. At every turn there is something bigger and brighter and more dazzling than the last thing you saw.

What's going on here? The casinos know that if you walk into their premises with money in your wallet, there's a good chance you'll leave some of it—maybe even all of it!—in their welcoming coffers. So they will do anything to attract your attention, get you to visit, have you linger briefly, and then maybe you will wander over and sit down for a moment at the gaming tables. Every casino's games are the same. The field of play in Las Vegas is creating something more spectacular than everything else, in order to grab people's attention, and in the process, the contents of their wallets.

For better or for worse, the whole world is becoming like Las Vegas. The one scarce resource in the economy today is attention. Adults can pay attention to only one thing at a time, and even today's multi-tasking kids have their limits. There is immensely greater demand for people's attention than there is time in the day. As a result, an inalienable part of life in contemporary society is choosing what to pay attention to from a relentless barrage of information and impressions.

A business cannot sell anything until it has first gained a potential customer's attention. Today just to get that it must pull out all stops. And more often than not, after it has won a sale, it's back to scratch in trying to attract the customer's attention again. Past the battle for attention is the battle for relationships. You may be able to attract someone's attention through the maelstrom, yet can you keep it? To do this, you must be part of the solution rather than part of the problem. Everyone is drowning in the flood of information overload, and those that can throw a useful lifeline will find ample takers.

We all demonstrate consistent patterns of behavior in the way we access and use information. And, in fact, all relationships can be thought of as simply a set of patterns or habits. When you repeatedly buy from a particular shop—be it online or one in which you can accidentally knock fragile things off the shelf—this is a pattern called a relationship. Now that information flow is at the heart of our world, our daily behaviors are increasingly centered on finding and using information. The patterns in how we access and use information form a central role in almost all business relationships. In many industries, the field of play has become the ability to form information relationships with customers, to be a regular and trusted source of information for them. This is now virtually the only way to maintain people's attention. You need both to continually improve at servicing your customers with high-value information, and to do it in ways that competitors will find difficult to replicate.

Personalization is the driver. If you can provide information that is more useful and relevant to an individual than he or she can find elsewhere, you will command his or her attention. There are powerful feedback loops at work here, as illustrated in Figure 4-1. Once you gain customer knowledge and the ability to personalize information effectively, you can capture more of their attention and interaction. This in turn—if you have effective systems—allows you to learn more about your customers and enhance your personalization. Since there are always greater demands on people's attention, you must continually build deeper information relationships in this way, otherwise you risk losing their attention completely. However if you are effective at this cycle, you can effectively lock your customers into your information relationship, as they will lose the invaluable personalized information your provide if they switch to a competitor. In Chapter 6 we will look in more detail at customer feedback loops, of which this is one example

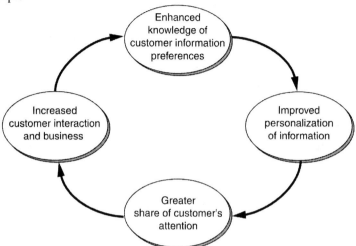

Figure 4-1: The feedback loop of customer attention and personalization.

Precision personalization

Step into the four-floor Levi's superstore in San Francisco, and among the many delights you will find some old personalization technologies. Customers can put on their new jeans, then sit in a tub heated to 100 F, thoughtfully provided with rubber duckies to play with as they wait. When the jeans have shrunk to fit them perfectly, they take them off and stick them into a nearby clothes dryer, and can stroll off home with jeans contoured to their body alone. Levi's and other clothes manufacturers are now investigating laser scanning booths, that will scan your body and produce specifications for custom-made clothes. These systems may produce better results than the old approaches, but they probably won't be as fun.

Personalizing information can be a little trickier. People often don't know what they're interested in until they see it. At the same time, while computers are marvellous at manipulating information in every way possible, they are far from being able to understand the content of documents. However the technology to personalize information is continually improving, and in any case the current state-of-art is greatly underexploited. There are three levels to technology-based personalization: profiling, inference, and agents.

• **Profiling**. My Yahoo! allows you to build a news page containing just the news sources and categories that interest you. Each of the categories has a little box next to it, and if you check the box by clicking on it, you will see all corresponding updates when you access the service. You can also receive e-mail updates of the news categories you select, as well as stories that match your selected keywords. In these cases, the personalized information sent to you is based on a profile you have defined. This simple approach to personalization can be very useful, however it is limited in that it can't suggest things you don't know about, and it doesn't have the ability to learn. Much of what many companies proudly call personalization consists of basic profiling.

• **Inference.** The reason many people choose to browse—and often buy—on Amazon.com is its book recommendation feature, which makes suggestions for books that may interest you, based on the books that you look at or buy. Inference systems observe your online behaviors and infer what else might interest you. This is usually done by comparing your behavior patterns with those of others. If many people that buy Stephen King books also buy Dean Koontz books, then if you buy a Stephen King book you may be sucker for a special offer on the latest Dean Koontz thriller. This is in fact a type of collaborative filtering—we are benefiting from the research and interests of people we have never met. Text categorization and search software Autonomy uses sophisticated algorithms to compare the word patterns in documents, so it can use what you read to infer other documents that may interest you, based on their content.

• **Agents.** Isn't it nice to have somebody—or something—to go and do work for you? Agents are software that act on behalf of a person by performing a specified task. A simple version can be asked to search online bookstores for a certain book, and tell you where you can buy it at the lowest price. More sophisticated agents can learn your preferences and over time improve at their tasks. However in order to learn your agent needs feedback. This can be *explicit*, in which you input information like "on a scale of one to five, the usefulness of this information is a four." Or it can be *implicit*, in which the software records data such as which files you open, how long you spend reading them, and what you do with them afterwards, without requiring any specific instructions from you.

Each of these three types of technology-based personalization has an important role to play in information relationships. However profiling is static, and can very easily be duplicated by going to another provider and creating the same profile. By now profiling is what it takes to be in the game, rather than providing any competitive differentiation. Inference engines can create substantial value, both by how they are implemented, and by combining the preferences of a particular group of well-informed people. Agents in particular have the potential to lock-in customers to your service. If a customer has spent time training an agent to deliver more useful information, sometimes simply by using it repeatedly, it can become hard to go without. You cannot recreate the ability of agents to personalize in the same way that you can through profiling. As such, agents can be a powerful relationship tool.

Integrating human and digital relationships

Geneva is evidently a place of tradition. The distinguished buildings along the lakefront are all five floors high, presenting a neat and tidy face to the tourists, diplomats, and mega-wealthy that frequent the town. Statues in the cobble-stoned "old town" commemorate how Calvin and other reformers came to the independent city-state to escape persecution. As you wander the streets, an occasional discreet doorway marks the private banks that have played such an important role in Geneva's history. Behind these doors, in this town of less than half a million inhabitants, 14% of the world's transnational wealth is managed.

Private banking offers a prime example of the meeting of tradition and the digital. Private banking relationships are clearly largely about close personal attention, yet at the same time money is information, and in many situations online services and reporting are far more useful than more traditional approaches to banking service. The key issues in this industry—and in many others—are defining the boundaries between digital relationships and full service, and effectively integrating digital and human relationships. Many online services for wealthy individuals have sprung up. JP Morgan provides a comprehensive suite of online reporting and portfolio analysis tools for its private banking clients. HSBC runs a service providing Internet-based financial services to affluent international investors. MyCFO competes with old and venerable institutions by offering a suite of largely digital services for the very wealthy.

The headlong rush over the turn of the century to establish Internet-based services has resulted in many companies having completely different strategies for their existing operations and their new online services. Online relationships and more traditional high-value relationships based on personal interaction are still often considered separately. For those firms that service high-value clients with dedicated relationship managers, the issue has become how to integrate human and digital relationships. It is essential to provide an extremely high level of personalization of service and information delivery to high-value customers. Successfully engaging in the positive feedback loop of gaining attention and improving personalization requires combining the capabilities of technology and professionals.

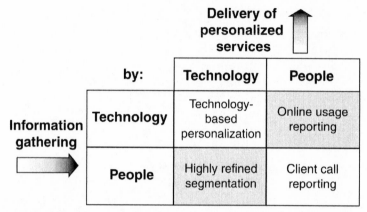

Delivery of personalized services

by:	Technology	People
Technology	Technology-based personalization	Online usage reporting
People	Highly refined segmentation	Client call reporting

Information gathering

Table 4-1: Personalization by integrating digital and human relationships

In order to personalize information flow and services for your clients you must continually gather and apply detailed information on their behaviors and preferences. As shown in Table 4-1, you can gather information in two ways: through technology such as websites or other interactive media, or salespeople's contacts with clients. This information can in turn be applied to the delivery of highly personalized services through both technology, and personal interaction.

There is nothing new about salespeople recording their client interaction and applying the insights to better service. Whether the information gathered is noted on 5" by 3" cards, or stored in a sophisticated customer relationship management (CRM) system, the principle is the same. You saw in the previous section of this chapter how technology-based personalization can be applied. These are both well-established fields of endeavor. What is still largely underaddressed by most companies is fusing people and technology to provide an extraordinary level of personalization to high-value clients.

One approach is to provide salespeople with detailed reports on how their clients are interacting digitally with the firm. For example, if a private banker sees that her client is reading research on a particular investment strategy, a swift phone call to discuss this could result in an order. However clients are increasingly sensitive to feeling watched as they browse on their suppliers' websites. Big Brother looms large for many. As a result, several large banks have told their large institutional and individual clients that they do not provide information on their online behaviors to their salespeople. Every company must establish clear policies for how it will or won't use reporting of its clients' use of its websites, and be prepared to communicate these clearly.

Business

Business.view, our online column on business, appears on Economist.com on Tuesdays. Past and present columns can be viewed at
www.economist.com/businessview

Online social networks

Everywhere and nowhere

SAN FRANCISCO

and privacy watchdogs cried foul. Mark Zuckerberg, Facebook's founder, admitted in December that "we simply did a bad job with this release" and apologised.

So it is entirely conceivable that social networking, like web-mail, will never make oodles of money. That, however, in no way detracts from its enormous utility.

on their users' information, to ensure that they keep coming back. As a result, avid internet users often maintain separate accounts on several social networks, instant-messaging services, photo-sharing and blogging sites, and usually cannot even send simple messages from one to the other. They must invite the same friends to each service separately. It is a drag.

Historically, online media tend to start this way. The early services, such as CompuServe, Prodigy or AOL, began as "walled gardens" before they opened up to become websites. The early e-mail services could send messages only within their own walls (rather as Facebook's messaging does today). Instant-messaging, too, started closed, but is gradually opening up. In social networking, this evolution is just beginning. Parts of the industry are collaborating in a "data portability workgroup" to let people move their friend lists and other information around the web. Others are pushing OpenID, a plan to create a single, federated sign-on system that people can use across many sites.

The opening of social networks may now accelerate thanks to that older next big thing, web-mail. As a technology, mail has come to seem rather old-fashioned. But Google, Yahoo!, Microsoft and other firms are now discovering that they may already have the ideal infrastructure for so-

books, in-boxes and calendars of their users. "E-mail in the wider sense is the most important social network," says David Ascher, who manages Thunderbird, a cutting-edge open-source e-mail application, for the Mozilla Foundation, which also oversees the popular Firefox web browser.

That is because the extended in-box contains invaluable and dynamically updated information about human connections. On Facebook, a social graph notoriously deteriorates after the initial thrill of finding old friends from school wears off. By contrast, an e-mail account has access to the entire address book and can infer information from the frequency and intensity of contact as it occurs. Joe gets e-mails from Jack and Jane, but opens only Jane's; Joe has Jane in his calendar tomorrow, and is instant-messaging with her right now; Joe tagged Jack "work only" in his address book. Perhaps Joe's party photos should be visible to Jane, but not Jack.

This kind of social intelligence can be applied across many services on the open web. Better yet, if there is no pressure to make a business out of it, it can remain intimate and discreet. Facebook has an economic incentive to publish ever more data about its users, says Mr Ascher, whereas Thunderbird, which is an open-source project, can let users minimise what they share. Social networking may end up be-

over the London Stock Exchange in 2005, triggering the resignation of Werner Seifert, the chief executive, and Rolf Breuer, the boss of the supervisory board.

German shareholders have more rights than investors in other European countries. In the Netherlands, for example, shareholders have "almost zero rights", according to Marco Becht of the European Corporate Governance Institute. But German shareholders are far less powerful than those in Britain, where investors need only a 10% stake in a public company in order to force an extraordinary general meeting of shareholders to vote on important strategic decisions or remove directors

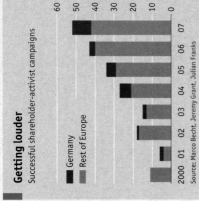

Getting louder

Successful shareholder-activist campaigns

Germany

Rest of Europe

2000 01 02 03 04 05 06 07

Source: Marco Becht, Jeremy Grant, Julian Franks

Raising their voices

Activist shareholders claim a rare victory

MICHAEL FRENZEL is remarkably resilient. The boss of TUI, Europe's biggest travel company, has been in his job since 1994. He has survived the slump in travel and tourism after the terrorist attacks in America on September 11th 2001; speculation about a takeover by a secret buyer through stake-building by Morgan Stanley, an investment bank; and fierce attacks on his strategy from shareholders. But in the past few weeks it seemed that the tenure of the longest-serving boss of a German blue-chip company was coming to an end at last. John Fredriksen, a Norwegian shipping tycoon who is one of TUI's biggest shareholders, and Guy Wyser-Pratte, an American investor, demanded the separation of Hapag-Lloyd, its container-shipping division, from the rest of the firm—and claimed to have the necessary support among other shareholders.

Mr Frenzel faced the choice between a showdown with shareholders at the general meeting on May 7th, or giving up his "two pillar" tourism-and-shipping strategy, which he has fiercely defended on the basis that shipping provides a hedge for the volatile travel business. He chose the latter course: on March 17th TUI said it was preparing to separate its shipping division. By giving in to shareholder pressure Mr Frenzel, whose mandate was recently renewed for another four years, has probably saved his skin. His concession was a rare victory for shareholders in a German company. But shareholders are starting to become more vocal and are making their demands in public, as Mr Fredriksen did.

"The example of the activism of London-based investors influences Germans," says Holger Schmieding, an economist at Bank of America. They regard the Children's Investment Fund (TCI) as a role model, after it forced the management of Deutsche Börse, Frankfurt's stock exchange, to abandon an attempt to take charge. Three years ago Mr Wyser-Pratte and other shareholders managed to oust Hans Fahr, the boss of IWKA, a German engineering and automotive supplier. Last year another foreign investor—Rustam Aksenenko, a Russian financier—led the successful campaign to topple Frank Rheinboldt, the boss of Escada, a fashion firm.

Meanwhile corporate Germany is fighting back. Big companies are pressing the government in Berlin and BaFin, the financial watchdog, to strengthen their defences by sharpening the definition of "acting in concert" in Germany's takeover law. The clause stipulates that if shareholders accounting for more than 30% of the voting rights are found to act in concert to push their agenda, they are required to launch a full takeover of the company or face a fine.

Mr Frenzel could have hoped for a decision by BaFin to investigate whether TUI's shareholders had fallen foul of this rule. Yet he preferred to placate his investors with the announcement of a sale of Hapag-Lloyd, which will not be easy. "We remain sceptical about any form of spin-off for Hapag-Lloyd, in the light of TUI's corporate history," says Carmen Hummel, an analyst at HypoVereinsbank. A few years ago TUI called off a flotation of Hapag-Lloyd because of weak markets. This could happen again, which means that this month's shareholder rebellion may not be the last under Mr Frenzel's stewardship. ∎

mean it is a business

A LARGE but long-in-the-tooth technology company hoping to become a bigger force in online advertising buys a small start-up in a sector that everybody agrees is the next big thing. A decade ago, this was Microsoft buying Hotmail—the firm that is the next big thing. A decade ago, this was Microsoft buying Hotmail—the firm that established web-based e-mail as a must-have service for internet users, and promised to drive up page views, and thus advertising inventory, on the software giant's websites. This month it was AOL, a struggling web portal that is part of Time Warner, an old-media giant, buying Bebo, a small but up-and-coming online social network, for $850m.

Both deals, in their respective decades, illustrate a great paradox of the internet in that the premise underlying them is precisely half right and half wrong. The correct half is that a next big thing—web-mail then, social networking now—can indeed quickly become something that consumers expect from their favourite web portal. The non sequitur is to assume that the new service will be a revenue-generating business in its own right.

Web-mail has certainly not become a business. Admittedly, Google, Microsoft, Yahoo!, AOL and other providers of web-mail accounts do place advertisements on their web-mail offerings, but this is small beer. They offer e-mail—and volumes of free archival storage unimaginable a decade ago—because the service, including its associated address book, calendar, and other features, is cheap to deliver and keeps consumers engaged with their brands and websites, making users more likely to visit affiliated pages where advertising is more effective.

Social networking appears to be similar in this regard. The big internet and media companies have bid up the implicit valuations of MySpace, Facebook and others. But that does not mean there is a working revenue model. Sergey Brin, Google's co-founder, recently admitted that Google's "social networking inventory as a whole" was proving problematic and that the "monetisation work we were doing there didn't pan out as well as we had hoped." Google has a contractual agreement with News Corp to place advertisements on its network, MySpace, and also owns its own network, Orkut. Clearly, Google is not making money from either.

Facebook, now allied to Microsoft, has fared worse. Its grand attempt to redefine the advertising industry by pioneering a new approach to social marketing, called Beacon, failed completely. Facebook's idea was to inform a user's friends whenever he bought something at certain online retailers, by running a small announcement inside the friends' "news feeds". In theory, this was to become a new recommendation economy, an algorithmic form of valuations depend on maximising their page views—so they maintain a tight grip

Coming up for air

But should users really have to visit a specific website to do this sort of thing? "We will look back to 2008 and think it archaic and quaint that we had to go to a destination like Facebook or LinkedIn to be social," says Charlene Li at Forrester Research, a consultancy. Future social networks, she thinks, "will be like air. They will be anywhere and everywhere we need and want them to be." No more logging on to Facebook just to see the "news feed" of updates from your friends; instead it will come straight to your e-mail inbox, RSS reader or instant messenger. No need to upload photos to Facebook to show them to friends, since those with privacy permissions in your electronic address book can automatically get them.

The problem with today's social networks is that they are often closed to the outside web. The big networks have decided to be "open" toward independent programmers, to encourage them to write fun new software for them. But they are reluctant to become equally open towards their users, because the networks' lofty

thriving ecosystem of small programs can exploit this "social graph" to enable friends to interact via games, greetings, video clips and so on.

The most important emerging domain in high-value relationships is applying salespeople's deep understanding of their clients to providing highly personalized technology-based services. Good relationship managers will know not just the concerns and issues their clients are facing, but how they are thinking about them, and what sort of approaches to presenting information will influence them. This must be applied to providing immensely customized service and information delivery.

Every firm providing high-value services must focus on integrating digital and human interaction to implement far higher levels of personalization. This is at the heart of their future competitiveness. XML is an immensely powerful tool to achieve this, because it can be used to break documents into their components, and then reconstruct them in whatever way is most relevant and useful to a particular client. Most firms try to implement CRM as a reporting tool. If it can be integrated with content management systems to provide high-level personalization, then it becomes possible for every client to receive a different document, designed to be directly relevant to his or her issues and thinking styles. To achieve this, not only new processes, but also new skills are required, and front-line professionals will need to shift how they work in this new environment.

WorldStreet Corporation is helping large financial institutions to implement these approaches, by providing peer-to-peer information exchange services for the industry. Companies such as Credit Suisse First Boston and WR Hambrecht use its systems to deliver customized packages of investment research to their major clients. WorldStreet's systems make it easy for salespeople to tailor the format and style of their reports to the client's portfolios and decision-making styles, and deliver them through whatever communication channel is most convenient at the time.

Vital Connections: Chapter 4

In this chapter you have seen how connectivity and integration are making trust and attention increasingly central to business relationships. Companies must focus on developing trust, and apply personalization to earn the attention of their clients and partners.

You have seen in Chapters 3 and 4 how information and ideas are flowing freely, and firms are collaborating ever-more closely. In Chapter 5 you will discover that innovation too must happen across organizational boundaries, and how the role of intellectual property in business is changing. New thinking and business models are required, so be an innovator! We all need it.

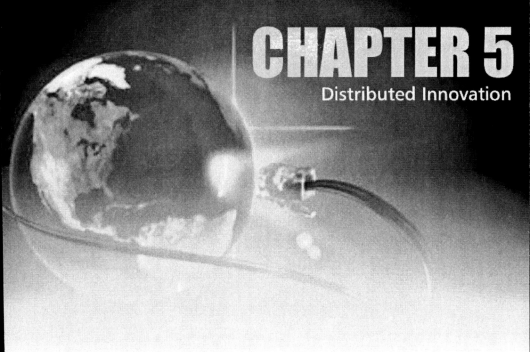

CHAPTER 5
Distributed Innovation

Intellectual Property in a Collaborative World

Innovation and intellectual property increasingly dominate the economy. As technology advances, no firm has the resources to stand alone, and collaboration with others is becoming essential. This means that new business models are needed for developing intellectual property and sharing in its value. Open source software provides us with valuable lessons that can be applied to many other aspects of business and innovation.

Does driving in the rush hour get you down? Don't worry. IBM's alphaWorks unit is market-testing Blue Eyes, which uses an infrared camera to monitor drivers' eyes and faces. It sounds an alarm if the driver closes his eyes or appears sleepy, and can make automatic adjustments to the mirror and seating position based on his retina signature. It can tell if the driver is smiling or frowning, and if he appears unhappy, the car can be programmed to play joyful, upbeat music.[1]

AlphaWorks is responsible for identifying promising technologies created by IBM Research's eight labs worldwide, and taking them into accelerated development of commercial products. To do this it gives open access to selected software at the early stages of development. A sophisticated community of software developers downloads the sample code, works to apply it in their own projects, and provides early feedback and participation on potential products. The technologies under assessment are available to the alphaWorks community for free under a special license, and 40% of those posted to the community have subsequently been incorporated into IBM products or licensed to third-parties. This is an impressive success ratio in a business where 10% is considered a good batting average.

Innovation is the throbbing heart of the twenty-first century economy, consistently pumping new revitalizing activity through the system. The opposing force is commoditization—probably the single most powerful force in business today—which rapidly takes what was distinctive and profitable and rapidly makes it commonplace and marginal, sucking out the vitality and profitability.

Unless you and your company can innovate consistently in every domain of business—creating valuable content and ideas, developing new products and services, enhancing client service, changing business models, and more—you are slowly dying. At best you are wheezing on a life-support machine, and that's not a fun existence. But as we shift into the living networks, there are four ways in which the whole nature of innovation and intellectual property is changing.

Innovation and intellectual property increasingly dominate the economy. For the last two decades copyright industries such as film, music, and software have grown at three times the rate of the rest of the economy. They added around $680 billion to the US economy in 1999, and generated more exports than aircraft, automobiles, computers, or agriculture. In 2001 the US Patent and Trademark Office granted over 166,000 patents, well over double the number granted in 1988.[2]

Greater complexity means collaboration is essential. To innovate today you must be increasingly specialized. With an exponential increase in the pace of innovation and depth of scientific knowledge you have to go correspondingly deeper in order to be at the forefront. Innovation—now more than ever—stems from bringing together different fields of specialization. In addition, the best individuals are often choosing to work independently or in small elite groups. The bottom line is you can no longer rely completely on your own resources to innovate. Even IBM, with an annual R&D budget of over $5 billion, and 3,400 research staff including five Nobel Prize winners, recognizes that it doesn't have the breadth and depth of expertise to innovate alone, and actively collaborates with partners and customers. The same issues apply within organizations. Research, manufacturing, marketing, and sales departments are all equally responsible for innovation, but in order to do so must work closely together, as well as with customers.

Changing flow is reshaping the role of intellectual property. If you can copyright it, someone can make it into a digital file. A file that flows ever-so-easily through the networks, creating perfect copies indefinitely. If you're in the music, publishing, or film industries, embrace change or be swept away. The world of patents has traditionally been one of the stickiest and most turgid, but the networks are promising to create the early eddies and flows that could turn it into a powerful economic torrent. And the rich collaboration that is at the heart of the living networks is enabling humanity to be immensely more creative, vastly enriching every sphere of innovation and intellectual property.

We need new business models. Most importantly, we need to find and apply new approaches to sharing the value created in collaborative ventures of all kinds. This is where the most wealth will be generated in the emerging economy. This may mean changing how intellectual property is applied, as in the open source software movement. It could result in networks of independent professionals playing a far larger economic role. It certainly will result in greater wealth creation for those innovators who are able to collaborate effectively.

Let us now explore these drivers in more detail, and what we need to do to be successful in this unfolding environment.

The brave new world of intellectual property

In 1421 the government of Florence awarded the world's first patent to Filippo Brunelleschi for a means of bringing goods up the usually unnavigable river Arno to the city. He demanded and was duly awarded legal protection for his invention, being given the right for three years to burn any competitor's ship that incorporated his design.[3]

Fast forward almost six centuries, and the global economy is dominated by intellectual property, and the flow of information and ideas. This "property" exists in the space of our minds rather than under our feet, yet it is by far the most valuable economic resource that exists today.

The US Constitution gives Congress the power "to promote the Progress of Science and useful Arts, by securing for limited Times to Authors and Inventors the exclusive right to their respective Writings and Discoveries." There are two key points here. Intellectual property gives innovators the right to benefit from their works. However the primary intent is to promote progress and the public good, thus giving legal protection for only a limited period, and also making inventions publicly available as a basis for further innovation.

Not all information and ideas are legally protected. The term "intellectual assets" is used to describe all valuable information and ideas. "Intellectual property" is the subset of information and ideas that can be and are protected by law. Every one of us has information or ideas that are intellectual assets. But they are only intellectual property if you can successfully sue someone for copying or using them without your permission.

There are four types of intellectual property, each with their own characteristics, and each of which is affected differently by the advent of the living networks. *Copyright* represents the world of information. Anything that can be digitally represented, including words, images, sounds, and software, can be copyrighted. *Patents* cover the universe of ideas. If an idea is novel, useful, and non-obvious, it can be patented. *Trademarks* are words and images that are associated with particular companies, and are protected as part of that firm's unique identity. *Trade secrets*, as the name implies, are protected by non-disclosure, and fall under a different section of the law to other intellectual property. To complement these core types of intellectual property, *contract law* is often useful for protecting the value of ideas when other legal remedies do not apply. In this chapter we will mainly look at the world of copyright and patents, as they are the most affected by issues of distributed innovation and collaboration.

The copyright battlefield

The Recording Industry Association of America (RIAA), in a belated response to Napster and other music file-sharing systems, in early 2001 announced with big fanfare a new system to protect digital music files called the Secure Digital Music Initiative (SDMI), at the same time offering a prize of $10,000 for anyone who could crack the technology. However the fine print of the competition stated that any successful attempts could not be publicly disclosed. As a scientist more interested in advancing his field rather than collecting prize money, Edward Felton, a professor at Princeton University, intended to present his crack of the SDMI to his peers at the

USENIX Security conference. The RIAA allegedly threatened to prosecute Felton, sparking off a long and complex legal tussle. Since then SDMI seems to have fallen by the wayside, with the music industry moving onto to new technology-based approaches to protection.

Copyright protects information. Whether the content is words, music, movies, software, or images, if they can be copyrighted they can be digitized. And as you know well, anything digital flows freely through the networks. The result is an ongoing battle engaging copyright owners, consumers, distributors, and technology firms, with all parties using both technology and legislation to further their cause.

It is networks created from immense connectivity that are transforming copyright industries. When content flows freely, new business models are required. Chapter 8 examines in detail the implications of the networks on content distribution, and proposes new approaches for these industries. In this chapter we will focus on how content and other intellectual property can be developed collaboratively.

Collaboration is the future of innovation. Those that excel at working collaboratively will win big in the unfolding world of intellectual property.

Patents run amok

Holger Balsum, a computer science graduate student at the University of Munich with a background in genetic sequencing, used his expertise to earn $10,000 for a couple of hours work, in the process throwing a wrench in the works of a major genomics firm. For an invention to be patented, it must be novel. This means that if anyone can identify work that predates a patent's filing, the patent may be rescinded. Internet firm BountyQuest offers cash bounties on behalf of its clients, to anyone that can identify this "prior art" on specified competitors' patents. When Balsum saw featured on BountyQuest's website a patent by Incyte Genomics on databases for storing genetic sequencing information, he immediately knew where to find the evidence needed to claim his reward. The networks had once again brought together highly specialized knowledge with its application.

As you saw earlier in this chapter, the intent of patents is to provide legal protection for useful and novel ideas. This rewards innovators, and society benefits by being able to use and build on the ideas. So far, so good. But the reality is sometimes a little different.

British Telecommunications holds a US patent for hyperlinks. In a world in which almost half a billion web surfers click on hyperlinks most days, it's a little like holding a copyright on the word "hello". The patent is being challenged in court, but for now it holds.[4] In a similar vein, in 1998 the United States Patent and Trademark Organization (USPTO) decided to allow patents on business methods. The most egregious examples of patents granted under this scheme include one for "one-click" shopping by Amazon.com; and a patent for reverse auctions, in which people nominate the prices they are prepared to pay, held by Priceline.

The heart of the issue is the quality of patent examination and grants. Specific inventions that are truly novel and non-obvious should be protected, but when mistakes are made and patents that are too broad in scope are granted, it can be both a license to print money for the grateful patent holder, and a severe dampener on innovation in the field. When in late 2001 President George W. Bush opened the way for federally funded research into stem cells, it came to light that a quiet biotechnology firm called Geron held patents that covered virtually all embryonic cell lines existing at that time, as well as the methods to produce them. As such, in principle they own the results of almost any future research in the field.[5] Recently the USPTO has promised to lift its game through hiring, training, and improved processes. That they and their sister organizations around the world do so is critical to global innovation.

One of the most important emerging issues in intellectual property is patent pooling. Increasingly, working technologies are based on whole sets of patents, that are often owned by many firms rather than just one. As such, unless these patent holders work together, technology users would have to get separate licenses from each company. This would be so complicated that the technologies would probably never be used, and all the companies would suffer. The solution is for the owners of the interlocking patents to pool them, and create a body that handles client licensing and payments to the patent holders.

This is not a new concept. In 1856, a pool of sewing machines patents was established by the Sewing Machine Combination.[6] However in a networked economy based largely on competition between standards, patent pools are becoming a critical tool. Recent patent pools include those for MPEG-2 video compression, the DVD-ROM format, and the 1394 high-speed bus that Apple has trademarked as FireWire.[7] This illustrates how collaboration in innovation can take place both before and after legally protected intellectual property is created.

The above examples illustrate some of the key facets of patent strategy. How can you convince the patent office to grant you an overly broad patent? How can you block your competitors? How can you draw together the range of patents necessary to implement advanced technologies? Strategic positioning in patents is becoming a driving factor for many companies' innovation programs. However collaboration is often becoming the centerpiece of that strategy.

Innovation and collaboration in the networks

On a stinking hot day the cool breeze of the airconditioner provides welcome relief. But ironically, until recently it has contributed to making the planet hotter. One of the prime culprits in global warming was Freon®, which for decades ran our refrigerators and air-conditioners, all the time contributing to the depletion of the planet's protective ozone layer. In 1990 a US federal law gave DuPont, which owned Freon, five years to develop and start manufacturing an environmentally-friendly substitute.

To meet this hefty challenge, DuPont's Center for Collaborative Research and Education created a global network comprising over 30 universities, laboratories, and corporates, allocating tasks among the participants and creating forums for them all to collaborate effectively. It took the network just four years to create not only a new refrigerant, Suva®, but also a new manufacturing process for the product. All the participants in the network received licensing streams from the results of the project.[8]

Collaboration is the future of innovation. Those that excel at working collaboratively will win big in the unfolding world of intellectual property. The advent of the networks changes how information and ideas—from their seminal conception to crystallization as legally protectable property— flow, merge, and evolve. First we need to understand some of the different forms and stages that innovation takes.

The different modes of innovation

Classical music and improvisational jazz are good models to understand the different modes of innovation. Classical music is almost always created by a single person, neatly and accurately written out, and then performed by an orchestra attempting to be faithful to the letter and spirit of the score. Jazz is volatile, created in the instant by a group. Traditional forms of jazz often involve musicians performing solos in turn to a backing structure. The more exciting and exploratory forms of jazz, funk, and soul music are created as a group, with no musical leader.

In my psychedelic funk band *Transceptor*, we generate all our musical ideas in completely improvized "jam" sessions. In any good jam, each musician listens to and responds to what the others are doing, and the music takes a life of its own, shifting unpredictably, with everyone contributing to the evolving shape. The musicians' laughter that often accompanies the end of a successful jam reflects the joy of being part of a spontaneous creative process that transcends what any individual could achieve. We later review our improvizations, and create albums by developing the best material into structured songs that are frequently remarkably close to the original jams.

This is exactly the way that creative teams need to work in order to tap the potential of collaboration. Ray Ozzie, when he conceived of the peer-to-peer software Groove, was explicitly trying to create a tool that would allow collaboration in the same way as jazz musicians find a common groove. In a world in which innovation is the primary field of play, we need to shift from idea generation by individuals to collaborative idea generation, simply because it makes so much more possible.

In exactly the same way as my band's process for creating music, innovation can be separated into two phases: idea generation and idea development. Collaboration is essential to both of these phases, but in quite different ways. Idea generation must be free-flowing, whereas idea development needs to be structured. We will look at some of the implications of this later in this chapter.

How the networks change innovation

In the US alone, there are over two million enforceable patents. Only around 5% of those make money. The rest sit dormant, the documents quietly gathering dust on a shelf for the 20 year duration of the exclusive patent rights, or lapse due to lack of maintenance payments. Some of those patents are not applied because they don't have a real commercial application. Probably many more are neglected because the patent holder is not interested in exploiting them, and they haven't managed—or perhaps even tried—to match them with a company that could profitably apply them and would be prepared to buy or license them. This is not just a problem for the company that forgoes revenue on its portfolio of patents. It also means that part of the intellectual property landscape is unavailable, potentially squelching innovation by other companies. Because of the complexity and sheer number of existing patents, information about intellectual property has tended to flow extremely poorly. The promise of the next phase of the networks is that this flow will become far more fluid, resulting in better exploitation of our existing intellectual property, and a faster pace of innovation.

The list of the 60 founding sponsors of virtual technology marketplace yet2.com reads like a who's who of corporate innovation, featuring firms such as 3M, Boeing, Dow Chemical, Du Pont, Ford, Hitachi, NTT DoCoMo, Philips, Procter & Gamble, Siemens, Toyota, and their global peers. Many of the members are primarily interested in selling or licensing their wealth of patents. Each of these firms owns literally thousands of patents, only a small proportion of which are being commercially applied.

To keep things simple Procter & Gamble has chosen to list every single one of its patents on yet2.com, so as and when anyone expresses interest in buying or licensing one, it can then decide what it wants to do. Procter &

Gamble's chief technology officer, Gordon Brunner, says he is trying to shift from Research & Development to "Connect & Development," facilitating connections both inside and outside the firm in order to accelerate the development and commercialization of intellectual property.[9]

Online exchanges facilitate the easy flow of intellectual property in many ways. A rival to yet2.com, Patent & License Exchange (PL-X), provides a wealth of tools and services that help decongest the traditional stickiness of the patent universe. Eastman Chemical was trying to conclude the sale of a patent to a German firm, but the buyer wanted assurance that the patent would remain valid after its purchase. Transactions on PL-X automatically include this insurance, so the firms chose to execute the sale online. Other PL-X tools include advanced intellectual property valuation models that help firms to negotiate prices more effectively, instead of being thrown by the difficulty of valuing these highly intangible assets.

The open source generation

Cybernovelist Neal Stephenson—who is also a software programmer—likens computer operating systems to vehicles. For Stephenson, Apple is like a sleek and stylish but expensive sedan, and Microsoft Windows an ugly and temperamental stationwagon. Linux, however, is a space-age tank that never breaks down, is easily maneuverable, and can drive a stack of miles to the gallon. To boot, these supertanks are waiting by the side of the highway with their keys in the ignition for anyone who cares to jump in and drive away, no questions asked and nothing to pay.[10]

Open source software is one of the most intriguing—and important—developments in recent economic history. Products based on highly-skilled labor working for free may have seemed unlikely to become a major force in a capitalist society, but that is exactly what is changing the entire shape of the software industry.

The flagship open source product is the Linux operating system kernel, which by 2000 had taken the number two position for computer server operating systems with 27% of the market, not far behind Microsoft NT. In fact in the important but less visible web server software market, open source software Apache is dominant, bagging over 60% of installations on active sites.

Open source software is a dramatic force in its own right, but what is most interesting is the model it presents for other parts of the economy. We will examine the defining characteristics that help us to understand how and why it works, and how it can be applied to other fields of intellectual property and business.

How and why open source works

The oft-told tale of how a young Finnish programmer called Linus Torvald revolutionized the software industry has already reached the status of a legend. Geeks talk with hushed reverence of the coder who in 1990 built a basic operating system kernel, informed people on a bulletin board of what he was doing, and started incorporating the best suggestions into his system. Within a few years the free software was one of the major players in its field. Source code is what programmers write. For a computer to run a program, the source code first has to be "compiled" into object code, in which form it cannot be read or changed. Commercial software is generally available only in compiled form, so it can be executed, but is inaccessible to programmers. In the open source software movement, a program's source code is distributed, so programmers can modify it at will.

The central point is that open source software is not given away, it is licensed. When you use open source software, you must abide by the terms of the license, just as with commercial software. The difference is that open source licenses specify that the software can be used without payment, and that any modifications made to the software must be distributed under the same license. You may have got the software for free, but if you make any improvements you have to give those away for free too. At last count there were 17 kinds of open source licenses in use, ranging from the radically libertarian (anything associated with this software will be free forever!) to more tempered ones that allow scope for commercial exploitation of some modifications. Heated debates rage within the developer community over which kinds of license should be used, however the core principles apply across all of them.

At this point we hear disbelieving mutterings. In our money-driven society, what on earth motivates skilled programmers to give away their time for free, to create something valuable without reward? There are different answers for each of the groups that participate in open source development. However the core driving motivation for most developers is very simple: they want to use the best possible product. This goes to the heart of the distinction between source code and object code, which is the ability to make modifications to software.

If you buy a commercial software package and it has bugs or doesn't quite do what you want, you can either live with it or complain to the vendor in the forlorn hope it will do something about it. On the other hand, if you have the source code, you can do what every natural-born programmer loves to do: go inside and tinker with it. Given the sense of community that software developers feel, it's only natural to share your improvements with others, because you know you'll be able to benefit from others' work. At that stage all it takes is using the right software license and having a system to coordinate people's work, and an absolutely fabulous product can be created. For example, systems administrators using the Windows NT operating system often get frustrated with its lack of stability. If they identify a bug and inform Microsoft, then in due course they might get a fix, together with an invoice for the new improved version. With Linux, they can fix the bug themselves, or alert a community that itself has a vested interest in fixing the bug. The accumulated result is the supertank that Stephenson describes—rock solid and admirably suited to its users' requirements.

Eric Raymond, the popular voice of the open source movement, famously declares that "given enough eyeballs, all bugs are shallow," meaning any problem is easy to fix with enough smart people looking at it.[11] This raises another critical aspect of the open source system—that it is extremely effective at improving an existing product, but not at creating a new one. Someone must establish a core product that is already sufficiently clearly defined and developed on which people will want to spend their efforts. Only this can create what Raymond calls the "plausible promise"[xii] that developers' contributions will result in an excellent and useful final product. In other words, a leader must create the initial project.

In the case of Linux, founder Torvalds did the development work that provided an initial foundation for the operating system. It was flawed in many ways, but it provided basic functionality, and there was indeed the promise that—given sufficient effort by enough talented people—it could become a viable operating system kernel, more powerful and robust than the alternatives currently available. The project did not emerge on its own, but was born from one person's inspiration.

It would be nice if all it took to get great software was to give it an open source license and throw it open to everyone in a free-for-all. But that would be a recipe for disaster. Everyone would develop their own versions with their own enhancements, and no one piece of software would take the best of what was developed in the community. Some kind of central process or leadership is essential. Just because someone offers a contribution **What has become clear through the increasing diversity of the open source movement is that intellectual property is not an all or nothing proposition. There doesn't need to be a stark choice between total protection, or release to the public domain.** to the software, doesn't mean it should be included. The best open source development is a strict meritocracy in which only the neatest bug fixes and most useful contributions are incorporated. That selection can be done by an "enlightened despot", as Linus Torvalds is often described, or committees formed by developers that have demonstrated their merit through the quality of their contributions. There is very strong structure in all good open source projects. Ultimately, participants need to respect the central figure; Torvalds and other successful open source leaders are often described as charismatic.

One of the core requirements of any distributed development project is that it can be partitioned into distinct, definable tasks. Software development meets the bill admirably, in which much of the work required is identifying and fixing specific bugs. These tasks can readily be done independently of any other project activities.

Commercial open source software

In mid-2000 Sun Microsystems announced it was transferring its office software suite StarOffice to an open source license, making 7.5 million lines of code freely available in the biggest open source release ever. This full-featured office suite includes word processing, spreadsheet, and presentation software, running on Windows, Linux, and other operating systems. Not only can it import and use files from Microsoft Office, but it also has an open XML-based file format that allows any other software package to use its files seamlessly. When a pre-release version of the software came out, incorporating open source enhancements, over 700,000 copies were downloaded in the first two months.

In this case, the strategic intent of Sun was pretty obvious: it wanted to break the Microsoft Office monopoly. A high-quality, robust software package, with files fully interchangeable with the market leader, is a pretty compelling proposition when it's free. Sun will open up many lucrative opportunities if it can break Microsoft's stranglehold on PC office software, and its associated grip on operating systems. When in May 2002 the renamed OpenOffice launched its solid version 1.0 for free download, incorporating the work of over 10,000 developers, Sun announced that it would sell a commercial version of the software, still named StarOffice.[13] For the extra $75, users get a few more features and better support. The reality is that many companies feel more comfortable paying for software, partly because it demonstrates that it's a viable proposition for the vendor, who will continue to support the product.[14]

It's not just software companies that get involved with open source. Dresdner Kleinwort Wasserstein (DrKW), the investment banking arm of German financial services giant Allianz, after spending $5 million and three years developing a systems integration toolkit called Openadaptor, decided to make it available under an open source license. Complex software applications sprout like mushrooms in investment banks, and integrating these both internally and with clients' systems is an ongoing challenge for the banks' IT departments. Opening the license for Openadaptor not only gives DrKW the possibility of tapping into external developer expertise, but it also makes the software something its competitors will consider for use.

It's not that they especially want to make life easier for their competitors, but if everyone in the industry uses the same tools to integrate with their clients' systems, then it saves cost and effort for everyone. And it doesn't hurt that they have more experience with the tools than anyone else.[15]

Both Sun and DrKW have engaged the open source software firm CollabNet to run their open source projects. This recognizes that open source projects do not happen by themselves, and require expert central guidance. For a start, software developers have literally thousands of open source projects competing for their attention and efforts, so projects need to be promoted to them effectively. Effective tools are required to allow developers to collaborate, and structure is required to ensure the best work is incorporated into the software project. Communities work best when they know what's happening and feel engaged, so clear communication helps to build a disparate group of programmers into something more like a coherent team.

IBM's alphaWorks, mentioned at the opening of this chapter, doesn't use an open source model, but still taps the expertise and input of developers outside the company. Promising early stage technologies are licensed on a free 90-day basis with no support, so clients and the developer community can find out what's coming, and start to integrate it into their development work if they find it useful. The value to alphaWorks **In order to attract this elite to participate in creating intellectual property, it is essential to offer them an appropriate share of the value created.** is firstly in the feedback and input they receive from their developer community, both in terms of how they want to see the software enhanced, but also simply in what generates the most interest. Also, releasing products very early in the cycle enables them to dramatically accelerate the product development cycle, creating software and tools that are the most relevant and suited to their clients' needs, far faster than through the usual channels. This dynamic unit, initiated in 1996, has just 10 staff, and is deliberately engineered to have a start-up mentality within an $88 billion company. Xerox has paid alphaWorks the compliment of copying its initiative, establishing its own alphaAvenue arm with the same business model.

Applying open source lessons to other fields

Innovation is being stifled by large corporations, overly restrictive legislation, and how technology is being implemented, according to Stanford University law professor Lawrence Lessig. Not just a persuasive speaker and writer, Lessig is taking concerted action to preserve the "commons" of ideas and innovation.

Lessig's latest initiative is Creative Commons, a non-profit organization that gives people free access to customizable intellectual property licenses.[16] These licenses enable writers, artists, software developers, and other creative people to choose the exact terms on which they make their work available. For example, they might specify that their work can be used freely, but only with full attribution and not for commercial purposes. Alternatively, they might make it available for free to non-profit organizations, but charge fees to corporate users. Just as in the open source model, these licenses will be legally binding to users.

What has become clear through the increasing diversity of the open source movement is that intellectual property is not an all or nothing proposition. There doesn't need to be a stark choice between total protection, or release to the public domain. The variety of open source licenses now available attests to that, as do examples like Sun's dual policy of selling StarOffice while giving away the source to create OpenOffice. Creative Commons has taken the concept of flexible licensing, applied it to every domain of intellectual property, and made it freely available to everyone. The result can only be a vastly more propitious environment for collaborative innovation, in which people can readily build on others' ideas and content rather than having it all locked away by rigid legal structures. At the launch of Creative Commons, technical book publisher Tim O'Reilly spontaneously announced that he would give all his company's authors the option of moving their copyright to the Creative Commons after 14 years.

Open source thinking can be applied to completely different domains in business. Rob McEwen, chairman and CEO of Canadian gold miner Goldcorp, believed his company's 55,000 acre stake had massive potential, but didn't know how to access it. When attending an information technology seminar at MIT, McEwen drew inspiration from the session on open source software. He did what was previously unthinkable in the mining community—exposing all of their geological data online, and announcing a competition for the best analysis of where they should mine next. All four mines the company has drilled on the winners' advice have hit high-grade ore.[17]

One clear application of an open source approach is to solve problems that can have massive benefits and inspire many to action, but don't interest large companies. In early 2000 a group of MIT Media Lab students proposed an initiative called ThinkCycle, that is dedicated to applying "open source problem solving" to help under-privileged communities. The cycle starts with getting clearly defined design challenges. These are often provided by non-governmental organizations who are familiar with the on-the-ground problems facing developing countries. A community website including collaborative tools provides a forum to provoke awareness of critical issues, allow design teams to form and work together, and propose workable solutions. One of the outputs from ThinkCycle has been a low-cost intravenous drip flow control system to facilitate cholera treatment.[18]

Often the most valuable interaction and interchange of ideas takes place before any legally-protectable ideas and content is created. Before the Internet was born, and way before it was accessible by the public, bulletin board systems (BBS) were the first technology tool that allowed a large number of people to gather "virtually" to exchange ideas and opinions. The name was apt, for the systems acted just like boards on the wall where participants could post notes, and respond to others' notes. Nobody could see the others stopping by to stick up their notes, but all could read what everyone else had written. Howard Rheingold, one of the first hosts of the early San Francisco online community The Well, evoked those early days in his book *The Virtual Community*, describing how "real" communities changed when they had an open, online forum for discussion.[19]

Online discussion forums have blossomed since the Internet became a popular tool, but many of the most dynamic and interesting are private, invitation-only forums. Rheingold's private Brainstorms community brings together some of the more interesting people on the planet—including many writers and authors—into a common space. One of the most basic principles of the community—and one that can only work in a private space—is "You Own Your Own Words" (usually abbreviated to YOYOW), which means no one can use others' words outside the community without permission. This rule allows writers to express themselves freely and bounce ideas around with others, without having to worry about their words being stolen before they can refine them into a form in which they can be sold.

As you discovered earlier in this chapter, open source is founded on users being the primary source of innovation. Open source software exists because users know what they want better than their suppliers do. They are the ones who are the first to discover problems, identify potential improvements, and develop ideas on what will work better for them. In Chapter 6 we will explore in more detail how to involve your customers in innovation processes.

Implementing distributed innovation and shared value

At a scientific convention in Hawaii in 1972, Stanley Cohen from Stanford University and Herbert Boyer of the University of California met for the first time in what proved to be the beginning of a long friendship and collaborative partnership. Their joint work on a process for cloning genes in microorganisms resulted in three patents that formed the foundation of the nascent biotechnology industry. Stanford University ended up as the sole owner of the patents, reaping over $150 million in royalties as a result.

The real reason for distributed innovation is simply that you can no longer be self-sufficient. You must bring together more and better resources than you can hope to have inside a single organization. This means that distributed innovation models must address how you attract the best people to collaborate with you in your projects. In order to attract this elite to participate in creating intellectual property, it is essential to offer them an appropriate share of the value created. Those that can best implement new models and approaches—both to organize work effectively, and share in the value created—will be the most successful in the network economy. There are five key action steps companies and individuals must take to implement distributed innovation, as shown in Table 5-1. We will examine these issues from the perspective of the individual in more depth in Chapter 10.

IMPLEMENTING DISTRIBUTED INNOVATION

1. Design processes to match the type of innovation required
2. Create structures to access and coordinate top global talent
3. Provide a share in the value created
4. Negotiate based on differing objectives, risk appetite, and power
5. Be open throughout the process

Table 5-1: Action steps to implementing distributed innovation

1. Design processes to match the type of innovation required

What are you trying to do? Do you need to come up with startlingly new and different ideas, or do you have to develop the seed of an idea into something useful and workable? Clearly both phases are necessary elements of innovation, but it is important to understand what you want to achieve, and then apply the appropriate approaches.

As you have seen, the collaborative structure of the open source model can be perfect for developing robust and refined products, but only once the initial core has been defined. MIT's ThinkCycle begins by establishing clearly formulated problems. Every open source project starts with an idea, an intention, and some code. Once a basic idea is in place, distributed development processes can bring a wide range of expertise to bear.

Idea generation is by its nature more unstructured, but systems and processes can help to create better results. British telecom firm BT implemented "BT Ideas" in 1996, providing a process and online forum for staff to submit ideas. This is being used in many ways, including focused idea generation campaigns around specific needs. When the CEO and directors spoke at one internal event, all were asked to end with a request for ideas on their chosen issue. The CEO received 100 sorted responses to his request within a few hours. BT now intends to get participation in the system from its partners and suppliers.[20]

2. Create structures to access and coordinate top global talent

Pharmaceutical giant Eli Lilly established InnoCentive LLP in order to tap outside talent in its research and development initiatives. InnoCentive takes research tasks that have been clearly defined by its "seeker" companies, which include Eli Lilly and other large firms, and posts them to a global community of thousands of scientists. Each problem has a specific reward attached. One graduate student at the University of Georgia won $30,000 for synthesizing an amino acid, while an Indian scientist earned $75,000 for his solution to another synthesis problem. Problem solvers must sign a confidentiality agreement, which gives them access to complete data and specifications on the problem, and hand over all intellectual property rights to the solution.[21] The seeker companies can access global talent to address specific research problems, match the reward to how much a solution is worth to them, and only pay if they get precisely what they need.

The heart of open source is bringing together vast global expertise in focused projects. Companies are now trying to implement similar approaches in their commercial research and development, and coming across the same challenges as open source. You need to attract the best participants. SourceForge, the largest site for open source software development, lists over 40,000 current projects. There is immense competition to get top developers to work on your project. In a commercial environment, getting the best people involved should be centered on financial rewards. However other issues can be highlighted, such as the opportunity to work with the best people on the most exciting projects, and personal career development. Innovation exchanges like InnoCentive will develop further, so it often makes most sense to access the largest pools of innovators rather than trying to create your own.

In addition you need to create structures that allow diverse groups to collaborate on projects. Fixing software bugs is eminently suited to distributed projects. In order to apply similar approaches in other domains, you need to be able to break down a project into clear and distinct tasks. For example, drug synthesis is usually a multi-stage process, so Eli Lilly and its peers in InnoCentive can isolate specific issues within the overall drug development process, and get outsiders to participate in these.[22]

Leadership is critical both in establishing the structures for the innovation process, and often in running projects. Linux and every other successful open source project has had a combination of a good leader or leadership team, and straightforward processes. The less that a distributed innovation team depends on an individual—usually working largely by force of personality—the more that clear structures and processes are required. CollabNet, mentioned earlier in this chapter, does very well by performing exactly that role for hire in software development.

3. Provide a share in the value created

There are basically two ways of getting rewarded for work. You can get paid for your input, for example by a salary, hourly rate, or fee for service. Or you can be rewarded for the value of the final output, such as a commission, profit share, or success fee. Things are relatively straightforward if you pay contributors to intellectual property by their input. Most R&D employees must sign over to their employers the rights to everything they create, and in return get paid a salary with probably a bonus if their efforts result in the company hitting the jackpot. Magazine journalists get paid salaries, or if they're freelance, by the word. However for distributed innovation, you are specifically trying to get the best to participate. They may want payment for their time and effort, but if they believe in their ability to create value, they will also demand a share in that to get their participation. Be prepared to offer specific reward models.

In the dot-com heyday, everyone wanted stock options. That was the way to get rich. But this is a very indirect way to profit from your contribution to intellectual property. As many discovered, it depends not only on the vagaries of the stockmarket, but also on the ability of the management team to run the company. Increasingly, top innovators are asking for a stake in the intellectual property itself. This means that if the company goes down the gurgler through no fault of their own, they still own a potentially valuable asset.

4. Negotiate based on differing objectives, risk appetite, and power

Money isn't always everything. Actor Keanu Reeves chose to forgo part of his profit-share in *The Devil's Advocate* in order to get the chance to work with Al Pacino.[23] Negotiation is based on the fact that different people and organizations have disparate motivations. This is what allows you to find win-win solutions. The greater your flexibility in creating value sharing agreements, and the more you recognize the different situations of the parties involved, the greater your ability to attract the best players to participate in your ventures.

The reality is that in any negotiation, the primary variable is relative power, which is basically how much one party needs the other. Today, many government organizations that issue tenders for consulting work specify that any intellectual property generated in the engagement is owned by the client. Take it or leave it. If you're a run-of-the-mill actor, musician, consultant, or programmer, you need the gig more than the project director needs you. However if you're a star in any of those fields, you can pick and choose between offers according to how much it pays and how well it progresses your career.

Any endeavor is risky. But when more than one player is involved, each has something different at stake, varied perceptions of how risky the venture is, and unequal appetite for that risk. Balancing participants' different attitudes to risk can allow the creation of innovative value sharing models.

5. Be open throughout the process
Humorist Art Buchwald sold the idea for the film *Coming to America* to Paramount Pictures in 1983. The agreement gave Buchwald a share of the film's net profits, as defined in the contract. Since the film grossed $350 million, but booked an official loss of $18 million, Buchwald felt he hadn't received his share of the rewards, and took Paramount to court. He lost the case, but the judge found the contract to be "unconscionable" in not representing the true profitability of the film. The studio's costs had been defined in the contract, and it was impossible to know its true financial situation.[24]

One of the most dramatic trends in a connected economy is towards transparency. Information always escapes, and attitudes around the world are rapidly shifting towards expecting and demanding transparency in all things. In the case of distributed innovation, it is essential to provide transparency in order to get the best people to participate. Trust is invaluable, but transparency can be almost as good. For example, the SKA Global consulting network, discussed in detail in Chapter 9, provides full disclosure of all accounts to its members. Patent pools are completely transparent to their members. Agreements must be unambiguous at the outset, so all participants are fully clear on what their responsibilities and potential rewards are. The more precise the contracts, the easier it will be to attract the best people to participate. Over time, it will become standard to have complete accounting transparency in any collaborative project.

Any network that forms to create valuable intellectual property will need to establish effective systems and approaches. Each industry is at a different stage in implementing shared-value projects. Before the advent of open source, the software industry was very much based on development within single companies, or sometimes by lone programmers. In consulting and professional services, these kinds of loose networks have been around for some time, but are just now beginning to become more common. However the industry in which these principles have been the most developed and used is movies, with profit-sharing contracts first implemented in the silent movie era, and featuring throughout its history.[25] Let's see what we can learn from Hollywood.

How Hollywood does it

Spike Lee, the first African-American film director to hit the big time, got his break in 1986 with his first commercially released movie, the critically-acclaimed *She's Gotta Have It*. To scrape together the funds to shoot the film, he managed to secure an $18,000 grant and brought in some private investors. However what really allowed him to produce a superb film on a shoestring budget was the time-honored tradition in the independent film industry of making deferred payments to his creative talent.

The life of an independent film producer is all about how to do a lot using very little money. You're very lucky indeed if you have enough money to pay the wages of the director, actors, camera operators, and technical and support crew. As an alternative you can offer deferred payments, which means the actors and crew get paid when you get paid. The film distributor sells the rights to screen the film, usually taking around a quarter to a third of the revenue as commission and paying the rest to the filmmakers. In most cases investors (and any outstanding invoices!) are paid until break-even point, with subsequent profit allocated between investors, the film producer and director, and the actors and crew.

The crux of the system is the order in which contributors are paid, and what proportion of any profits people receive. Sometimes these are dealt with by oral promises, but any producer that wants to attract good creative talent will have to offer contracts that specify payment priorities and profit shares.

In this system of deferred payments in independent films, the producer plays the central coordinating role, designing a set of offers of later payment or profit share to his or her creative team that attracts the desired talent, but doesn't exceed the pool of benefits available. In order to do so, the producer must consider the motivations and risk appetites of each member of the team. Some need to pay the rent, so are only interested in payment now. Others are looking for the big break in their career. A deferred payment system, however, requires trust in the producer. If it does well, will we get paid? The movie industry is a very tight community, and everyone will know others who have worked with the producer before. The relative power in this situation depends on whether the film has been pre-sold, looks like it's likely to get good distribution, or somehow inspires people's belief. Spike Lee's faith never wavered through all his trials in funding and filming *She's Gotta Have It*, and his passion carried his entire team with him.

Turning to films produced by the major studios, we see very similar approaches, except for the relative power and risk appetite of the participants. Film studios have plenty of dollars to spend—in fact arguably a large part of the role of studios is providing financing. As such, most of the workers on a major production will be contracted on a daily rate. The studio has the negotiating power, so they choose to take on the risk and potential upside on the film, and pay whatever fixed cost is required to get a talented crew. The story changes once we get to the stars who can make or break a film, and hold the power in a film.

The field of movie profit-sharing contracts is extremely complex and contentious, but also highly instructive. As you saw in the case of the Buchwald film, so-called "net profits" contracts define a profit-sharing pool, not by the true profitability of the film, but by taking the revenue to the studio net of distribution fees, and subtracting specified costs, usually print production, advertising, overheads, and interest expenses. The director, actors, and crew are allocated "points" which entitle them to a share of the profit-sharing pool. In most major productions offers of profit-sharing are an addition rather than replacement for upfront payments, demonstrating its nature as an additional incentive.[26]

You know you're a big star when you can negotiate a "gross" contract. In its simplest form, this pays a fixed percentage of the gross revenues from the box-office and other sales, either from the first dollar or after a certain threshold has been reached. As such, this is at the top of the hierarchy of payments being made to contributors, and forms part of the costs deducted from the profit pool, which leaves lower-ranked participants with less to share.

The variety of possible ways of allocating revenue or profits in the film industry allows for fine-tuning of the risk and reward. The producers of *Forrest Gump* tried to sell the film to the major studios with no success until its star talent—director Robert Zemeckis and actor Tom Hanks—unusually agreed to work for no upfront payment, but in return demanded a share in the "first dollar" gross. Paramount was happy to fund the film with the lower amount at risk, and in return was prepared to forgo part of the profit.[27] Zemeckis' and Hanks' belief in the film was rewarded when it grossed $660 million at the box-office. On the other hand, those that were due to share in the film's net profits lost out—according to Paramount's accounting system there were none.[28]

Vital Connections: Chapter 5

In this chapter, you have seen how the world of innovation and intellectual property is shifting in the networks. Ideas flow freely, both before and after they can be legally protected. New approaches such as open source software provide models that business can adapt in order to successfully implement distributed innovation.

In Chapter 6 you will discover how in the living networks, an organization is its presence in the flow of information and ideas. Marketing, customer feedback, sharing knowledge are becoming new domains at the very heart of organizational success. Other pressing issues concerning intellectual property and sharing value will be explored later in this book. In Chapter 8 we will examine in detail the new world of content distribution, Chapter 9 will cover how professional networks work, while Chapter 10 will look at capturing the value of intellectual property from the perspective of the individual.

arnessing the Flow of Marketing, Customer Feedback, and Knowledge

Today, your company's success depends on how well it builds its network presence in three key domains:

- *Marketing*, which is now mainly about influencing the flow of messages through consumer networks;

- *Customer feedback loops*, that tightly link a company and its customers, enabling them together to constantly create more value;

- *Work processes and knowledge*, that flow through the networks of workers within and beyond the firm.

J.R.R. Tolkien's epic saga of Middle Earth, *The Lord of the Rings*, was first published in 1954, accumulating tens of millions in sales over the coming decades. As the foundation for a vast subculture, and an entire associated industry of fantasy books and games, the book still plays an important role in many people's lives. When New Line Cinema, a division of AOL Time Warner, began work on the *Lord of the Rings* film trilogy that would be the first to use digital technologies to bring the books to life, it recognized the value of tapping the existing communities of die-hard fans. Other film studios have closed down fan websites so they can control marketing, including a different division of AOL in the case of the Harry Potter films, but New Line decided to actively work with the more than 400 existing fan sites.

The keys were maintaining an official film website so exciting that other sites would publicize its activities, and providing fan sites with their own material to keep their audience returning and interested in the films. When New Line's LordoftheRings.net was launched almost three years before the first film's launch, sporting not much more than early notes and sketches, it attracted several hundred thousand hits on the first day. Since then the website has been consistently updated, and will continue to be until the last film of the trilogy is released on video in 2004. The wide network of fan sites ensures that any major releases on the site, such as short clips on the film's making, are quickly accessed. The first movie trailer was downloaded 1.7 million times in its first day on the site.[1] This successful film promotion drew on how deeply people are connected today, how they spread news through their personal networks, and how communities of like-minded people gather to share information.

Just for a moment, think of how you fit into the global networks. You are at the center of a vast network of connections with other people, consisting of everyone you have ever known and communicated with. As a consumer, most of the messages that contribute to your buying decisions come from this network, from the people that are in some way part of your life. As a worker, your ability to connect usefully with people inside and outside your firm is increasingly the foundation of your ability to create value. Each of the people you touch in your life is at the center of their own rich set of connections, together weaving the immense web of humanity.

A meme is the cultural equivalent of a gene: an idea, belief, or behavior that has a life of its own, and spreads from one person to another by how it influences its carriers.

Within the networks that constitute society, communities emerge that feel they have something in common, something that draws them together. These communities can be based around an interest like the Lord of the

Rings, values such as ecological activism, or professional expertise like waste-water engineering. Whatever it is that brings people together, the result is that each member knows what others find interesting, and will actively pass on and exchange information. There is a sense of affiliation that leads to sharing, and even from self-interest, people know that those who add value to communities tend to get back a lot more in return as others provide them with useful information and insights. John Hagel and Arthur Armstrong first brought home the business implications of Internet-enabled customer communities in their book *Net Gain*.[2] Communities have become even more important today because they are so central to global information-sharing activities, but it is also essential to understand that they are just a subset of the personal connections that constitute the global networks. Nurturing communities of workers and customers are invaluable management practices, as you will see. However, this is just part of the picture.

In an economy based on the flow of information and ideas through networks, a company is its presence in these networks. There are three primary aspects to a company's network presence. Marketing is now primarily concerned with the flow of messages between networks of consumers. Companies must build customer **Today only the very fittest memes thrive, though if they do they can almost literally conquer the world. The rest die ignominiously.** *feedback loops*, that connect them closely with their customers and allow them to enhance the value they offer. Within companies, work *processes and knowledge* flow through the networks that connect workers. These three key domains to companies' network presence are illustrated in Figure 6-1.

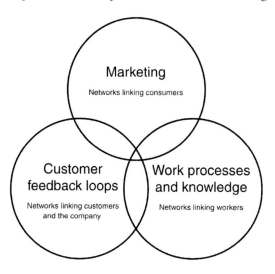

Figure 6-1: A firm's network presence covers three key domains

These three domains are deeply related. Marketing is oriented to both existing and potential customers, while customer feedback is focused on creating more value for current customers. The connection of useful knowledge with its application within organizations is how this value is created. In order to achieve a more powerful presence in the networks, companies must address all three issues. The three related sets of action points companies must implement to build their network presence are shown in Table 6-1.

BUILDING NETWORK PRESENCE

Marketing
    1. Design for propagation
    2. Foster network effects
    3. Create interaction
    4. Choose fertile territory
Customer feedback loops
    1. Monitor customer communities
    2. Get faster, richer feedback… and use it
    3. Involve customers in innovation
    4. Use input for customization
Work processes and knowledge
    1. Identify and empower network hubs
    2. Nurture communities of specialists
    3. Create adaptive systems
    4. Develop a collaborative culture
    5. Foster external networks

Table 6-1: Action steps to building network presence

Marketing in the networks

You may have once opened your e-mail to find a movie depicting a bear fishing in a pristine mountain river. After the bear catches a large salmon, a man comes up and in unarmed combat demolishes the bear, running off with the fish, leaving the logo of British canned food maker John West. Leo Burnett in London had created the humorous ad for television, and apparently simply posted a compressed video of the ad on an industry website for feedback. Viewers immediately e-mailed it to their friends, sparking a flurry of distribution that was estimated to reach 15 million people within 24 hours. The award-winning commercial had a far bigger impact through its free e-mail distribution than its expensive television screening.

One of the most useful tools to understand the new world of marketing is the idea of the meme. A meme is the cultural equivalent of a gene: an idea, belief, or behavior that has a life of its own, and spreads from one person to another by how it influences its carriers. A catchy jingle that people hum, virus hoaxes that ask to be sent on, and flared trousers coming back in style are all memes. Perhaps the best example is the idea of the meme itself. Coined in 1976 by evolutionary biologist Richard Dawkins to help explain his ideas, it rapidly took on a life of its own, spawning millions of conversations, a small library of books, scholarly journals, and now many hundreds of websites. All ideas that flow through the networks, including marketing messages, are memes. Their breeding grounds are people's minds, and they spread from one mind to another by speech, behavior, and increasingly digital communication. Just like genes or anything living, some are more successful than others.

We know that the propagation of ideas has become immensely easier. Memes have never before had the potential to spread so fast to so many people. It's as if rabbits could suddenly breed with any other rabbit around the world, and produce offspring in seconds. Certainly a great leap forward for rabbit-kind. But, to continue the analogy, rabbits are not the only animals that can now breed prolifically. Suddenly every animal has the ability to create a massive population overnight. All of these animals may be able to procreate almost infinitely, but in a world of limited resources, only a few will survive. In the case of memes, their common living territory is people's minds. This, fortunately or unfortunately, is a limited space. With a million memes—and more every day—trying to come to roost in our minds every day, only a few will succeed, let alone motivate us to pass the meme on to others. Certainly memes have the potential to propagate incredibly fast and wide, but the competition is remorseless. Today only the very fittest memes thrive, though if they do they can almost literally conquer the world. The rest die ignominiously.

This is the world in which marketers live today. Their ideas have the potential to be immensely successful, accessing tens of millions across the globe, yet it is far harder for them to be heard at all, usually stifled before infancy by the vast population of competing messages. Designing memes for marketing success requires paying attention to four key success factors.

1. Design for propagation
The Wall Street Journal, no less, expressed its admiration for the smooth disco dancing moves of President George Bush, as shown in the popular interactive software "Dancing Bush". The clip's designer, Miniclip.com, makes interactive games using Flash software, that are around a tenth of the size of short video files. This makes it easy for the majority of Internet users that still use dial-up access to access the clip or forward it to friends.

Now almost any interesting information, video, music, or games can be passed on to others with minimal effort. It is by now standard practice to put "E-mail this to a friend" buttons on websites, allowing people to spread the word at the click of button. Recommend-It's free referral service is used on over 140,000 websites, enabling webmasters to easily incorporate the feature. Visitors can spread the word about the site, enter promotions and contests, and all the while the website earns revenue for each person who uses Recommend-It's services from its referral.

Since it has become so easy to forward messages, the primary issue has become how to motivate people to pass something on. Movies, as in the John West example, have successfully spread because they can be very entertaining. But attention spans are short, especially in the demographics usually targeted by this kind of marketing. *Zeitgeist*—a word neatly stolen from German—means "the spirit of the times". As the pace of cultural change accelerates, the job of marketers is precisely to tap the zeitgeist, to create messages that people feel represent the cutting-edge of society and culture.

Flat Eric was a marketing phenomenon unleashed by Levi's Europe. Three brief television advertisements showed an outsized yellow sock puppet dancing to techno music in a car. The Internet version of the movies spread like wildfire, a cult movement was created, the Flat Eric single reached number one in the UK and Germany, and Flat Eric went on to take Japan by storm, despite the advertisements not being screened there. Levi's UK advertising agency Bartle Bogle Hegarty, in its regular trawling of underground art, had seen a short movie created for $2,000 by French director Quentin Dupieux, decided it had street-credibility, recreated it as an advertisement that barely referred to Levi's, and saw it spread like wildfire.

Marketers are now engaged in a battle to create more virulent memes than anyone else. This is far more art than science, because the cultural environment is changing so quickly. Something that excites people one day may seem boring a month later. Creativity in marketing—and an associated ability to be on the edge of trends—is becoming more rather than less important in the networks. In this book's Postscript, we will look at the future of the propagation and filtering of marketing messages.

2. Foster network effects
Let's say you receive an e-mail that says "You've Got Cash!" All you need to do is open a free no-obligation account, and you can claim the payment. It's a pretty easy decision to make. Paypal, a company that enables anyone with an e-mail address to send money electronically, has designed a business model that has built over 16 million users with almost no traditional marketing or advertising.

Paypal is trying to create the dominant network for Internet payments. It's a classic example of network effects: people will tend to use whichever system is used by the most other people. Paypal has to make it easy and worthwhile for users to sign up for its payment system and spread the word. It got started with a straightforward proposition for potential users: sign up for an account, and we'll pay you $10. Initial subscriptions were healthy but not earth-shattering. Then participants in online auction site eBay came across Paypal, realized it was the easiest way to make payments online, and by using it introduced it to others who were regularly sending money to many people. In early 2000, Paypal's user base grew by 7% to 10% every day. Since then Paypal has reduced the payment for user registration to $5, and introduced conditions that help ensure that the user will be profitable. It also runs a user-referral scheme, whereby whoever introduces someone who is eligible for the $5 bonus, also receives $5. Certainly one perspective on Paypal's initiatives is that it is implementing aggressive pricing models to build the network, however the whole structure of its business model is based on exploiting network effects to their fullest.

Any information-based product or service has potential network effects, and marketers need to take full advantage of these. Companies need to assess precisely how their customers may benefit as the network grows larger. Out of this can emerge a multitude of potential strategies to engage customers in promotion on your behalf… and their own. You must communicate effectively the benefits to users of building the network, and make it easy for them to do so. A simple example is how cell phone providers offer extremely low rates for calls to subscribers on the same network. Customers will actively want to get their friends to use the same mobile provider, because it means they will have to pay less for their calls. The users of Apple computers have always understood the importance of spreading the word, and Apple has done what it can to help them. Guy Kawasaki's job as Chief Evangelist at Apple was largely to assist the missionary efforts of its customers. One user designed a "Made With Macintosh" logo to be placed on websites, clearly explaining to Mac users why they should want to proactively promote the platform in this way.

3. Create interaction

If you watch MTV, how often do you wish you could put on your own choice of music? If you live in Europe, you can. Viewers do the programming on MTV's VideoClash. The audience uses voice telephone, mobile text messaging, or the MTV website to vote on what music video should be played next, so even the producers don't know which video will be broadcast until 15 seconds before it goes on screen. The great success of the initial program in the UK has resulted in VideoClash being rolled out in local language versions across Europe.

The new game is creating interaction. Increased interaction between you and consumers results in a stronger brand presence, additional marketing opportunities, and more information about your current and potential customers. At the same time, the more interaction there is between your customers, especially if it's related to your offerings, the more likely positive messages will spread. The more your target market is connected, the better for you.

Instant messaging and text messaging are at the vanguard of how the flow of messages is changing. In early 2002 there were already well over 75 million users of instant messaging in the US alone, and the number looks set to soar as the technology becomes integrated into websites. Instant messaging "buddy lists" that show people's chat friends are now starting to include automated conversationalists. Activebuddy is helping companies like eBay and Ellegirl magazine to create instant messaging buddies that interact with their customers by answering questions and chatting. Another firm, Facetime, is helping companies like Dell and FAO Schwartz to use instant messaging to communicate with their customers.

In Europe, text messaging is now part of everyday life for many people. A few marketers are trying to send advertising messages to consumers' mobile phones, but this is more likely to turn people off than attract them. However it creates a new medium for interaction. A UK campaign for Cadbury's chocolates put a code number on the wrapper of 65 million chocolate bars. Customers sent a text message of the code for a chance of winning major prizes, bringing a wide-ranging response of people who not only provided their mobile phone number, but yield extremely detailed information on distribution and consumption previously unavailable to manufacturers.[3]

4. Choose fertile territory

Research in Motion (RIM) was a relatively unknown Canadian company in early 1999, when it launched what it believed had the potential to be a hot product—a mobile pager and e-mail device called the BlackBerry. It didn't have the budget for a massive advertising campaign, as many of its peers were undertaking at the time, so it sought to tap the opinion-makers in its target community. RIM recruited around 50 "wireless e-mail evangelists", whose job was to visit Fortune 500 companies, and set up BlackBerry pilot programs that offered free trial pagers. These evangelists focused on accessing mobile professionals such as salespeople and consultants, and staff in the companies' IT departments, because they knew that these were the ones likely both to take to the device, and spread the word to their peers.[4]

Since messages increasingly spread by word of mouth, marketing campaigns need to be designed to tap those groups that are most likely to spread the word, and be influential in the target market. Sometimes the relevant communities will be obvious, for example in marketing baby products. In other cases it may be necessary to tap related groups. Wherever possible you want to gear your promotions to the people who are the most connected, both technologically and socially. Absolut Vodka initially focused on the San Francisco gay community in its US promotions, because it is a well-connected trend-setting scene, not because it was the target market.[5]

Marketing is increasingly about spreading messages within broad communities of consumers, who may or may not be customers. It is designed to generate positive impressions, attract interest, and hopefully create customers. Once they are customers, the critical network is the one that connects them with the company. Here we will explore how to create customer feedback loops.

Building customer feedback loops

Consumer expectations have soared over the last years. In a world of digital connections, customers take for granted virtually immediate responses to their problems and desires. For the last few years companies have been working hard to improve their service response, by creating new service delivery channels, building sophisticated automated response systems, and enhancing call center processes. The intent is to respond to customers' issues quickly and efficiently.

What companies now need to do is to close the loop. This means using feedback to change *how* things are done. What customers tell you should result, not just in fixing a problem or trying to keep them happy, but actually in enhancing services, products, and their delivery, and swiftly getting feedback on those changes. This creates a living cycle that builds powerful relationships, and a level of value to customers that can be hard to equal.

Applying customer feedback to improving how business is done is not new. What is new is how communication technologies enable companies to integrate input and feedback so quickly that the customers become deeply involved in the company's core processes. This tight customer feedback loop is illustrated in Figure 6-2.

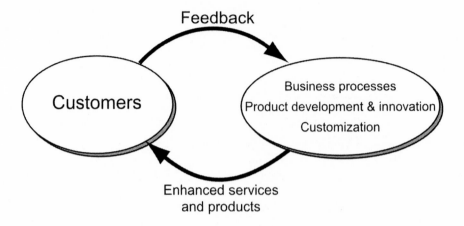

Figure 6-2: Customer feedback loops

The heart of the issue is how customer feedback is used. It's easy today to gather feedback quickly and effectively through Internet focus groups and by monitoring online discussions; but unless that input is applied to make things different, it is wasted. It is only when customers' feedback results in changes that they can notice that there is a true customer feedback loop rather than simply a response to complaints. There are four key steps in bringing these customer feedback loops to life, and in the process creating true competitive advantage.

1. Monitor customer discussions
Many people who would never have complained to a company are happy to express their thoughts on PlanetFeedback.com, a website where consumers can share their experiences and views. It's easier and less confrontational than writing a letter or making a telephone call, consumers feel that their voices are heard because at least their peers will read their opinions, and they understand the power of numbers in attracting the attention of corporations. In a typical story on a similar Australian website, aptly named notgoodenough.com, one user found the manufacturer of a faulty heater responded with alacrity when his complaint was posted in a public forum, after getting no answer to letters and e-mails.

The new forms of dialogue that have emerged in the Internet Age present a massive opportunity for companies to gain a deeper insight into their customers' views and opinions. Chat and discussion forums are the new agoras—public, open spaces in which everyone can hear what others are saying and join in with their own thoughts. The proliferation of these means that far more of the world of customer interaction is visible, but it is harder to monitor everything that is going on. Companies like eWatch, a division of PR Newswire, scan public activity on the Internet and report to their clients on any references to their company and products. However these services are promoted mainly as a means of identifying and dealing with negative messages. For example eWatch also offers services such as getting forum hosts to delete messages, and tracking down anonymous posters. There may be times when these are useful, but monitoring what is being said about the company is far more than a public relations tool. It should be one of the primary inputs into everything the company does, and how it tries to continually improve what it does. Staples.com has a "service improvement" team that uses feedback directly from customers as well as from third-party monitoring sources to enhance the website and service.[6]

Customer communities often provide the best source of direct input, because participants expect the company to be monitoring discussion, and are more likely to make constructive comments. Unfortunately, there are quite a few customer forums that provide customers with a chance to interact, but their comments are either left unread, or are not acted on in any form. This is a big missed opportunity.

2. Get faster, richer feedback… and use it

Procter & Gamble now does almost half of its product tests and focus groups online, allowing it to get feedback on new product trials within a few days rather than months. Every one of the more than 250 brands within the company's vast empire of consumer products regularly runs focus groups, so the shift results not just in cost savings but also probably more importantly a substantial acceleration in the feedback and product development process.[7] In a similar vein, every day eBay e-mails thousands of customers that have been in touch with the company within the previous 24 hours to invite them to respond to a detailed satisfaction survey. Companies

The challenge for companies today is to find effective ways of involving their customers in the innovation process, rather than simply seeking feedback or market testing along the way.

can now swiftly get far more detailed feedback from their customers. The obvious first step is to take advantage of communication technologies to tap that faster, richer feedback. The initial problem is that there is now often far too much information. In addition, business processes must change in order to take advantage of the new wealth of feedback.

Clearly one of the richest channels for customer feedback is a company's salesforce. The challenge is taking the immense wealth of information potentially available and making it useful and actionable, without disturbing salespeople from their primary duties. Companies can get their salespeople to contribute ideas or snippets of information into an online system. This is only worthwhile if a streamlined filtering mechanism is in place to ensure action is taken, however this also means that salespeople can be rewarded for valuable contributions. Innovation processes such as the BT Ideas systems referred to in Chapter 5 can be adapted to tap customer feedback. One company provides a different topic each week for its salespeople to focus on in gathering customer feedback.

In technology product development, traditionally alpha testing is an early stage process performed inside the company, while beta testing gathers feedback on a pre-release version from potential customers. It is now possible to rapidly get input from a very broad range of external beta testers, but doing this effectively is becoming an enormous job. BetaSphere, a company that provides software and services to incorporate customer input into product development, has attracted clients such as Palm, Cisco, HP, and Federal Express. These companies need to recruit a broad and representative range of testers; work with them to ensure they are providing useful, timely information; and collate their input into reports that developers can apply directly in enhancing products. Taking full advantage of the new possibilities of information flows requires applying effective processes. In addition to making beta testing far more valuable, the development of the networks means that even very early stage alpha testing can include customers. This is exactly what IBM's alphaWorks unit does, as described in Chapter 5. Customer involvement can shift from product development to innovation—generating the ideas that drive a business.

3. Involve customers in innovation

United Parcel Service (UPS) regularly visits its largest clients, sending teams that include product development, strategy, and innovation executives, as well as the account manager, to meet its clients' senior management for up to a day, presenting and discussing forthcoming UPS initiatives. Everything from recently launched products through to very early stage concepts are brought to the table to see what may strike a chord with the clients. In one of these sessions with Gateway, UPS proposed the idea of merging goods in transit. This meant that UPS would put together the shipments from all of Gateway's suppliers as they were being transported, to result in regular deliveries of all the required goods for production, rather than a multitude of uncoordinated parcels coming into the dock. Gateway expressed enthusiasm at the idea, worked with UPS to refine the concept and implementation, and was the first to adopt this new service that was subsequently offered across all of UPS's major clients.

Customers always have and always will be the greatest source of innovation. That doesn't mean that companies can simply ask their customers what they want, and give it to them. Innovation stems from the interaction between a company and its customers, bringing different perspectives together both to come up with novel ideas, and develop them into a useful form. The challenge for companies today is to find effective ways of involving their customers in the innovation process, rather than simply seeking feedback or market testing along the way. The potential power of this is unleashed in a networked world. British consultancy KSBR works with major firms such as Lloyds TSB to identify customers who have complained vocally. It asks these customers to develop ideas to help the companies improve their service, and gets them to present their ideas to company executives in highly interactive forums or on video. KSBR finds that most customers who complain have very constructive ideas, and actively want to help companies to perform better.

Lucas Arts asked its customers to help develop its game "Star Wars Galaxies". A year before the planned release date, the developers launched a website specifically to get broad participation in the design process. As the game was developed, updates were posted to the site, participants were asked their opinions on design issues, and the lead designers answered questions from the community. Die-hard fans were able to debate issues dear to their heart, such as whether any player should have the ability to achieve the ultimate Star Wars gaming ambition—to become a Jedi Knight. Clearly the exercise was valuable for its promotional value, but as importantly, it resulted in an award-winning, top-quality game that was truly designed from the perspective of the user.[8]

In Chapter 5 you saw how open source software demonstrates the power of customer innovation, as well as the distinction between idea generation and development. This helps frame how you can involve your customers in innovation. Focus on getting ideas directly from customers, as well as gaining insights that will spark your own ideas. Actively engage in dialogues about their needs and issues. Get designers and product developers, not just marketers, to interact directly with customers. And design development processes that involve customers throughout. Customer testing is not enough—you have to get them involved earlier. That is what creates winning products and services.

4. Use input for customization

The product designers who spend a day at GE Plastics' Customer Innovation Center in Selkirk, New York, can leave the premises not only having developed the exact color and effects they require for a new product, but toting home in their luggage an initial batch of color resin and sample plastic parts in their very own custom color. If the library of 20,000 standard colors isn't sufficient, customers can create a new one, within a few minutes produce plastic samples to view under a range of lighting conditions, and then if they have brought plastic molds, can evaluate how their own product looks in the selected color. For those who prefer to avoid leaving the office, an online service allows a similar interactive process for color development, producing small lots of the customer-designed color within 48 hours. The customer colors are held in the system, and an extranet gives customers a secure way to share color information with third-party designers and manufacturers.[9]

Billions are spent annually doing customer surveys, yet many of these focus mainly on asking customers how satisfied they are with different aspects of service. This feedback certainly can be useful, but far more valuable is applying information directly to customizing service and products. Consider how you can build this approach into your business model, as GE Plastics has done.

Many companies have missed much of the potential value in how they have implemented customer relationship management (CRM) systems. These systems can only ever be as valuable as the information they contain. As firms gather information on all of their interactions with customers, they can learn a great deal on how to service them better, and what sorts of offers they are likely to accept. However, whether you interact with your customers online, through call centers, or through dedicated salespeople, you have an opportunity to ask them questions. So given your customers' limited attention span, what few questions do you want to ask them?

Rather than asking your customers whether they are satisfied with your service, try asking questions that will enable you to customize what you do for them. In Chapter 4 you saw how this kind of approach can be applied in high-value services relationships, but it is just as relevant in every industry. Depending on your business, you might ask what communication channels they prefer, whether they prefer a large typeface, what operating system they use, or the configuration of their loading docks. Customers recognize that this sort of information enables you to provide them with better service, so they are usually very open. The trick is designing your CRM system so that it can both accept this sort of information, and apply it directly to customized service. If the system is designed with this in mind, then it can prompt customers or relationship staff for the information, and then immediately demonstrate to customers that you are listening to them, by using it to directly enhance service. This can do an immense amount in making them more open to sharing information with you, creating loyalty, building rich customer feedback loops, and uncovering far more revenue-generating opportunities.

Customer feedback loops link the people inside an organization with the most important people outside: the customers. However in order to be able to respond effectively and create the service levels and innovation that will delight customers, the workers in a company themselves need to be closely networked. Let us examine the flow of knowledge and work within organizations.

The flow of work and knowledge

While a Shell affiliate was developing an oil well near Damascus, a drilling tool become stuck near the surface of the well. The cable had snapped, wrapping around the tool and making it unable to be moved in any direction. No one at the facility or in the local Shell country operations knew how to fix the problem. At the same time as considering whether they would have to abandon the well, they promptly sent a message to Shell's Global Network covering expertise in well operations. The person with the greatest experience in the field was usually located in the Netherlands, but was currently in Bangladesh. After being contacted and put in touch with the local well-drilling team, he was able to run simulations and suggest different equipment to use, enabling the tool to be freed and the well to resume production.[10]

How do you connect knowledge with its application? Every company confronts the same issue. However Shell provides a particularly pointed example, with 81,000 people around the world each developing highly refined expertise that can be of value across the organization. Shell has focused on developing networks of experts in a wide range of domains. It also collects documents and models that can be valuable to others around the world, but it recognizes that in the case of highly-specialized knowledge, it is most valuable simply to connect people. Shell Exploration has developed three core global networks focused on technical disciplines, as well as a number of other ones covering business issues such as procurement and competitive intelligence. The basic functionality of the systems is to allow anyone to post questions, and get responses from anywhere in the world for possible solutions, or who or what might provide an answer. Often users find that others have already asked similar questions, and can find the answers posted. In many cases the exchange simply helps the people who have a problem to identify those that have the relevant knowledge, and they can then continue discussions by e-mail, telephone, or if necessary by travel. Another initiative called "Global Consultancy" provides a "yellow pages" directory of leading subject experts throughout Shell's worldwide operations that can be contacted and brought in for short-term assignments to different locations and divisions.[11]

The challenge of accessing and applying knowledge within organizations can be met through two main approaches. People's knowledge can be embedded into documents, models, and software, so that many others can use it. And staff can be connected directly to others with relevant experience to apply their knowledge to a specific issue.[12] These two strategies— sometimes called "collections and connections"—are relevant to every business. However, increasingly, providing connections to others is becoming the dominant tool. One reason is that in today's business environment innovation is essential. Following processes effectively is important, but the greatest value is created by enhancing how things are done, and this is almost always a complex, collaborative task.

As you saw early in this chapter, communities are a subset of networks. The idea of "communities of practice", that bring together the practitioners of a technical or work domain into collaborative groups, has recently attracted enormous management attention. In a business world increasingly based on applying specialist knowledge, this must be a primary emphasis, but it is easy to overlook the reality that most work today is multi-disciplinary, and so it is frequently the connections made across fields that are the most valuable. Building communities focused on specialist topics is invaluable, but what is more important is the bigger picture of creating a deeply networked organization. Managers must take the following five key steps:

1. Identify and empower network hubs
Look at just about any kind of network you can think of—for example the Internet or social connections—and you will see that a relatively small number of "hubs" account for the majority of connections. In the case of companies, there are always a few particularly widely-connected people who not only know what is happening and who has expertise in their own division, but also have valuable contacts in other parts of the organization or other locations. These people are the hubs who make the organization a network.

It's great to have an online system that lists the resumes and experience of every person in the company. "Yellow pages" initiatives of this kind, similar to that described in the Shell example above, are often one of the first in any internal knowledge sharing program, as they're relatively easy to implement, and can have immediate benefits. However, they by no means reduce the importance of network hubs in connecting people. Having a personal introduction often makes a tremendous difference. Someone calling you because they've seen your name on a database is likely to elicit a different response than if they say they're calling on the suggestion of a trusted mutual contact. One of the reasons is that knowledge networks are in effect marketplaces—you trade your knowledge for other benefits, largely the ability to draw on others when needed. The more that social networks are involved in this process, the more readily the company can become an effective knowledge market. In addition, the network hubs know who really is the best in their field, who is likely to help, and how best to approach them—all information that is never shown on a database. In addition to providing online means of connecting people, companies need to identify the people who are already acting as network hubs, and help them to be better at this invaluable function.

BP Amoco actively develops individuals who are well-connected across the organization. Employees contact these widely-connected hubs when they need to access expertise and resources, but don't know where to find them in their far-flung organization. The managers of these network hubs try to ensure they have the time available to fulfil this role in addition to their normal responsibilities. Connecting people becomes an informal part of their jobs.[13] Many firms now use network analysis software to identify who are the network hubs for valuable information flow, and use this to nurture people in these roles or to promote better working structures. Deloitte Touche Tohmatsu Australia has used network analysis for some of its service lines to identify which people are most useful in winning business, and the most generous with their ideas, time, and contacts. This helps individual practice groups and partners to develop more effective strategies for working within the broader firm.

2. Nurture communities of specialists
Montgomery Watson Harza is one of the world's largest environmental and infrastructure engineering firms, engaged in projects such as building the world's biggest centrifuge to treat digested biosolids (let's keep that in engineering-speak) for the City of Los Angeles, and constructing wastewater treatment facilities for an Intel chip plant in China. Since its work depends on highly specialized engineers spread across more than 30 countries, it has placed a strong emphasis on developing focused knowledge communities. Its initial work concentrated on identifying those groups who already had substantial useful interaction, and providing them with the tools and resources to work more effectively. For each identified community a "knowledge leader" was chosen, who commands the respect of his or her peers, has the necessary social skills to form cohesive and productive groups, and very importantly has personal ties to key knowledge leaders, especially in other regions of the world. These nominated leaders are given both classroom and online training courses on how to run effective communities, and are supported by dedicated staff in their community leadership roles. Technology plays an important role in being able to intermediate communication, but the role of face-to-face contact is clearly recognized. Community members are provided with the budgets to meet regularly, as a complement to their online activities.

Any firm that doesn't actively nurture connections with the broader community of its clients, suppliers, partners—and even competitors—risks isolation from the vital flow of information and ideas through the economy.

Even though nurturing communities of specialists is only one element of creating the effective flow of knowledge and work in an organization, this often provides an essential linchpin for all efforts to build knowledge networking. The affiliation felt by people who have a common field of expertise or practice can be very powerful—they usually want both to learn from their peers and to actively share their knowledge. These initial networks can help to seed broader-based initiatives and collaboration.

Organizations should begin by identifying the informal communities, the groups that communicate and get together for no other reason than because they find it a valuable part of their work and personal development. They often don't think of themselves as communities, but they're likely to be quietly doing marvelous things for the organization. If a community is already thriving, allow it to continue, but offer resources such as communication tools, recognition, and possibly a formalization of its role. Since most workers are short of time, it can be very useful to make it part of key members' job descriptions to participate in internal communities.

One of the most important success factors for communities is leadership. The reality is that effective groups are almost always centered around a person or small group who moderates, encourages, connects, seeks resources, and generally makes a disparate and often distributed group cohesive. There are a clear set of skills required, and training in community leadership for those who are nominated or fall into that role is invaluable. At the same time, good leadership requires respect from the community members. Schlumberger, a large oil services company, has placed a strong emphasis on connecting its technical experts and field engineers in communities. Community leaders are formally elected by the members, ensuring that the leaders are trusted by their peers, and virtually always well-connected. The voting turnout for community leaders exceeds 50%, reflecting the importance members place on the issue.[14]

3. Create adaptive systems
Too much structure in trying to enhance internal networks and collaboration usually results in the unforeseeable—and most valuable—interactions never happening. On the other hand allowing things to happen by themselves usually means that very little happens. How can you tread the delicate boundary between creating enabling structures and ways of working, without stifling the unpredictably useful connections from emerging?

Eli Lilly's Research and Development group has implemented an internal collaboration system designed by CompanyWay, a start-up that applies to collaboration the principles of how swarms of insects can demonstrate organized behavior. The system allows a broad range of participants to propose ideas, add comments, and assess the value of each others' ideas and comments. As discussion on a particular topic proceeds, the groups' collective judgment is applied to determining whether to pursue or abandon the idea, and how best to modify and apply it. Over time, the contributors whose comments are consistently rated highly by their peers gain privileges in the discussions. Throughout the process participants are allocated "credit" points depending on how their contributions are assessed. One of the most useful aspects of Eli Lilly's implementation of the system is that a number of users who were not formal experts made some of the most valuable contributions, as assessed by the group. Ideas are the true currency, and leaders emerge through the quality of their input rather than their titles or qualifications.

The networks are alive. So we need to treat them as living systems, allowing behaviors to emerge rather than imposing rigid structures. When ants forage for food, they lay down a pheromone trail. When they are in new territory they walk around more or less randomly, but when they stumble across food, they will take it back to the nest, and return for more. Since ants will tend to follow paths that have stronger pheromone trails—that is have been walked along by more ants—other ants will discover the path and go to the food, further reinforcing the path and bringing other ants to take the spoils. What the ants are doing is actually collaborative filtering, in which the best discoveries of individuals are made known the group. Building these principles into collaborative systems, as CompanyWay and others are doing, creates dynamic ways for the intelligence of groups to emerge.

4. Develop a collaborative culture
In 2000 Buckman Laboratories was named the Most Admired Knowledge Enterprise. It could bask briefly in the accolades, but it had been a long hard slog, and it's by no means over. As chairman Bob Buckman noted, 90% of the work in building its famous knowledge-sharing capabilities was in shifting the company's culture. Its online knowledge-sharing system, called K'Netix, is world-class, but as anyone who has worked to implement collaborative systems knows, the technology is the easy part.

In the early 1990s Bob Buckman in his then role as CEO played a leading role in transforming the company's culture. The bold move to make information openly available at all levels of the firm was embraced by some, however many middle-managers were unenthusiastic, while others were openly hostile, going so far as to forbid their staff to participate in the systems. Without initially providing explicit rewards or censures, it began to become apparent to staff that those who actively shared their knowledge gained better opportunities, whereas the recalcitrants stagnated in their careers, and were sometimes visited by the chairman for a quiet word. Continued initiatives including a knowledge-sharing conference helped to cement the message over time, but perhaps most important was the obvious positive impact of the evolving culture on the success of the firm. Many Buckman employees refer to the firm's Code of Ethics to provide a clear direction for their daily work. The new CEO Steve Buckman led an 18 month effort to bring together input from across the company to develop a simple list of guiding principles. Management sees the Code as a foundation for building the culture the company requires to succeed.[15]

Buckman Laboratories' experience illustrates many of the issues of building a collaborative culture. Enabling connections between staff is of little use unless they are willing to collaborate by sharing knowledge and actively working together. Whatever a company's current situation, it needs to improve collaboration in order to succeed in a hyper-networked economy. There are no silver bullets, just an ongoing commitment to basics. There is no substitute for clear leadership. If those at the top of the firm continually reaffirm the importance of effective collaboration, this provides a platform for change. Messages need to be repeated and consistent. All communication programs should be designed to convey the importance of collaboration. And remuneration and recognition programs must reflect personal contributions. Many firms, for example Siemens, Xerox, and IBM Global Services, have implemented processes to reward people depending on how much they contribute to knowledge systems, however these are easily abused and don't change underlying attitudes. Collaboration in some form must be a component of employee assessment, and even more importantly promotion opportunities must be linked to behaviors. One uncooperative person progressing successfully in their career can undo the benefits of an entire communication program. However the crux of the issue is people realizing that their ability to do their own jobs well depends on effective collaboration from others, which in turn relies on how well they contribute.

5. Foster external networks

When Bristol-Myers Squibb, a $16 billion pharmaceutical company, examined the relative success of its research divisions, it found that its oncology division had performed especially well for an extended period. The major difference between the researchers in this division and those in others—and the likely reason for the better performance—was the span and richness of their networks and interaction outside the organization.[16] Other pharmaceutical firms, such as GlaxoSmithKline, have also placed an emphasis on building active communities and interaction beyond the boundaries of the organization.

Any firm that doesn't actively nurture connections with the broader community of its clients, suppliers, partners—and even competitors—risks isolation from the vital flow of information and ideas through the economy. No firm today is self-sufficient in knowledge and ideas—specialists must engage with others outside the firm. And as you saw in Chapter 3, work processes are now often distributed over several companies. Those who work together within that process are a community, whether they recognize it or not.

Every effort should be made to get your staff to actively engage outside your company. Provide the communication tools for your specialists to create communities with their peers. Encourage staff to get involved with academic groups, through teaching or research. Sponsor informal gatherings with the primary intent of building useful dialogue within your broader community. Assisting company alumni associations can help build broad external connections for the firm, among other benefits. It has always been important to hire people with strong personal networks and the ability to form wide connections, but this is now becoming a dominant factor in staff selection.

Vital Connections: Chapter 6

In Part 2 of this book, we have examined how organizations change as the networks come to life. As the boundaries between companies blur, firms must demonstrate leadership with their partners and within their industry. Relationships can quickly grow deeper and broader in a digital world, however the constraining factors are trust and attention. Innovation is increasingly a collaborative discipline, creating a whole new world of intellectual property issues. Today, an organization is its presence in the flow of information and ideas, in which marketing, customer feedback loops, and knowledge must all be connected in rich networks.

In Part 3 we will examine how strategy is evolving. Business is now conducted in the flow economy, which is the convergence of every industry that is driven by the flow of information and ideas. The distribution of digital content, including entertainment and high-value information, is quickly shifting, while the world of services is already an intrinsic part of the flow economy. Finally, we will examine the strategies that individuals must take to participate successfully in the living networks.

PART 3: Evolving Strategy

Today's connected economy is dominated by the flow of information and ideas. This affects not just the most obvious industries of telecoms, technology, media, entertainment, financial services, and professional services. Every company in every industry is finding its ability to succeed is founded on how effectively it positions itself in this emerging "flow economy".

In Part 3 of *Living Networks* you will discover how strategy changes in our hyper-connected world. Chapter 7 describes the foundations of the flow economy, and provides action steps for companies to develop powerful new strategies. In Chapter 8 I examine how the world of content distribution is changing as information flows freely, and effective strategies for participants. Chapter 9 looks at the new world of services, including both digital services and evolving strategies for professional services firms. In Chapter 10 I go on to look at the connected economy from the perspective of free agents, and the strategies they must take to succeed.

Part 4 briefly examines the future of business in our networked world, presenting 10 predictions for what awaits us.

Opportunities and Risks in the New Convergence

Devices, communications, and industries are all converging into one vast space for doing business. This is the flow economy, in which almost all value is based on the flow of information and ideas. Companies must continually reposition themselves in this flow economy, both to meet new competitive challenges from unexpected quarters, and to take advantage of the massive emerging opportunities.

For a few years there in the mid 1990s Japan seemed to be lagging in the uptake of mobile communications. Then suddenly it exploded, and everywhere you looked there were mobile phones, from the giggling girls sporting tiny toy-like devices on wrist straps to the dark-suited office workers muttering earnestly into their phones as they bustled by. At the heart of the phenomenon was NTT DoCoMo, which launched its i-mode service in February 1999, to see almost 20 million paid subscribers snatch it up within two years.

What has made NTT DoCoMo such an enormous success, and its glitzy showcase offices in Tokyo a Mecca for pilgrimage by telecom executives from around the world, is simply its business model. It wanted to make the service fun, easy, and inexpensive, and to do that it had to create the conditions for excellent content providers to want to participate. It passes on to providers an amazing 91% of what it bills its customers for content usage, but in return it has strict quality control standards, first in vetting the up to 100 proposals a week it receives from content providers, and then in monitoring the content, usability, and pricing on an ongoing basis.[1] As a result, it boasts over 50,000 high quality content sites, ranging across news, horoscopes, karaoke, multiuser games, and far more.

DoCoMo gives access to this vast array of content and services by providing its customers with mobile always-on connectivity and the required interfaces. The firm doesn't manufacture the i-mode handsets—these are made by the likes of NEC, Panasonic, and Sony—but it works with them to define the device specifications, and sells the handsets directly to its customers, all clearly emblazoned with the NTT DoCoMo logo and no other. DoCoMo has announced plans to publish the technical standards for the i-mode service and to open the network to other providers, after initially keeping the standards closed. However DoCoMo's powerful relationships with its close to 30 million customers place it in an extremely solid position moving forward.

What Japan's leading mobile telephony firm has done is positioned itself to provide each of the elements that enable far richer and easier flows of information and ideas. Back not so long ago, a large proportion of the value in industrial economies was in tangible flows, like transport, water, and electricity. In the early 19th century canals dominated global stockmarkets, with railroads taking their turn a little later. These new, efficient modes of transport enabled the flow of goods on which the rest of economy depended. In the first half of the 20th century many of the largest companies were those that provided the infrastructure and distribution for flows of water, electricity, and oil and gas, again providing a foundation for other economic activity.

Today, economic flows consist overwhelmingly of information and ideas. However, now these flows provide far more than just an underlying infrastructure for other industries. They are intrinsic to almost every aspect of the economy. We now all work and do business in the emerging *flow economy*. Business strategy must be reinvented in this new world. In this chapter you will discover the shape of this converging economic landscape, and steps to position your organization effectively within the flows.

The convergence of convergence

It's hard to read a business or technology magazine these days without seeing the 'c' word splattered around like the victim in a Quentin Tarantino movie. However "convergence" has many different meanings. The term is primarily applied to how devices, communications, and industries are each becoming unified. These three major convergences are themselves coming together to create a new convergence that is giving birth to today's flow economy.

Device convergence

Humanity is just beginning to emerge from a strange phase in its technological evolution, in which people have carried a multitude of separate digital and communications devices for different purposes. Over the last years it has not been at all unusual for people to carry a cell phone, personal digital assistant (PDA), and pager. Many have also been squeezing into their bulging pockets or handbags a mobile e-mail device like the RIM Blackberry. It seemed like the more technology progressed, the more devices we had. So will our glorious techno-future give us yet more things to carry around?

For years now, PR and media hype have promised better, but only now are we finally getting there. In the spring of 2002 several players, including Motorola, Handspring, and start-up Danger Inc., launched what were billed as the ultimate in handheld devices. These lightweight devices combine mobile phone, e-mail, Internet browser, and a calendar, all literally in the palm of your hand.[2] It is becoming increasingly difficult to sell portable digital devices that do not cover the spectrum of functionality.

Devices are converging, not just in our palms and pockets, but also in our homes. The convergence of PCs and TVs has been far slower than the evangelists of the 1990s proclaimed, but each is gradually taking on some of the functionality of the other. People watch DVDs or news broadcasts on their PCs, and interactive TV is offering Internet-style services. Game consoles are emerging as powerful multimedia platforms that have the potential to play a central role in home entertainment. A battle royal is under way, and the winners in this space will win big.

Communications convergence

When you pick up the telephone and dial a friend's number, you are quite possibly using technology that dates back to the 19th century. The public switched telephone network (PSTN) establishes a circuit directly between two people, tying up bandwidth for their conversation. Through much of the 20th century telephone companies gradually upgraded their networks to cope with growth in voice communication, a business that still earns more than the US national defense budget. Then in the 1980s and 1990s telecommunications companies built new kinds of networks to carry the massive explosion of data communications. Different networks again were deployed for the boom in cable television. Some large telecom firms found themselves running over a dozen distinct networks, each based on different infrastructures and technical protocols.

Now this multitude of voice, data, and video communication networks is converging to a single network. Internet Protocol—usually called IP—is the clear winner as the most effective and versatile communications framework. It needs to be adapted for some uses, like voice, but in essence a single communications protocol and network can be used for all telecommunications. The major telecom companies are still in the process of phasing out old networks and replacing them with IP-based systems, and it will take many years for the transition to be complete, but the shift is by now inevitable. The implication is that telephone, television, Internet, and all other digital flows can be carried through the same pipes, potentially merging these businesses.

Industry convergence

In Tampa, Florida, a single building houses Media General's three operations: the *Tampa Tribune* newspaper, NBC affiliate WFLA-TV, and the Tampa Bay Online website. Newspaper reporters become talking heads in front of the TV cameras, television staff write stories for the paper, and material from both media is adapted to become online content. Across the nation, over 50 companies and partnerships are merging what were traditionally distinct media into single operations.

In companies representing almost every sector of the economy, boardrooms are hot with talk of "industry convergence". Each industry is experiencing convergence in a different form, but in each case it is driven by similar issues of deregulation, the increasing information component of business, the desire to maximize customer value, and companies seeking to leveraging their strengths into new domains.

Take a look at the financial services sector—including the banking, securities, insurance, and funds management industries—which has been the scene of a mating frenzy since the early 1990s. When financial firms' appetite was unleashed by the abolition of Depression-era regulations, they sought desperately to gain economies of scale on their massive investments in technology, cross-sell products to their customer base, and globalize their businesses. These powerful drivers were exemplified by the birth of colossus Citigroup, formed by the merger of Citibank and the Travelers Group, which itself had recently digested investment bank Salomon Smith Barney and insurer Primerica, among others.

Now the financial services sector is itself converging with other industries. Every major British retailer offers a broad range of financial services, while in Germany Volkswagen Bank has diversified from providing auto finance to now offer credit cards and mortgages. Banks too are extending their tentacles. Spanish bank BBVA joined with the country's leading telecoms firm, Telefónica Móviles, to form Móvilpago, that provides mobile payment facilities in Spain and 30 other countries. Barclays Bank and investment bank Nomura jointly own Shopsmart, Britain's largest online shopping site. The shift to defined-contribution health plans in the US is resulting in a convergence of health care, insurance, and other financial services. Accenture's relationships with health care firms are managed by its financial services group.

Other examples of industry convergence include pharmaceuticals, biotechnology, and medical devices, which have seen a flurry of mergers as the distinctions between their industries blur. In energy, the synergies between different sectors have became apparent, resulting in 17 mergers between gas and electricity firms in the US in the four years up to 2000. Even automakers are seeing their offerings overlapping with other industries. The Mazda MP3 is a sound system on wheels, while General Motors and Fidelity Investments have allied to provide real-time trading and financial information through GM's OnStar communications service. Later in this chapter you will discover new approaches to business strategy that cut through traditional industry boundaries.

The new convergence

Today, these three powerful convergent trends are themselves converging. As the economy becomes increasingly dominated by the flow of information and ideas, all boundaries between sectors are dissolving. Business now exists within a single convergent space, and the very concept of an "industry" is losing meaning.

It is not just the more obviously information-based sectors such as telecommunications, technology, entertainment, media, and financial and professional services that are participating in this new convergence. Many manufacturing, mining, energy, utility, transport, and retailing firms are also finding that much of the value they create is in the flow of information and ideas. Their strategies must become increasingly similar to those of more typical information-centered companies. As you saw in Chapter 4, companies selling manufacturing inputs such as Dow Chemical, Buckman Laboratories, and FMC Corporation are making information flows the heart of how they differentiate themselves from their competitors. FedEx, American Airlines, and Cemex are just a few of the firms that would appear to be firmly rooted in the physical economy, yet have been lauded as paragons of information-based businesses.

There are two key implications of this emerging convergent space. The first is that all companies are experiencing many new threats to their established businesses. The melting of traditional industry boundaries means that competitors can—and do— emerge from what not long ago seemed like totally different fields. In Europe, banks have seen new competitors spring up from department stores, supermarkets, car manufacturers, airlines, a furniture retailer, a semiconductor firm, and an oil company, among others.[3]

The second implication is that massive new opportunities are emerging as firms suddenly find that they can parlay their existing strengths into new and profitable domains. Gas and electricity utilities are piggybacking their existing relationships and infrastructure to provide communications services. Banks are jumping into retailing, online exchanges, media, software sales, and many other pursuits. Transport firms are becoming telecom providers, consultants, and logistics outsourcing firms. Every company must think of itself as no longer belonging to any particular industry, but simply a participant in the flow economy.

Every company must think of itself as no longer belonging to any particular industry, but simply a participant in the flow economy.

The six elements of the flow economy

In 1958 Tokyo Tsushin Kogyo, unheeding of advice from its bankers and partners that it shouldn't throw away an established and well-recognized brand, changed its name to Sony Corporation. At that time its product line consisted primarily of transistor radios and audio tape recorders. Over the following three decades Sony created, or was first to market with, many of the devices that have become an intrinsic part of our lives: color television, the video-cassette recorder, the Walkman personal cassette player, the CD player, and 8mm video.

Then, in 1988, Sony dramatically shifted its strategy, buying CBS Records, and the following year Columbia Pictures. It had moved from selling physical products that provided an interface to entertainment, to owning the entertainment itself. When you bought a CD Walkman, you might also pay Sony for the music that you played on it, and the videos you played on your VCR might be from Sony's extensive movie catalog. At the time, the business world was sceptical, casting doubt on the ability of a Japanese product manufacturer to manage creative businesses, and questioning that there really were any synergies between entertainment content and electronic goods.

Sony has in fact been biding its time, running its consumer electronics and content largely as separate businesses. Now is when broadband connectivity and the true birth of the networks is enabling its long-held vision to come to fruition. Howard Stringer, the CEO of Sony Corporation America, notes that until now Sony's millions of electronic devices have been bought without Sony ever having any knowledge or connection with its end-customers. Now it will be able to reach, identify, and connect those customers, providing them with not just interfaces to the networks, but also the content they access.[4] In Japan, Sony has an alliance with NTT to provide broadband access to users of its Playstation2 game console. Sony generates more revenue from online games than anyone else in the world, boasting 300,000 subscribers paying $10 per month to play its *EverQuest* multi-player game. In Japan, Sony offers stock trading and auto insurance through its website.

Sony's positioning illustrates many of the key principles of business in the emerging flow economy. Rather than thinking about traditional industry definitions, firms must position themselves relative to the flow of information and ideas. There are six elements of the flow economy, as shown in Figure 7-1:

- Standards
- Interfaces
- Connectivity
- Relationships
- Content
- Services

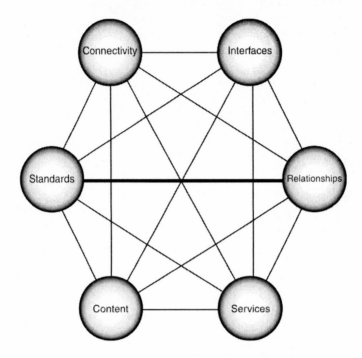

Figure 7-1: The six elements of the flow economy

The primary axis in the flow economy is that of standards and relationships. In Chapter 2 we introduced the basic drivers and strategies of a world increasingly built on standards. In Chapters 3, 4, and 6 we explored the role of relationships in the connected economy, and how this is intertwined with that of standards. However there are four more "flow elements" that combine with standards and relationships to form the landscape of the flow economy. These are connectivity; interfaces; content; and services.

Each of the six flow elements can act as a stand-alone business. However the greatest value is unlocked in how they are combined. Only a handful of firms—most obviously Microsoft, AOL Time Warner, and Sony—have the wherewithal to attempt to play in all six elements of the flow economy. Even then they must rely heavily on alliances. Companies must understand what flow elements they currently provide, and how they are positioned relative to other providers. This allows them to build on their existing strengths.

In this section we will look briefly at each of the six primary flow elements. We want to understand how each can be a business in its own right, and the fundamentals of how it can be combined with the other elements of the flow economy. In the following section we will present the key steps to reposition your company in the emerging flow economy.

The power of standards

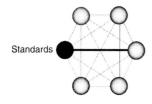

Whenever you click on a website to listen to audio or watch video, you are using streaming media, the technology that is enabling the Internet to begin to compete with radio and television. The streaming media market is a true David and Goliath battle, pitting RealNetworks against Microsoft. At the time of writing, the market is relatively balanced, with similar numbers of users for each system.

Streaming media is a classic standards battle, as discussed in Chapter 2, driven by the preferences of both consumers and distributors. As in every standards war, success breeds success. If one clearly dominates, then content providers will offer streaming in only that format, resulting in less interest by consumers in other choices, and thus a reinforcing feedback loop leaving just one winner. Given the current even-handed battle, most media sites must offer streaming in both formats. As befits a winner-take-all struggle, the two companies are waging a bitter war. Microsoft takes advantage of its operating system domination by bundling Windows Media with Windows XP, while RealNetworks has cut deals such as paying Major League Baseball $20 million for three years of exclusive Web radio broadcast rights.[5]

Standards are at the heart of the connected economy, as you saw in Chapter 2. Because of the forces driving towards open, accepted standards, it is increasingly difficult for a single company to run a standard as a stand-alone business. It is more viable for a consortium of powerful firms to establish and license a standard, but it is still challenging to run a standard purely as a business. If the owners try to make too much money from the use of a standard, more open—and less expensive—standards stand a good chance of attracting users. The MPEG-4 video compression technology—which is owned by 18 patent holders—is attempting to become a widely accepted standard, however it is jeopardizing that effort by charging steep licensing fees, as we will explore in more detail in Chapter 8.

In the case of streaming media, Microsoft and RealNetworks are battling over establishing a technological standard. However they don't make their money from the standard as such, but how it enables them to control the customer's interface to the networks, and thus form powerful relationships.

Most companies are in the situation of requiring standards in order to participate effectively in the flow economy. The value they provide is in the other five flow elements. As such, they would prefer to see open standards that enable greater flow that they can exploit in other ways. Wireless Application Protocol (WAP)—a kind of wireless version of the Internet—was developed by a broad range of companies in the wireless industry, because they could all benefit from the business opportunities enabled by an open standard. In all cases, companies must understand the current state of play in the standards that underlie their participation in the flow economy, and follow the action steps proposed in Chapter 2.

Relationships rule

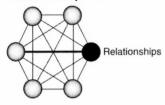

In 2001 Virgin Mobile was rated #1 in customer service for mobile telephones in the United Kingdom, despite not operating any telecommunications capacity.[6] It set up shop in August 1999, selling wireless services supplied by One 2 One, and became the fastest growing operator in the market, chalking up a million subscribers in less than one year. Virgin Mobile is in the business of relationships alone—all the other flow elements that comprise the total offering to the customer are provided outside the company.

As standards and networks rapidly become more open—and thus it becomes ever-easier for customers to change affiliations—relationships are becoming the primary source of value. In just about every case, whoever controls the relationship, controls the value. If you provide other flow elements, without the relationship, your business is very likely to become commoditized. However, the other flow elements can be used as tools in order to establish and build relationships, as you will discover later in this section. For example, the use of a network interface like a web browser or cell phone can be used to build relationships.

As you saw in Chapter 4, relationships can be thought of as habits or patterns of behavior by customers. These will include both digital and real components. Yahoo! gets more Internet visitors than any other company in the world, yet its audience is always literally just a click away from going to a competitor. Much of its efforts have gone into developing services such as Mail, Chat, Finance, and Photos that promote "sticky" relationships, that is require a significant effort to switch to other providers.

In the vast chain of video production and distribution, it is Blockbuster Video and its peers that control the final customer relationship. Blockbuster's relationships with its customers are less virtual than Yahoo's, as they usually physically visit its stores, and are offered various schemes and incentives—financial and otherwise—to come back regularly. However as a result, they know who is hiring videos, can learn their habits and profile, and regularly initiate direct, personalized communication.

Connecting the world

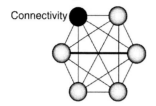

Connectivity

Communications bandwidth is a commodity. Global Crossing, founded in 1997, raised over $20 billion and ploughed it into fiber-optic cables providing digital connectivity around the world before filing for bankruptcy protection in early 2002. What it hadn't counted on was the rapid drop in prices for global bandwidth, meaning it couldn't reap a decent return on its massive investment. Global Crossing tried to build direct relationships with corporations by providing value-added services, but this market was dominated by AT&T and WorldCom, and Global Crossing found it could only sell its bandwidth wholesale.

As standards and networks rapidly become more open—and thus it becomes ever-easier for customers to change affiliations—relationships are becoming the primary source of value.

The commoditization of pure connectivity is amply demonstrated by the emergence over the last years of Band-X and a number of other bandwidth trading exchanges. Bandwidth trading is like the stockmarket. You can buy or sell, make money by day-trading, and not care who you're dealing with. However one big difference is that over the long-term equities prices will always go up, while Band-X's pretty colored charts show how the price of bandwidth seems to be heading just one way: down.

Despite the challenges of providing connectivity at a wholesale level, it can be very powerful when used to create relationships with consumers. Those firms that provide their customers with the famous "last mile" that connects their home to the global networks or cell phone to the local transmission tower are potentially in a very powerful position. Cable providers are clearly in the core business of providing bandwidth. However the real value in this business is in the relationships, and tapping the resultant business opportunities effectively.

Our interfaces to the networks

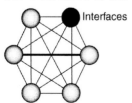

Interfaces

Buy a Logitech keyboard for your PC, and you will find it studded with a series of buttons that give you access to a range of Internet sites and services. Logitech, the world's largest maker of computer interface devices such as mice and keyboards, is leveraging its position to become part of the relationships that are at the foundation of the flow economy. Its alliance with Google means that the

Search button on its keyboards takes users to the Google Web site, going via its own Web site so that the two firms can keep track of the value of the well-positioned button. Other buttons on Logitech's keyboards—in their default configuration—lead users to Amazon.com, Citibank, and other service providers.

Interfaces are the bridge between people and the networks. Many of these are the digital devices discussed earlier in this chapter, including cell phone, PDA, PC, TV, game consoles, music players, video recorders, and so on. Web browsers too can be considered as interfaces to the networks. Microsoft's aggressive bundling of its Internet Explorer Web browser into the Windows operating system—which is at the heart of the Department of Justice's antitrust concerns about the company—demonstrates the very high value that Microsoft places on mediating people's access to the Internet. Web browsers can be set up so that users find it easier to access some services than others, thus channeling their attention and potentially spending. This illustrates how controlling people's interfaces to the networks can be used to create massive value.

Every aspect of the flow economy is ultimately accessed through an interface of some kind. Many businesses don't need to care about this—as long as their customers have PCs and Web browsers they are happy. However especially now that information flow is shifting to wireless channels, businesses need to understand how they can effectively deliver value through an entirely new set of emerging interfaces. For those firms that are playing in the interface space, the issue remains how to gain a solid user base, and leverage that hold into other flow elements, especially in helping to create or develop relationships.

The magic of content

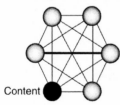

Content

On October 9, 2001, Disney released its classic *Snow White* on DVD, selling over one million copies on the first day. This provided a tidy addition to the more than $1 billion the film has earned Disney since it was first released in 1937. This is the kind of tale that has led to the constant refrain heard at every bar and party in Los Angeles: "content is king".

Content creation can certainly be run as an independent business, as long as it can generate sufficiently strong demand. If it does, then the providers of other flow elements will be eager to use the content to attract customers. Cable television companies attract subscribers on the basis of their quality of content, even though their core business is actually connectivity and relationships. By becoming increasingly involved in broadcasting and distribution, Disney has chosen to more directly exploit some of the opportunities created by the strength of its content. However content is not always the magic bullet. UK digital television firm ITV Digital collapsed in early 2002, largely as a result of having committed to pay £315 million over 3 years for soccer broadcast rights. Content providers on the one hand, and those providing the connectivity, interfaces, and relationships that channel content to customers, are involved in a complex dance to appropriate value for themselves.

People talk about "content" very loosely, but it important to understand that there are many different kinds of content, and that the appropriate strategies for each can vary widely. There are two key variables in content: *shelf-life*—that is how long the content remains valuable—and *audience focus*—which is how narrow or broad is the range of intended viewers. Figure 7-2 shows how these dimensions can be used to classify content. Entertainment tends to access broad audiences, and almost always attempts to have a long shelf-life. Disney has a clear policy of not overexploiting its most valuable content, in order to extend its shelf-life. In contrast, high-value information such as customized investment strategies, industry analysis, or strategy recommendations, gains its value specifically by being directly relevant to a very narrow group, or even an individual client, and its value usually falls rapidly over time. News is by its nature fleeting, but can become more valuable by being tailored for a particular group, or compiled into archives. In Chapter 8 we will discuss detailed strategies for content providers in the flow economy.

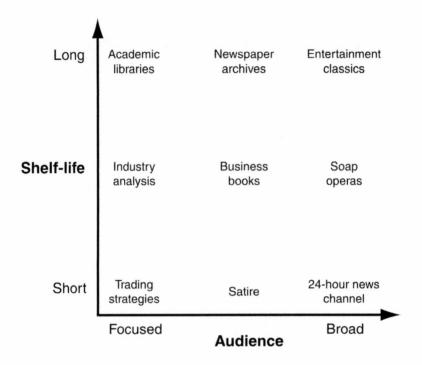

Figure 7-2: Classifying content by shelf-life and audience focus

The services that surround us

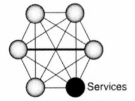

Unless you pull a crisp bill out of your pocket and hand it to someone, you have no way of making a payment without in some way using the banking system. Our entire economy is based on a set of networks that enable banks to transfer funds between accounts. You may have the best products or services in the world, but to make any money from them you are completely dependent on the banking system. In a networked world, financial services—not just payments but also credit, investment, insurance, and more—are fundamental to the flow economy.

Services—which are things that are done for you—are fundamental to the flow economy. They underpin much of the value of the other flow elements. As you have seen, financial services are necessary for all flows of value. We still live in a physical world, so the logistics of moving goods is a key part of the flow economy. In addition, increased connectivity allows a far broader range of services to be delivered online. Services are now often provided by software. In other cases, people still provide services such as consulting or even mowing the lawn, but we are connecting to those service providers by purely digital means.

Services can usually be run effectively as an independent business, and simply rely on the other flow elements being in place to deliver these effectively. In some cases, providing services can allow firms to leverage themselves into new types of business. Some financial services firms have done this effectively, as we'll see later in this chapter. UPS, Fedex, and their competitors, have all sought to move into entirely digital businesses such as secure document delivery, based on their existing positioning. However, as always, relationships are what enable services to be customized rather than become commoditized. In Chapter 9 we will explore in more detail the new world of services, focusing on digital services including software, and the evolution of professional services.

Strategic positioning in the flow economy

Walk into a youth hostel or budget hotel in any exotic country around the world, and you're more than likely to see someone reading a guidebook from Lonely Planet, the dominant global brand in budget travel. From its birth in the early 1970s, when Tony and Maureen Wheeler found so many people asking how they'd travelled overland from London to Melbourne that they decided to publish a book about it, the company has grown and repositioned itself neatly in the flow economy. The core of Lonely Planet's business remains the publication of over 500 regularly-updated travel titles, however that is now complemented by a broad range of other business initiatives. The firm's website attracts over two million unique visitors a month, providing free downloads of book updates that enhance the attractiveness of the guides, direct book sales sent from distributors worldwide, a highly popular discussion forum where readers share travel experiences, and access to Lonely Planet's other services.

Lonely Planet launched CitySync in January 2000, providing in-depth guides to four US cities plus Sydney for mobile devices running the PalmOS operating system. The software and content, including interactive maps, can be downloaded on the Internet or purchased on CD-ROM or preinstalled modules. In addition to integrating city maps with reviews of hotels, restaurants, and nightlife, it integrates with other Palm functionality and enables users to add their own comments. As with Lonely Planet's guidebooks, updates can be downloaded for free. Lonely Planet's customers are by their nature on the move, so it seemed a natural fit to offer telecommunications services. Its eKno service provides not just low-cost international calls, but also global voicemail, faxmail, and voice notification of emails. In addition, Lonely Planet licenses its brand for a television travel series that is screened worldwide, and now it even publishes world music CDs. From publishing books, Lonely Planet has successfully diversified into providing telecommunications services and software in addition to a very wide range of content, and in the process built powerful direct relationships with its end-customers, which it never had before.

New approaches to business strategy are required as the economy begins to reshape itself. Almost every strategic tool in use over the last couple of decades is based on the increasingly dated concept of industries. Tools such as Michael Porter's five forces model of competition are still applicable, but their value is fading because they are based on the concept of an industry as something static and defined.[7] You must now consider your firm as a participant in the multi-dimensional space of the flow economy, rather than belonging to a particular industry. As you saw in Chapter 3, the issue is now how to extract value from your participation in a deeply integrated economic lattice made up of many players.

Earlier in this chapter we described how in the new convergence of the flow economy every organization will face new competition—often from unexpected quarters—and immense opportunities will unfold for those that recognize them. Firms must go through a constant process of strategic repositioning, founded on opening their thinking to dramatically new possibilities. Far more than at any time before, companies can participate in shaping the evolving structure of the economy. There is now immense scope for creative thinking—and leadership—in conceiving and forging entirely new forms of business. There are three core steps to this process of strategic positioning in the flow economy. We will study these steps, and then examine how to bring the strategic process itself to life.

STRATEGIC POSITIONING IN THE FLOW ECONOMY

1. Define your space
2. Redefine your space
3. Reposition

Table 7-1: Action steps to strategic positioning in the flow economy

1. Define your space

To know where to go, first know where you are. Every company and industry will face different challenges and opportunities. Each firm must ask a number of strategic questions that will enable it to establish and implement a clear strategy. The key strategic questions for defining your current space in the flow economy are shown in Table 7-2.

STRATEGIC QUESTIONS FOR POSITIONING IN THE FLOW ECONOMY – I

Define your space

- What is the "total customer offering" in which you participate, and what is the value created for the customer?

- Who provides each of the flow elements that comprise the total customer offering, and what is the competitive landscape within each flow element?

- Which flow elements do you provide, and how are they combined?

- Are there any non-information elements to the offering, and who provides these?

- What alliances do you have with providers of other flow elements?

- What are your organization's distinctive competences and strengths?

Table 7-2: Strategic questions for defining your space in the flow economy

The starting point is to define the "total customer offering" in which you participate. Since at this stage of the process we are examining the current strategic space, this should be the most obvious articulation of what customers receive. Only rarely do firms provide the entire customer offering. For example, newspaper publishers may frame their businesses as providing news to end-customers, and selling access to end-customers' attention to advertisers. The other participants in this offering include newsagents, delivery services, and newswires; and if the newspaper has online services, a far more complex array of providers. Digitally-based customer offerings will always draw on every flow element in some form.

Let's illustrate the strategic positioning process by taking a brief look at one major player in the flow economy, addressing the key strategic questions by examining each of the flow elements in turn. Nokia—and its peer mobile handset makers—at first view is a participant in providing the customer offering of mobile connectivity and services. Standards are the very basis of this mobile connectivity. Some standards—such as GSM (Global Standard for Mobiles)—are set by non-aligned industry bodies, and as such are essentially in the public domain. Nokia participates actively in the standard-setting process, both in order to have input to the technology, and to be fully informed on developments. It has made a strong public commitment to open standards, and has often worked closely with competitors and partners to initiate and develop other standards such as Wireless Application Protocol (WAP), that have promised to expand the use of mobile services. It is also a strong proponent of RosettaNet, described in Chapter 3. In most cases Nokia doesn't provide connectivity; this is the role of its close partners, the telecom firms. Relationships with the end-customers are usually controlled by telecom providers, since they usually sell the handsets, and while Nokia has a powerful brand, it often has little or no information on the end-users of its handsets. Nokia, as many of its peers, outsources the actual manufacturing of its products.

The heart of Nokia's participation in the total customer offering is the interfaces, in the form of mobile handsets. Both content and services are important parts of the total customer offering, and it works hard to make it easier for its partners to deliver these. It understands that the better the total offering, the bigger the space will become, and it will benefit along with all of its partners in providing the total customer offering. Nokia has also established "Club Nokia" in 26 countries, in which it provides services such as customer support, games, and ring tones exclusively to Nokia handset owners. The strategic benefit of this initiative is in fact at least as much in establishing direct relationships with the owners of its handset as in service provision.

The idea of a firm's distinctive competences and strengths of course has been central to business strategy for over a decade now.[8] In defining a company's current strategic space, in most cases the existing understanding of the firm's competences will be adequate, though this may be reframed in the process of redefining the space. Nokia's core competences and strengths can be considered to be telecommunications expertise, brand and market presence, global presence and scale, and its relationships with telecoms firms.

2. Redefine your space

Having defined the strategic space in which you are currently participating, you can now begin to redefine that space. Selected strategic questions to reconceive your space, and your position within it, are shown in Table 7-3. The creative scope and active challenging of assumptions required by this phase means that highly participative—and provocative—approaches are often useful.

STRATEGIC QUESTIONS FOR POSITIONING IN THE FLOW ECONOMY – II

Redefine your space

- How is the flow of all information and value changing in relation to your current and potential customers, suppliers, and competitors?

- How can you reframe the total customer offering?

- How are market dynamics changing within each of the flow elements?

- Are there flow elements in which you do not participate that influence your ability to extract value?

- How can you leverage your existing strengths in the flow economy into new sources of revenue or value?

Table 7-3: Strategic questions for redefining your space in the flow economy

A very valuable early exercise is simply mapping the current flows of information and value within your strategic space. This can help to uncover new ways to participate in existing flows, and elucidate how they are changing, particularly from the perspective of your current and potential customers. Formal processes, such as Verna Allee's approaches and tools for mapping value networks, can be very useful.[9] Understanding the current status of each of the flow elements provides a foundation for identifying potential strategic moves for your company.

American Airlines was a very early leader in redefining its participation in the emerging information flows in the economy. Starting in 1959, working with IBM, it established the Sabre airline information and reservations system, which at one stage was the largest private real-time computer network in the world. In the 1990s Sabre generated more profits than its parent, playing a dominant role in one of the most information-intensive industries in the world. Now one of six global computer reservation systems, Sabre is continuing to reposition itself, having taken a 70% stake in Internet travel agency Travelocity and providing software to other airlines on an applications service provider (ASP) model.

Another example is provided by how corporate banking is redefining its scope. The family tree of JP Morgan Chase is long and distinguished one, bringing together a multitude of firms such as Manufacturer's Hanover, Chemical Bank, and of course John Pierpont Morgan's eponymous institution, all of which have provided financial services to the corporations of America and the world since the 19th century. JP Morgan Chase no longer provides just financial services to its traditional client base, but is now seeking to take a commanding position in the information and value flows between corporations.

Electronic Invoice Presentment and Processing (EIPP) is a digitally-based process by which firms present invoices and make payments in business-to-business transactions. At its most basic, the field is about providing electronic notifications to suppliers and clients of order status, and making the related payments. However to implement these systems effectively when there are a multitude of complex processes including internal approvals, partial shipments, returns, insurance, and far more, ultimately requires integrating the accounts payable and accounts receivable systems of the firms involved. For consumer goods companies, these systems can extend as far as providing accounting systems and payment options to retailers, while for other large firms, they can cover all aspects of procurement, including integration into online marketplaces. This emerging space is attracting competitors from all fronts, including software vendors such as SAP, start-ups such as Billpoint, and banks like JP Morgan Chase. The only part of the EIPP suite of services traditionally provided by banks is payments—a very low-margin and commoditized business. However JP Morgan Chase has redefined the scope of its business to encompass a far larger proportion of customer value.

3. Reposition

Once you have determined your new strategic space, you need to decide how you will reposition your company. You have the usual range of strategic options available, as illustrated in Figure 7-2. You can:

- **Build.** Create the capabilities you require, by internal development and hiring.

- **Acquire.** Identify and merge with a firm with complementary capabilities and positioning.

- **License.** Implement technologies or processes others have developed.

- **Form Alliances.** Create shared business models with other organizations.

- **Virtualize.** Outsource business processes and functions.

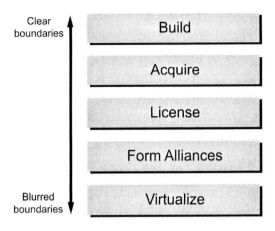

Figure 7-3: Strategic options for repositioning

Traditional approaches to corporate strategy remain useful in assessing this range of options. Depending on the specific situation, some of the issues to be taken into account include the degree of integration required, financing costs, the importance of market dominance, intellectual property, cultural fit, industry barriers to entry, and so on.

At the same time, it's important to understand how the rapidly shifting dynamics of the flow economy change repositioning decisions. As you saw earlier in this book, companies can now easily integrate their processes and operations to a far deeper degree. This means that it is increasingly possible and relevant to shift towards options that require blurring the boundaries of the organization. You are severely limited in what you can achieve if you simply buy or build capabilities internally. Those firms that actively engage in the more challenging approaches of drawing on external intellectual property, forming alliances, and allocating business processes inside and outside the organization, will have immensely greater flexibility in their strategic positioning. In Chapter 3 you saw that companies today participate in a broad network of value creation, and position themselves to extract value from that. The greater your versatility in fine-tuning your positioning relative to other firms, the more accurately you can conceive and implement your strategic vision.

Those firms that actively engage in the more challenging approaches of drawing on external intellectual property, forming alliances, and allocating business processes inside and outside the organization, will have immensely greater flexibility in their strategic positioning.

Lonely Planet, discussed at the beginning of this section, clearly started with its primary strength in content creation, combined with a strong brand. In seeking to develop direct relationships with its end-customers—which most book publishers don't have—it chose to develop its own capabilities for the Internet and online community development. However for its other new ventures it has formed alliances with a telecommunication provider, television program producer, software developer, and personal organizer makers to leverage its content and brand. In all cases it ensures that it controls the customer relationships—and thus the majority of the value creation.

Microsoft has never hidden the fact that its Xbox game console is in part the first step of a strategy to be at the heart of all home entertainment. As such it needed to create a standard. It could have done that through alliances with established players, but it decided that it wanted to completely control this business. Despite being historically a software firm rather than hardware vendor, it was easy for it to outsource manufacturing of the console. However for a game console to be massively successful it needs a large range of quality games to be available, so in addition to providing its own games, it allies with third-party game developers.

Strategy in the flow economy is also about positioning relative to your competitors. Microsoft is a powerful player in many of the flow elements, however one of the elements at which it is currently weakest is connectivity. It's happy if the market is open and competitive, but if there is a dominant player, especially combined with relationships with end-players, it could throw a wrench into its plans. So, when AT&T's cable television business was auctioned in late 2001, Microsoft was desperate for it not to fall into the hands of its arch-rival AOL Time Warner, as it would have doubled the firm's broadband reach to 26 million subscribers. Accordingly, Microsoft chose to bankroll Comcast's bid for the cable networks, thus averting the powerful hold its competitor may have gained on customers' access to digital broadband services.[10]

In this chapter we have looked at strategic positioning at a very high level. In Chapter 9 we will look briefly at the implications of web services in creating modular organizations. This allows firms to define what they choose to locate inside and outside at the level of specific business processes. We will conclude this chapter by examining how firms can bring the strategic process to life inside their organizations.

Creating participative strategy

The Work-Out process is one of General Electric's standard practices. This brings together 40 to 100 people in a "town meeting" to discuss specific issues, and make firm recommendations. Once the issues that need to be addressed have been identified, these are clearly defined by a team, and attendees for the meeting are selected from a range of functions and managerial levels. The team meet in an offsite location for usually three days, commencing with a briefing by the relevant executive, who then leaves. The participants break into a number of teams, and in a structured process come up with clear recommendations. At the end these are presented to the senior manager, who must make a decision on the spot whether to proceed. Work-Out sessions are routinely run across General Electric's divisions, and often include customers and suppliers.[11]

This participative approach to strategy—which permeates General Electric's culture and practices—has become imperative in the flow economy. Most importantly, strategy development must happen in real-time, rather than at the traditional annual off-site strategy review. In the same way as any form of innovation, it must draw on the broadest possible spectrum of experience and perspective available in the organization. This is required by the increasing complexity of technology and the economy. In addition, strategy must be communicated meaningfully to all employees and even partners, as it affects day-to-day business decisions. In short, strategy must draw in the participation of people across and sometimes even beyond the firm, rather than be set by senior management behind closed doors.

Clearly there are limits to the ability to distribute strategy formation through the organization. Leaders must assess rapidly-changing situations and make quick decisions. Confidentiality is often an important issue, especially regarding acquisitions and major strategic moves. Most employees cannot afford the time for deep consideration of strategic issues. However firms that use these issues as excuses to keep strategy an isolated exercise will be severely disadvantaged. There are three key steps companies can take to rapidly and effectively build participative strategy.

BUILDING PARTICIPATIVE STRATEGY

1. Develop an iterative strategy process
2. Link to innovation processes
3. Use scenarios

Table 7-4: Action steps to building participative strategy

1. Develop an iterative strategy process

Most company employees will be all too familiar with the strategy roll-out session. A roll of drums, death by Powerpoint, and perhaps an appearance by the CEO, then everyone files back to their desks, deeply inspired by the bold vision they have just been presented, and already forgotten. People cannot have a sense of ownership when they are presented with a finished product.

An effective iterative strategy process cycles back and forth between the strategic planning group—that can put in the effort required to research key issues and develop strategic frameworks—and the broader employee community, that can take on early stage frameworks and be given an opportunity to provide input and perspectives. In most cases these sessions will result in valuable input to the strategy development process, and they will always generate a far greater sense of participation and involvement. Perhaps the most important success factor is presenting a strategic framework that is both readily understood, and has clear dimensions for input and discussion. For one global financial services firm, I designed a process that included framing the organization's strategy in a format suitable for employees to provide input, and applying the output from these discussions into high-level strategy and innovation sessions. In this way an iterative strategy development cycle could be begun.

2. Link to innovation processes

Over the last few years many organizations have implemented formal innovation processes. In their simplest form, these enable employees to submit ideas to an assessment panel that selects the most promising for allocation of funds or other resources to develop the innovation to fruition. During the dot-com era, innovation processes often focused on ideas for ebusiness start-ups, functioning much like venture capital firms, however the focus for these initiatives is increasingly applied to issues such as product development and process enhancement. It can be very valuable to link innovation processes with participative strategy initiatives. Most companies that have implemented innovation programs have found that after an initial flurry of ideas, submissions dry up. People need to be challenged in structured ways to provoke new ideas. For example workshops that work through how value flows within and across industries are shifting often stimulate new thinking in those that have extensive experience in the field.

Royal Dutch/ Shell's Exploration & Production division has been running an innovation process called GameChanger since 1996. It is essentially an internal venture group, reviewing proposals for new technologies and strategic visions that can come in from anyone, anywhere, anytime. It typically approves initial funding for successful ideas within one month, but if ideas are proven worthwhile they are then passed on to operating units within the Shell group for full commercialization. At the end of the last decade, four of the top five growth initiatives in Shell had emerged from the GameChanger process. While the GameChanger team is open to all ideas, most stem from innovation workshops that are run both within Shell, and at universities and institutes worldwide. These focus on stimulating different perspectives on where new revenue streams can be exploited in what appears to many to be a mature industry.[12]

3. Use scenarios

I have consistently found that scenario planning is the single most powerful tool for developing participative strategy processes within an organization. The process of scenario planning develops a small number of realistic, complementary, and relevant future scenarios for the organization's environment, that are used to establish a robust yet flexible strategy. One of the key advantages is that the scenario development process is inherently iterative, and so can very easily be adapted to running broad participation sessions, interspersed by focused development and research by a specialized team. By their nature, scenarios are easy to communicate, and the development process generates frameworks that provide a solid foundation for rich discussion.

Since 1995 Morgan Stanley has used framework scenarios as a foundation for strategic thinking across its businesses, involved more than 3,000 executives worldwide. The strategic fields to which it has applied scenario planning include technology, international expansion, and the changing nature of its institutional and retail clients. The scenario development processes are specifically designed to gain useful input from a diverse range of internal and external thinkers, and to give key stakeholders a sense of ownership and participation. To do so, initial scenarios are created that provide valuable perspectives on the future of the business in question, while still clearly being not in final form. This enables participants in the process to contribute effectively, gain a deeper understanding of the issues underlying the resultant strategies, and be clear on their role in successfully implementing the strategies.

Vital Connections: Chapter 7

In this chapter we have looked at the development of the flow economy, in which almost all value is based on the flow of information and ideas, and traditional industry boundaries are dissolving. Companies must understand the six flow elements that comprise this emerging flow economy, and take the necessary steps to position themselves effectively as competitive dynamics change.

In Chapter 8 we will explore in-depth strategies for content providers, while Chapter 9 covers the pressing issues in the new world of services, including online services and professional services. Chapter 10 will go on to examine strategy in a networked world from the perspective of individuals.

CHAPTER 8
Next Generation
Content Distribution

Creating Value When Digital Products Flow Freely

In a hyper-connected world digital products flow freely, unless safeguards are put in place. Providers of content— including entertainment and high-value information— must balance protection and promotion to maximize value. All content industries are in a state of massive flux, and evolutionary strategies are required to succeed in this time of transition.

One of the early digital devices that gave consumers greater control of their entertainment was TiVo, the digital video recorder that allows viewers to easily search for and record multiple shows, and pause and rewind live programs. In 2000 TiVo developed an advertising campaign featuring a television network executive being thrown out of a window, but for some reason CBS felt the commercial was inappropriate, and declined to show it.[1] When SONICBlue released ReplayTV 4000, a next generation digital video recorder that not only allows users to delete commercials automatically during playback, but also to share recorded programs with friends, apoplectic broadcasters petitioned a federal court to stop sale of the device.[2]

The content and entertainment world is perhaps the aspect of today's economy that is the most dramatically impacted by the advent of the digital networked world. The vast content industry—including music, film, software, books, market research, images, and more—is undergoing a seismic shift that will eventually result in a very different landscape. Throughout the extended transition period, powerful vested interests in existing industry structures will battle hard to slow the pace of change. There will be many winners and losers along the way, as the business of content—which is increasingly the business of distributing digital products—reshapes itself.

There are five core drivers that are transforming content distribution:

• **Lower distribution costs.** It is no longer necessary to manufacture and distribute physical goods such as CDs, books, and packaged software. Digital distribution can be done at almost negligible cost. Distribution currently accounts for 60% and sometimes far more of the total cost of creating and delivering content.[3]

• **Ability to tap a far larger market.** Any digital product can easily be made available to a global market. The value of controlling physical distribution channels is eroding, and companies of any size can now access either large or niche markets effectively.

• **Benefits to customers.** The many advantages of digital products include immediate availability, the ability to quickly search for and find anything you want to purchase, instant access to anything on your entertainment system without having to handle CDs and tapes, and the availability of customized products.

• **Digital products can be copied, protected, and cracked.** Digital products can be copied indefinitely, with every copy equal in quality to the original. Rights management software can make it difficult for users to copy content, but it currently appears that all content protection can be cracked.

- **Products and messages flow in the networks.** Today's communication networks mean not only that products can be delivered digitally, but also that they can readily flow both to friends, and your millions of acquaintances on peer-to-peer networks. In addition, information about what is worthy of attention flows ever-swifter.

Perhaps the most important single factor in determining the new landscape—and the least predictable—is consumer attitudes and behaviors. During the initial boom phase of the Internet, people grew to expect to get things for free. A multitude of free services such as e-mail accounts, news, and share portfolio analysis were quickly taken for granted. Then Napster and its successors made high-quality music available for free to all comers. Not only is a whole generation growing up knowing nothing other than free music, but a broad swathe of their seniors have swiftly adapted to downloading tunes at will. At the same time, many still get a little niggling in their conscience, and would prefer not to steal from the artists they admire. The problem is, the only alternatives are at best immensely inconvenient. Going to a music store and sorting through racks of CDs seems like a waste of time if you're just going to rip the songs and transfer them onto your portable MP3 player, and it's hardly any better to have to download an array of different types of software and scour through a range of online music services to find which one has the songs you want. The future landscape for the distribution of music—and all other forms of digital content—will ultimately depend on how consumers' behaviors evolve in response to the range of choices of differing convenience and legality that are available. This is very difficult to forecast in detail, and many firms have foundered on bold—and inaccurate—predictions of their customers' responses to changing technologies.

The other vital issue is the development of legislation on content protection. As you will see later in this chapter, major content companies are pushing for legislation to be embedded into technology. The decisions of lawmakers may have a dramatic impact on the future of the flow economy.

Despite Napster and its contemporaries, the promise is that content industries can make more money—maybe even a lot more—than they have in the past. The simple reason is that they have the potential to provide far more value to consumers. Total demand increases if consumers can easily access a broader selection of entertainment.

Collaborative filtering means that consumers are becoming aware of many things that they like and want to buy

Amazon.com has increased the total size of the book market by 15%, partly through making it very easy to buy almost any published book.[4] Back catalogues of music, film, and books can become big money-spinners. "Alternative" content may be a small proportion of the total market, but it can become far bigger if its audience can access it easily.

The ready flow of messages through the networks means that people are getting more recommendations from friends than before. Even more importantly, collaborative filtering means that consumers are becoming aware of many things that they like and want to buy, but didn't know about before. We have been living in a world in which music labels, film studios, book publishers, and their peers act as the filters that select what consumers are able to choose from. We are now shifting to an era in which everyone can access all creativity. Clearly this results in a massive excess of choice. MP3.com alone gives access to over 800,000 songs. Part of the continuing value of the major distribution firms will be to help people select what is outstanding from an overwhelming range of choices. However they overstate their case when they assert that this is an essential function. Plenty of people will want to find quality beyond what is approved by these self-appointed arbiters of taste.

The immense value of the collaborative filtering systems described in Chapters 1 and 4 is that they bring the highest quality material to the fore. This broadens the spectrum of what is available, and increases demand as people find what they like far more easily. The recommendations features of Amazon.com, Yahoo!'s Launch.com, and their peers are already playing an important role. As more sophisticated collaborative filtering systems are developed and widely used, we will be able to tap the collective experience of the many people that have similar taste to us, but we will never meet. Collaborative filtering company Media Unbound asks users to answer questions about their music taste, rate music, and give ongoing feedback on the music it plays them.[5] Major music website Pressplay, among others, has implemented Media Unbound's software as part of its service.

These twin powerful trends of greater access to content, and increased awareness of quality content, can result in greater revenue for these industries, but new business models are required. For example, US music consumers currently spend on average $60 a year on CDs—equivalent to perhaps four albums. If each of those consumers were given the option to pay $10 per month, and in return get all the music they wanted, it is safe to predict that most would take it up, feel they are getting great value, and the industry would double in size.[6] Unfortunately, implementing this attractive vision is easier said than done. Let us examine first the impact of digital rights management on the world of content, and then move on to how the content distribution landscape is evolving, including the action firms should take to shift their business models and approaches.

Rights, rules, and balance

You would have to search long and hard to find someone who has never made a cassette or digital recording of a CD for a friend, used unregistered software, photocopied a magazine article, or otherwise broken copyright laws. While in many cases these acts are trivial, in others they are theft, pure and simple. However it would be wrong to see the issue in stark black and white terms. If copyright holders sometimes benefit when people copy or pass on their content, by gaining more sales, earning revenue from other sources, or increasing market presence and awareness, should they demand that the law be enforced regardless?

Copyright owners can sell the right to use their content in specified ways. For example, if you buy a physical book, you are given the right to read it as many times as you like, to lend it to others, and to sell it, but not to copy or store it in any form. Purchasing a CD is understood to give you the right to make a copy for your own use, but not for others. Those are your legal rights, however even if you happen to know the specific boundaries of those rights, there is nothing stopping you ignoring the law and copying at will.

However now that content is becoming largely digital, everything changes. When you purchase a digital product, it is possible to control down to the minutest detail what rights you do or don't have. You may be given the right to read a document on your PC only, use software for 30 days, watch a film three times, or listen to music only at a low quality level until you pay more. Suddenly content distributors can specify to whatever degree they wish the "business rules" of how their content can and cannot be used. This gives them incredible flexibility in how they approach distribution and pricing. However as Lawrence Lessig eloquently points out, in some cases the digital rights given to consumers do not even match their legal rights, such as copying for personal use.[7]

Digital rights management (DRM) is the domain of using software to give customers specified usage rights to digital content. A plethora of vendors, from IBM and Microsoft to endless start-ups, are competing vigorously in this space. There are significant direct revenues at stakes, but far more importantly, whoever owns the standard DRM system in a content market has the potential to leverage that to control a very broad space in the flow economy. Later in this chapter you will discover why firms like Microsoft are so aggressively pushing their DRM offerings, in its case Windows Media.

The reality is that most DRM systems are a pain in the ass to use. Let's say you have a choice in how you access content. You can be forced to hunt around a variety of sites to find everything you want, and have to download and familiarize yourself with a range of unwieldy programs in order to access the content. On the other hand, you can go to one site and get everything you want with no hassles, with the additional upside of it being free and downside of it being illegal. In the case of digital music, many people are choosing the latter option—that is downloading files from the peer-to-peer music file sharing systems. The inconvenience of many DRM systems is tipping the balance to make people choose the easier option. There is a clear trade-off between protection and customer convenience.

The other key factor is that no digital content protection system is fully secure, as you saw in Chapter 5. The very fact that entertainment needs to be converted to sounds or images in order to be used means there is always a point at which encryption can be broken. If hackers can break DRM to create unprotected content, then it's back to having to compete with alternatives that are far easier to use, and free to boot. However if consumers need to use software or systems to crack protected content, not only does it become inconvenient, but it also emphasizes to them that they're indulging in illegal activities, meaning far fewer are likely to do it. As many industry executives have noted, most people prefer to think that they aren't pirates, and are willing to pay for what they use, as long as the prices are reasonable and the systems are easy to use.

The turning point in how content industries are trying to protect their goods was perhaps the cracking of the so-called Secure Digital Music Initiative, discussed in Chapter 5.

Given that software doesn't seem to do the job, the industry is trying to implement more draconian measures. For example, they suggest that if every CD player, PC, and other consumer digital device manufactured were equipped with mechanisms to prevent them playing protected content, everything would be fine. These proposals are deeply flawed, and not only because many perfectly legal activities would also be prevented and consumers would ultimately bear the costs. Technological innovation on many fronts would be stifled, and more importantly, the entire flow that the emerging economy is based on would be dampened. These industries must realize that their future is based on richer and faster flows of information, and not stagnation.

Of course the issues with DRM and distribution depend strongly on the nature of the content. If content is very high-value, for example research reports, then customers will download them infrequently, usually be happy to go to a particular site for what they need, and is unlikely to be worried about minor access requirements. For instance TechSearch International produces reports on semiconductor packaging trends, priced at $4,000 apiece. Its clients wanted the convenience of receiving reports in digital format rather than on paper, so TechSearch has chosen to use DRM protection on the files it sells. This works perfectly well for both the content provider and its customers.

The yin and yang of content marketing

When Radiohead released its album *Kid A* in October 2000, it went straight to the top of the Billboard charts, despite there being no promotional video or big tour. EMI label Capitol Records, three weeks before it released the album, launched an iBlip, an interactive mini-site that fans could host and forward to their friends. It contained access to the entire album in streaming form, an MP3 track download, content on the band, and the ability to add other content. The more than 900 Radiohead fansites—not to mention radio station websites and online retailers—were eager to host the pre-release album and other features, as it was cool and drew people to their sites. The iBlip allowed Capitol Record to syndicate content from its own sources and the many very professional fan sites, so it was continuously updated wherever it was accessed, also allowing local sites to add their own content. On average the fans forwarded the iBlip to two friends, astounding when at a time when a 5-10% pass-on rate was considered good. Another part of the campaign was the Googly Minotaur custom buddy, which fans put on their instant messaging lists to receive updates on the band and album. Over 300,000 messages were sent to the buddy on the day after it was launched, with the chatter of instant messaging pals around the world sparking almost instant global awareness. For the promotion, Capitol Records became the first from the five major record labels to collaborate with the loathed music file-sharing networks. It offered to Aimster users a Radiohead "skin", or interface design, which gave them access to the Radiohead website. At the same time, Capitol knew that the album's tracks were readily available for free download on Aimster, Napster, and other services, yet understood that this could boost sales rather than dampen them, as indeed turned out to be the case.[8]

> If you go too far either way—in protecting content at the expense of promotion, or promoting it without generating revenue—your returns will suffer. What is required is a mentality of not just balancing promotion and protection, but integrating the two sides.

Many content owners' inclination is to protect at all costs people from stealing what they see as rightfully theirs. Unfortunately this is not necessarily the best way of making the most money, which is probably what copyright holders really want. In an economy based on the flow of information and the scarcity of attention, focusing too much on protecting digital products can greatly hinder promoting them effectively. In Chapter 6 you saw how positive awareness is increasingly developed through the flow of messages in the networks. This requires both offering something of value that people want to pass on to others, and making it as easy as possible to purchase the product and let others know. Of course we must also keep in mind that the dot-com experiment has shown us that giving everything away for free is rarely a sustainable business model.

If you go too far either way—in protecting content at the expense of promotion, or promoting it without generating revenue—your returns will suffer. What is required is a mentality of not just balancing promotion and protection, but integrating the two sides. To whatever degree possible, you need to make them complement rather than conflict with each other. The old Chinese yin-yang symbol, shown in Figure 8-1, represents the balance and harmony that marketers must seek. Capitol Records' Radiohead campaign illustrates how not being afraid to experiment with reduced protection, and integrating that into effective promotion, can result in more dollars in the door. Capitol uses similar approaches with those of its artists that are willing to try new approaches. When you log onto rocker Dave Navarro's website, an audio streaming of all tracks on his latest album automatically pops up.

Figure 8-1: The yin and yang of content marketing

It's not so long since Disney was all but unknown in China. When a few Disney cartoons started airing on Chinese television in the mid-1980s, it coincided with the birth of VCRs, and pirated and often dubbed copies of Disney's classics flooded the Chinese market, with Disney none the richer. The rampant unlicensed production of Disney merchandise in China was a thorn in US-China relations throughout the 1990s, with constant threats of economic reprisals for China's blatant disregard for intellectual property. Now that China is seeking to open its economy internationally, manifold opportunities are opening for Disney. It has cut a deal for Mickey Mouse to reach 225 million Chinese television-viewing households in kid's prime time, is opening a theme park in Hong Kong in 2005, and considering opening another park in Shanghai. It is also reviewing its merchandising opportunities on the mainland, especially now that it can more readily apply pressure on the government, given China's role as the largest legitimate producer of Disney branded goods and a proud new member of the World Trade Organization.[9]

Disney executives would probably never admit it publicly, but its current business opportunities were only made possible by the rampant pirating of the previous two decades. If every Disney product ever sold in China was legally licensed, the pricing would have been prohibitive, people wouldn't have been exposed to Disney's lovable characters, and Disney's brand in China would be worth a fraction of what it is today. The strategy was hardly deliberate in the early days, but now more firms are recognizing that over-protection of intellectual property can be counter-productive.

The world of the digital affords many opportunities to integrate promotion and protection. *Superdistribution* may sound like something out of a comic book, but it simply means people sending digital products on to others. If people like a song, video, or book, they can easily forward it to their friends and contacts, who can in turn pass it on. This is a type of viral marketing, however it uses DRM to incorporate a way of generating revenue as each person along the chain uses the product. This works by putting the product in a "wrapper" that encrypts it, gives specific access rights, attaches an identifying code, and can also include free material such as low-quality previews or video clips. This means that when people send this package, recipients can look at the free material, and perhaps listen to or view the product once or twice, but must pay in order to keep it. The identifying code means that the vendor can tell who originally sent the product. They can reward them, for example by giving them the product for free if 10 people they forwarded it to pay for it, or even establishing a multi-level marketing plan in which people get small commissions for everyone that pays for a product along an entire global chain.

The evolving landscape of content distribution

Ten years from today, how will the total book market be shared between paper books and their digital counterparts? How about in twenty years? These questions are guaranteed to spark lively—and often heated—debate among book lovers. Without tempting fate with a specific forecast, we can safely say that a large proportion of books will be digital, certainly within twenty years, and probably within ten years. This will be driven largely by the development of ebooks that mimic many of the useful characteristics of paper books, while providing additional advantages afforded by digital products, not least of which is packing hundreds or thousands of books into a single handy volume. What is far harder to predict is who we will be buying these ebooks from—be it authors, bookshops, online vendors, or others—and what the landscape of standards and ebook devices will look like.

As the shift to the digital reshapes the content distribution landscape, it is worth distinguishing what we can say about the future with some assurance, and what is less predictable. The reality is that we are in the early stages of what will be a breathtaking shift in the world of content. In each content industry, we can actually get a reasonable idea of what will drive the market once the majority of the transition is through, be it in five years, ten years, or more. What is far harder to discern is the results of the jockeying for position in the meantime. There will be big losers, as some of the current giants fail to adjust effectively, and there will also be massive winners, as existing and new players position themselves to take a large chunk of the value in the new market. Without being able to pinpoint who will win or lose, we can at least understand what will drive success and failure as intense battles are waged to stake a claim to riches.

Let us first consider what we can foresee in the longer-term future:

• **Almost all content will be digital.** In software, music, and high-value information first, then in images, films, and books, almost all content will be distributed in digital form over networks. In some cases the complete transition will require wide availability of high bandwidth access, in others better interfaces. In time, these will be available, heralding the final arrival of the digital content world.

• **Content will be largely available on demand.** As the next generation of broadband becomes available in both the home and through wireless, there will be less reason to store most forms of digital content. Content will be accessible wherever you are, through whatever device you are using at the time. Internet radio is a predecessor of that nirvana, allowing anyone with an Internet device to listen to any of thousands of radio channels around the world, wherever they are.

• **Content creators will have more choices.** Musicians, artists, authors, and film and game-makers will no longer be beholden to publishers and studios. Publishers will often have to offer more value to attract star creators to work with them, including financing and promotion. The implications from the perspective of creative individuals will be covered in detail in Chapter 10.

• **Physical retailers will exist, but in a different form.** It's an inescapable fact that people like shopping. However as content becomes increasingly digital, retailers will have to rely on providing fun experiences and useful ways of finding good content to entice consumers through their doors.

• **Industry revenue and profitability will depend on the adoption of standards.** The actual benefits gained by consumers and producers of digital content will depend on the widespread adoption of standards for technology and interfaces. The potential value of controlling these standards will lead to bitter battles, but if no consensus or clear winners emerge, everyone will lose.

Studying the longer-term future of content distribution is an exercise in exploring how value will be reallocated between participants. There will be a different array of participants, including both existing and new players, and how each creates value will change. The high degree of uncertainty means that scenario planning is a very useful tool to explore the long-term dynamics of any particular industry. However the reality is that many strategic decisions today will be driven by short-term considerations, as firms jockey for position in a rapidly evolving space. Dealing with issues such as evolving standards and changing control of customer relationships requires tactical expertise as well as long-term vision.

Applying the flow economy framework

The flow economy framework presented in Chapter 7 provides a valuable approach to analyzing the content distribution landscape. The six flow elements are at the heart of how the content distribution landscape is changing. Considering these in the context of a particular industry can enable the development of refined strategies. Firms must examine in detail how they should position themselves within each of the flow elements, how the flow elements combine and interact, and especially how to reposition themselves by leveraging strengths in one element into others.

The music industry is the case study for digital content distribution that everyone is watching. While there are many different factors at play in other industries such as film, TV, and books, the evolution of digital music distribution is still highly instructive for all content providers. The five major record labels have demonstrated they have essentially a two-pronged strategy: stamp out all other attempts to distribute music online; and establish their own online music distribution.

The recording industry's immediate response to the stunning rise of Napster was to strive to destroy it. Having succeeded at stopping it in the courts, the established players then looked up to see other peer-to-peer networks mushrooming on all sides, some of them distributed networks with no central server to shut down. After realizing that they had to respond to consumer demand or lose a large part of their revenue, the major labels finally took action. Vivendi Universal and Sony joined to create online retailer Pressplay to sell their music, while Warner, EMI, and BMG established MusicNet, along with RealNetworks and Warner's parent, AOL

Time Warner. Later in this chapter we will examine some of the issues in this creation of two separate alliances to aggregate content to customers. The biggest problem the two alliances and their consumers face is that they have adopted different standards for their music distribution. Pressplay has established a broad-ranging agreement with Microsoft, that

No single business model is likely to be effective indefinitely, as technology progresses and consumer behaviors and attitudes unfold.

entails providing their music through Windows Media technology, and includes distribution through the MSN Music website. In the other corner, Microsoft's arch-rivals RealNetworks and AOL Time Warner are using their own incompatible streaming and encryption technologies. While these giants posture and feint at each other, Napster—backed by its part-owner BMG—is still endeavoring to rise from the ashes to establish itself as a legal subscription service that will cover all music. At the time of writing, both Pressplay and MusicNet were finding business very slow, perhaps even to the extent of putting their future into question. By the time you read this, the next chapters in the saga will have been told.

This very brief case study shows many of the dynamics at work in the evolving content distribution landscape. Microsoft's positioning—as always—is intriguing. It aligned itself with Pressplay largely as a means of promoting its Windows Media platform, which encompasses both DRM and audio and video streaming. Microsoft recognizes the potential power of dominating DRM standards, which it could leverage into receiving ongoing licensing revenue for all content. In addition, by gathering customer information and providing customized offerings from other parts of its substantial and growing empire, it could controlling customer relationships.

There are four key steps that content distribution firms must take to position themselves effectively as the new industry landscape evolves in the coming years, as shown in Table 8-1.

POSITIONING FOR CONTENT DISTRIBUTION

1. Build evolutionary business models
2. Define and refine strategies for standards and interfaces
3. Develop and implement aggregation strategies
4. Enable versatile syndication models
5. Rework your product versioning

Table 8-1: Action steps to positioning for content distribution

1. Build evolutionary business models

By 2001 analysts were growing concerned that Microsoft's revenue stream could falter, as the IT managers at large corporations began baulking at upgrading the software on all their PCs every time a new version of Microsoft Windows or Office was released. The software titan was finally galvanized to implement the strategy it had been musing about for years—switching to licensing its software as an annual subscription instead of a one-off purchase. Its new Software Assurance program gives users the right to receive all upgrades released during their subscription period, and includes support services. It seems few customers were delighted by the change, partly because for many their licensing costs increased, and Microsoft was forced to backtrack slightly, including extending the initially planned five month transition period to well over one year. Microsoft is already thinking of how it will further shift its business models to accommodate its .NET strategy, which will be described in Chapter 9.

Business models must be engineered to evolve in response to shifts in the landscape. As the flow of information and ideas grows ever-more fluid, the balance between protection and promotion will change. No single business model is likely to be effective indefinitely, as technology progresses and consumer behaviors and attitudes unfold. There are two key steps to building evolutionary business models: actively experimenting; and considering not just how to manage the transition into the new business model, but also how that model can later transition into another.

The truth is, no one can accurately forecast what will and won't work in content distribution. Firms must experiment, try variations, see what consumers do and don't respond to, and do it in a way that allows them to readily shift and try other possibilities. Pressplay, established by Vivendi Universal and Sony, in its initial launch offered four different pricing options, each offering a different combination of music streaming, downloads, and CD burns. As they monitor consumer response to this array of options, they can establish what pricing mix is most attractive.

One of the marking experiments for content business models was made by novelist Stephen King. He offered his book "The Plant" in installments, bypassing publishers completely and selling directly to readers from his website. People could freely download each installment, but were asked to pay a small amount for each part. King said he would continue writing the book if sufficient readers paid. By the fourth part, just 46% of readers paid for the download, and in November 2000 the author announced he would stop working on the book indefinitely, having reportedly earned almost a half million dollars after costs in the process.[10] As an independent author, Stephen King had the latitude to experiment more than large firms might, however by stopping mid-stream he has made it harder for others who want to try variations on his experiment, for example using DRM to protect content. He probably also had not fully thought through the consequences of stopping the experiment. Many of those who have paid $7 for the first half of a thriller probably no longer consider themselves Stephen King fans.

2. Define and refine strategies for standards and interfaces
Imagine, as you watch a video being able to click on the actors' clothes to buy them, to zoom in when you want, or to get further information on locations in the film. No doubt you've read about this marketer's dream. This can in fact be done today on the Internet, enabled by MPEG-4, the compression technology that is intended to succeed earlier standards including MP3. But the technology hasn't taken off yet. In early 2002 MPEG LA, the licensing body formed to represent the 18 firms holding the patents that underlie MPEG-4, announced its pricing plans. The proposed fees—that included per-minute fees for all streaming video—created an uproar as market participants struggled between wanting to use a powerful technology, and not wanting to pay what they saw as excessive ongoing fees for its use. The Internet Streaming Media Alliance (ISMA)—an industry body seeking to establish open standards in the field, and representing over 30 major firms including Apple, Cisco, IBM, and Philips—weighed in with their concerns over the pricing scheme. Taking advantage of the brouhaha, On2, a small video compression firm, offered the use of its technology to ISMA for free.[11] In the meantime, the primary competitor to MPEG-4 is Windows Media, with Microsoft carefully steering clear of alliances in this field.

This snapshot of intrigue demonstrates many of the key standards issues in the world of digital content. Reflecting the basics of standards strategy outlined in Chapter 2, it is clear that firms can choose between establishing and profiting from standards, or promoting fully open standards that benefit the industry but level the playing field. Those who play little role in standards setting, but use standards in their business (as do all content businesses), have to decide whether a particular standard is likely to succeed, the costs of implementing and using it, and whether to back just one horse or several. Firms that wish to offer full-featured video over the Internet need to consider whether to invest in aligning their efforts with MPEG-4, Windows Media, or the other alternatives available. Firms need not only to place their bets judiciously, but also to make sure they are able to switch courses mid-stream if necessary.

There are similar issues with the interfaces that enable access to content. As with standards—and indeed all of the flow elements—controlling these can allow firms to reposition themselves in the content distribution market. Gemstar eBook is now one of the major players in the ebook market, with two of its early moves acquiring Nuvomedia, which makes the Rocket eBook, and Softbook Press, the maker of the Softbook Reader. The original Rocket eBook worked by transferring ebook titles from PCs by serial cable after they had been downloaded from the Internet. Gemstar eBook redesigned the next version of the Rocket eBook to include a modem, which enabled users to get dial-up access to an interactive catalog, and and purchase books directly from the device maker. Gemstar eBook had neatly shifted from controlling the interface to moving into the content distribution business.

Content providers and interface makers are often involved in intricate mating dances. Content firms generally would like to make their offerings available through all devices, but sometimes they can benefit by aligning themselves with a particular interface. In order to help establish standards, companies will offer lucrative deals to get exclusive content.

3. Develop and implement aggregration strategies
No doubt Mark Getty was thinking of the awesome riches accumulated by his grandfather—oil monopolist J. Paul Getty—when he set out with the intention of buying and building a business. He openly admits he was searching for a fragmented industry that he could come to dominate. What he found was stock photography. Today Getty Images is the largest player in a \$2 billion industry, the product of 17 acquisitions made since 1995.[12] Getty and his colleagues had realized the value to its media, advertising, and corporate clients of being able to go to one source for their images rather than having to scour through many suppliers. The advent of the Internet and high-quality digital photography has vastly simplified the process of searching for and obtaining images, but the same simple dynamic applies: if you can go to one source rather than many you can dramatically reduce your transaction costs.

One of the greatest boons of the Internet to business and consumers is the ability to bring together information in one place. At the same time as buyers have gained access to many more suppliers, they are now able to consolidate and compare information on all offerings, and go to just one place for all their purchasing activities in any area. That's the theory, anyway. Certainly B2B exchanges such as Free Markets allow purchasers to access global suppliers for complex offerings, AOL's shopping channel brings together retailers of all stripes, and websites like mySimon.com compare the prices of any given product across all online retailers. However because the position of aggregator is so powerful—in many cases essentially controlling the relationship with the end-customer—the battle to become the predominant aggregator in any market is often fierce, reflecting many similar dynamics to standards wars.

The Pressplay and MusicNet case provides a great illustration of the issues. The reality is that all the five major labels would benefit if they provided one site for consumers to access all music. They have split into two competitive camps, even though consumers will never settle for music from just one group of labels. This is different from other markets, for example cable TV, in which customers are likely to choose the set of channels they prefer rather than needing to access everything. When these aggregators were being formed the question for each label was whether to participate, and if so which group they wanted to join. Each of the major labels is powerful by right of representing top artists that people want to listen to, thus forcing consumers to come to their aggregator site. EMI, a member of MusicNet, has hedged its bets by also making its music available through Pressplay. This means that it is potentially diluting the value of its stake in MusicNet, but accessing a broader market. Independent labels that wish to distribute through these sites may choose to go through both—depending on exclusivity negotiations—but if so must bear the cost of providing their content under multiple formats.

In the meantime, the peer-to-peer file sharing networks are effectively aggregating music from all labels, thus making them attractive to users. Napster is now seeking to position itself as a legal subscription service providing access to all content. The major labels want to avoid licensing their content to others, so that customers are forced to go to their online retail units, however this raises antitrust issues. Aggregators have the potential to combine market power to the detriment of consumers, and the Department of Justice has investigated numerous B2B exchanges as well as the music labels' online efforts.

4. Enable versatile syndication models
In 1865 the young newswire started by Paul Julius Reuter got its first big scoop when it broadcast news of Abraham Lincoln's assassination before anyone else in Europe. Today, when you point your browser to AOL, Lycos, MSNBC, Yahoo!, or almost any of the other top new sites on the Internet, and you will see news provided by Reuters. The global information provider feeds multimedia content to more than 1,000 client websites, packaged to target specific regional and industry audiences.

The Reuters content is delivered in NewsML—an XML format that allows its clients to select and present the information however best suits their websites. Part of the power of NewsML is that it allows stories to be reformatted for different situations, for example using shorter titles for display on mobile devices, or changing references if used in different countries.

Syndication is one of the best-established business models for content. By the early 1900s there were over 150 comic strips in syndication,xiii and the business model is central to newspapers, radio, television, and just about every other form of content and media. However, in a hyper-connected world, the drivers and nature of syndication are changing. The global scope of distribution means it is difficult to negotiate with all end-users yourself, so syndicating intermediaries like iSyndicate, ScreamingMedia, and Factiva have a vital role to play. The key role of customized content in relationships—as you saw in Chapter 4—is making access to useful, regularly updated content critical. The increasing cost of developing high-value content means syndication must be a core component of the business model. CBS Marketwatch.com makes close to one third of its revenue from licensing charts and articles to other websites, as well as newspapers and wireless networks.[14] Salon.com has reversed the traditional flow of content by syndicating its material to print newspapers and magazines.

The variety of content formats and breadth of distribution possible today means that technology is at the heart of effective syndication. Ad-hoc solutions will not scale effectively. In order to provide content in ways that can easily be used and customized by customers and different media, XML formatting such as that used by Reuters is almost essential. Companies that have a wide range of existing content need to convert it to common formats so it can be used in many forms of distribution. EMI Music Distribution has established a system in which 135,000 items, including songs, videos, lyrics, and cover artwork have been digitized as master copies, which can be converted for use in any media from CDs to mobile phones. These kinds of enabling infrastructure provide a foundation for firms to be flexible in implementing syndication business models as the environment shifts.

The scope of syndication is rapidly broadening. Providing information such as product catalogs to distributors and exchanges is effectively a syndication process. As we will see in Chapter 9, syndication is increasingly relevant to services as well as content.

5. Rework your product versioning

One of the essential excursions for any youthful visitor to London is the Ministry of Sound nightclub, established in 1991. The owners have parlayed the nightclub's success into one of the premier youth brands in the UK and worldwide, encompassing the world's bestselling dance CD, around 200 dance events annually around the globe, a popular monthly magazine, a radio station, merchandise and more. In its latest addition to its portfolio of businesses, it is launching a digital music store in conjunction with Peter Gabriel's OD2, offering a massive library of dance recordings and videos from major record labels. It provides three services to its subscribers. They can purchase and download individual tracks that can be kept, burned to CDs, or transferred to portable devices. In another service, top DJs compile the latest sounds into monthly music programs that provide unlimited access to streams and downloads, but the music files can only be used for 30 days. Finally, a personal play list gives users each month unlimited access to streams or downloads of their choice of tracks. Again, these can be played for just 30 days.

Versioning—releasing content in a range of versions with different features or at different times—is one of the core strategies in the business. Books come out in hardcover before they are released as paperbacks. Major films are released first in movie theatres, then in turn on DVD, video, cable programming, and free-to-air TV. Financial market quotes are free if they're delayed 20 minutes, but you can pay hefty subscription fees to receive real-time data. Software is often available in both a full-featured version, and one with reduced functionality that is cheaper or sometimes free.

As the content distribution landscape shifts to the digital, versioning becomes if anything more important. However the old approaches are often not the best suited to the new environment. Most importantly, both promotion and protection have become more important, and the balance between them is shifting.

Clearly the ability for users to pass on digital copies, sometimes after cracking the protection, has become a dominant factor. Film and TV content owners are often reluctant to release their programs onto digital TV, because they can be readily copied and shared. The entire economics of the film industry are built around the staged release of movies in different formats, with the premium revenue movie-theater release going first. For now, film studios are doing everything they can to maintain their current system, partly by avoiding any form of early release that could possibly be cracked and made available on the illegal market. However if consumer attitudes to file sharing and broadband technology advance faster than copy protection technologies, it is possible that content owners will have to rethink their versioning strategies.

Vital Connections: Chapter 8

Digital content flows freely, so in a hyper-connected world, content industries including entertainment and high-value information are being transformed perhaps more than any other. They must balance protection and promotion, and implement new strategies to maximize the value of their products.

One of the primary driving shifts in the economy for over a century has been the move from products to services. In Chapter 9 we will examine the rapidly expanding world of online services, and the new strategies required for professional services providers.

CHAPTER 9

The Flow of Services

Reframing Digital and Professional Services

Digital connectivity and integration are dramatically shifting the role of services in the economy. Software is being provided as a service, business processes are readily outsourced, and the functions of the firm can be broken down into defined modules. Professional services now range across a spectrum of business models ranging from digital services to traditional face-to-face delivery. The same drivers are resulting in the rise of professional networks as viable competitors to established firms.

In September 1998 John "Launny" Steffens, then vice-chairman of Merrill Lynch, was quoted as saying that Internet trading represented a "serious threat" to the financial well-being of Americans. A 38-year veteran of the firm who had started as a broker in Cleveland, his emphatic stance was supported by the 15,000-odd brokers who clearly saw the Internet as a threat to their own financial situation. Merrill Lynch's clients didn't see it quite the same way, and made their feelings known, often by setting up online accounts with the brokerage firm's rivals. Just over a year after Steffens' widely-publicized comments, the online broking service Merrill Lynch Direct was launched, garnering an award from the financial weekly Barrons as the number one online stock trading site within six months. The supertanker had begun to turn around, with Merrill Lynch shifting to actively present itself as an innovative provider of information-based services to its individual and corporate clients.

In order to transform itself, Merrill Lynch is using technologies that can embed business processes into software. You learned about web services in Chapter 2. These are the most important technology bet Merrill Lynch is now making, according to its chief technology officer, John McKinley Jr.[1] The firm is running literally hundreds of initiatives based on web services, helping both to integrate internal systems and to provide services to clients. One of its projects is a portfolio analysis system that integrates disparate account and product information from within Merrill Lynch, and market data from external partners. This assists its brokers in providing effective recommendations to their clients. However it goes beyond this. Selected clients are also being given access to the new systems, offering real-time analysis and insights on their portfolios directly over the Internet. The broker sitting in Merrill Lynch's offices no longer acts as an intermediary to these high-value services, and top clients are now receiving a whole spectrum of services, including both interaction with highly-skilled advisors and a suite of online offerings.[1]

In this chapter we will examine the evolving world of services. Digital services—those that can be delivered online—are becoming central to the economy. Connectivity is allowing both software and business processes to be delivered as services. Now the development of web services is creating a new modular world of business, not only making it easier for companies to fine-tune the selection of what they perform in-house and what they outsource, but also enabling firms to become both consumers and producers of services and business processes. The world of professional services is closely linked to the rapid development of digital services. Professional services strategy must make traditional face-to-face services and new online services fit together seamlessly. Professional networks, that bring together best-of-breed experts from around the world in tightly-knit teams, will become increasingly important in the economy, and challenge traditional business models.

Services go online

Submitting travel and entertainment expense claims is the bane of every businessperson's existence. For the companies that employ them, it is a time-consuming, error-prone process that takes valuable resources from more productive efforts. Application service provider (ASP) Outtask— among its comprehensive suite of online services—allows its clients to automate the entire process, from entering the expense claim to reimbursement, and subsequent integration with the company's accounting systems. Employees can access the system wherever they are, whenever they want, and the company can concentrate its efforts on what it does best.

This is a simple example of how the blossoming of digital connectivity is transforming how services are delivered and used. As companies and consumers get access to reliable and secure bandwidth, whole new worlds of possibilities open up. As you have seen earlier in this book, software is increasingly being delivered as an online service, and it is becoming far easier to outsource business processes while keeping them closely integrated with the organization's core activities.

The shift to providing software as an online service rather than as a packaged product has been driven by both vendors and clients. Software firms—and often their shareholders—prefer receiving ongoing revenue rather than the intermittent lump sums resulting from major sales or the pressures of quarterly reporting. Clients can often reduce costs—especially for the initial capital investment—and free up management to focus on core issues rather than technology. Our ability to connect to the networks almost anywhere and anytime means that using software over the web is an increasingly viable alternative to having it installed on our computers. Service firm Always-on—and a multitude of competitors—provides Microsoft Office software as an online service, available for a monthly subscription fee. Services such as Yahoo! Calendar or Hotmail fit the same model of giving online access to computing resources, except that they are available for free.

The pace of the shift to providing software applications as an online service has been slower than some early evangelists proclaimed. One of the major concerns of potential clients has been their dependence on connectivity. If communication goes, so does their access to software. The other vital issue is the ability to integrate external applications with internal systems. Both of these are becoming less problematic over time. Networks are becoming more resilient and robust, with uptime almost always exceeding that of in-house computer systems, and as you have seen through this book, systems integration is swiftly becoming easier. However it means that many ASPs are starting to include integration services as a core part of their business, rather than simply providing their clients with access to software.

The only services that can't be delivered via digital connectivity are those which require physical presence. Installing PC boards, haircuts, and massages all require—at least for the meantime—a person to be there. High-value professional services are also commonly based on face-to-face interaction, as we will discuss later in this chapter. However all other services can be provided online. You probably only communicate with many of the departments of your company through e-mail or telephone. When was the last time you went to visit your accounts receivable staff? As connectivity and integration drive business, it now makes virtually no differerence whether a business process is performed inside or outside your company.

Outsourcing business processes

Automatic Data Processing (ADP) set up business in 1949 to provide outsourced payroll operations. Clients provided information in print or on the telephone, and keypunch operators entered this onto cards for processing by mainframes. Payroll quickly became widely outsourced, because it was a highly information-intensive process that only needed to be performed fortnightly or monthly, thus making it suitable for the early batch-processing systems. Now connectivity has enabled the explosion of business process outsourcing, commonly abbreviated to BPO. Just about every business function can be performed outside the company, even those that require both constant access and deep integration into other parts of the firm. Not so long ago the accounts department was a staple of every organization. Now not just accounting functions such as order entry, purchasing, and billing are being regularly outsourced, but also other operations usually considered a core part of companies, like human resources and even sales, are being executed externally.

Business functions are increasingly automated, but they also often require people. When in 1999 BP Amoco and Pricewaterhouse Coopers announced a billion dollar outsourcing agreement, it included the transfer of 1,200 finance, accounting, and IT professionals.[3] However the defining issue with most BPO is that the primary interface with the client organization is digital, which enables it to be easily integrated. As the ability to integrate systems improves further, companies will be able to select far more precisely what is a core competence of the firm, and what is better done outside.

The other key issue is transparency, which enables companies to get full and free visibility of operations, even if they are run externally. Flextronics, a contract electronics manufacturer that makes equipment for firms such as Microsoft, Ericsson, Cisco, and Motorola, provides its clients with total transparency into their outsourced manufacturing operations. As Flextronics manufactures Microsoft's Xbox game console in its plants in

Mexico and Hungary, Microsoft executives are given a single real-time view into global operations, down to the details such as shop floor data and inventory turns. Essentially they are able to see the same degree of information on production and order fulfilment as Flextronics executives. The operations may be outsourced, but the degree of transparency and integration means there is virtually the same information flow as if they were performed in-house.

The new modular world of business

Norwegian insurer Storebrand runs the pension plans of over 390,000 staff for 6,500 firms, which means that its records for every one of these employees must be updated whenever his or her salary or personal details change. The system used to be that companies sent in data changes by file transfer, mail, or fax, and Storebrand's customer service representatives would then enter these into the central database, creating a substantial drain on resources for both the insurer and its clients. Since the required information was already on Storebrand's clients' human resources systems, it made sense to transfer this electronically, however it seemed a hopeless task to try to integrate Storebrand's mainframes with thousands of different computer systems.

Web services, as you saw in Chapter 2, are standards for how applications can find each other and integrate seamlessly. Storebrand worked with IBM to design and implement a new web services application. This enables its clients to update Storebrand's records on their employees from within their own payroll applications. The insurer is now looking to register the web service it has designed on a public directory, so other insurers or distributors can find the application and license it for use within their own applications, thus generating additional revenue for Storebrand.

The heart of web services is breaking down what used to be monolithic software packages and business processes into a set of modules. This is only possible because web services architecture allows these modules to integrate perfectly into each other, requesting information or tasks to be performed as if they were part of the one program, whether they are running on the same computer or on systems on opposite sides of the world. What may initially seem a relatively minor adjustment in fact has revolutionary implications for business.

Inside the organization, web services can change how the business processes and software that are the foundation of the company are developed and implemented. Flexible modules can be built, and then reused in other applications, or simply reconfigured to mean software functionality can evolve with minimal effort. Outside the firm, this powerful new set of technologies has the potential to allow totally seamless integration of internal and external processes, vastly accelerating the blurring of organizational boundaries, and creating the potential for almost unlimited flexibility in designing and implementing the corporation. Companies must implement four key actions to take full advantage of the new world of web services, as shown in Table 9-1.

BENEFITING FROM WEB SERVICES

1.Use web services to integrate internally and externally
2.Modularize your business
3.Be both a consumer and provider of services and content
4.Experiment with new business models

Table 9-1: Action steps to benefiting from web services

1. Use web services to integrate internally and externally
The government of New Mexico has used web services to integrate a wide variety of existing systems to provide its employees with a single interface to all of their personal information. iv One of the greatest boons of the technology is the ability to give almost any range of systems a common interface so they can be easily linked together. Not only are significant costs saved in performing the integration, but any future initiatives to link data and systems internally can be vastly accelerated after the initial conversion.

Often even larger benefits come from being able to integrate with the systems of external partners, who frequently use completely different hardware and software. Dell uses web services to publish updated manufacturing schedules on its extranet every two hours. This allows all of its suppliers to readily take this information and integrate it directly into their own systems, which helps to bring Dell's plant inventory to sometimes as low as three hours. Another service implemented by Dell generates automated queries to its suppliers' systems on order status. This results in maximum visibility of the supply chain flow for all participants.[5]

Clearly it is not always straightforward to integrate applications across organizations. Companies like Grand Central and Bowstreet represent a new sector that provides the infrastructure and services to facilitate process integration between companies. This helps ensure reliability and security in business transactions, while taking full advantage of the power of the new technologies.

2. Modularize your business

Ford Credit provides online financial services to 12,500 car dealerships and 10 million individual car owners around the world, giving them access to account information, online payments, loan applications, and a wide range of other services. By early 2002 its developers had created 23 reusable web services that are combined into customizable applications. The modular designs have created an estimated $15 million in savings. One of Ford Credit's largest software applications provides services to 5,000 branch offices. In shifting these applications to a browser-based environment that requires less computing power in the offices and allows workers to access services from wherever they are, Ford Credit has again taken a modular approach, saving costs and dramatically improving efficiency.[6]

The most powerful wave of emerging information technologies does not just enable a business to be broken down into distinct mix-and-match modules, it makes this a clear and powerful path to make a company far more efficient, and immensely more flexible. While the tools to achieve this are software-based, the design for this must be done at the level of business processes. Every company must start thinking about its operations in a new way. What are the distinct business processes that make up your organization? Which of those processes might you want to reuse in a different context? What elements of larger processes could be valuable as stand-alone processes or as part of other processes, either inside the firm or in other organizations?

These are key strategic questions for any company, and today, you have the ability to act on the answers to those questions. The issue of distributing specific business processes inside and outside the firm is at a lower level than the broad strategic issues discussed in Chapter 7, but the birth of the modular organization has a major impact on what strategic options are available to companies.

The flexibility of web services means that existing resources can be easily redeployed in any number of new ways. What is now required is the imagination to conceive and implement new business models.

3. Be both a consumer and provider of services and content

As it becomes increasingly easy to construct applications and business processes from modular components, companies can decide for each one of those modules whether to source it in-house or externally. In addition, if useful business processes are built inside the firm, these can then be sold to third-parties. GMAC Mortgage developed web-based applications for its own use that it has now chosen to provide externally, generating incremental revenue for work it has already done.[7]

Web services is comprised of a set of open standards. Most of the standards focus on how applications effectively send messages and integrate their functions in a secure fashion. However the web services modules that together create applications need to find each other. This is the function of the standard called Universal Description, Discovery, and Integration (UDDI). This is essentially a global database of web services, which allows anyone to search for modules that match specified requirements, identify where they are located, and immediately integrate them into their applications. All that is required is for companies to register their web services in the central UDDI database. Storebrand, mentioned above, is registering its services so that anyone worldwide can find and use them. This central repository of web services means that any firm can easily find and use the best services available, and in turn—if they are the best in their domain—to sell their services to a global market.

4. Experiment with new business models

Commercial real estate broker Collier International is using web services to integrate information on properties and clients from more than 250 offices worldwide. This makes it far easier for salespeople to pull together deals, and also creates a new, valuable resource that can be easily reconfigured. Collier plans to sell selective access to the global database to third parties.[8] The flexibility of web services means that existing resources can be easily redeployed in any number of new ways. What is now required is the imagination to conceive and implement new business models.

These new technologies allow companies to think about services in a similar way to content. You can widely distribute and redistribute services, just as you can with information. Syndication, which as you saw in Chapter 8 is a well-established business model for content, in an intensely networked world is also an increasingly relevant model for other businesses. The development of web services means that anyone can be a publisher at minimal cost, gaining incremental revenue or enhancing brand by providing content or services for broad distribution. Even using existing approaches, new service models are possible. ASP Outtask, mentioned earlier in this chapter, distributes its travel booking services through travel agent Kintetsu, among others. Since compact web services modules can be easily found and used by third parties, companies will have to develop new approaches to pricing these effectively. Again, syndication business models provide a useful basis for experimentation.

Web services and the flow economy

When Bill Gates repeatedly says that he is betting the future of Microsoft on web services, you know there has to be a good business in there somewhere. Given the potential position of web services as providing the glue that holds together the entire world of commerce, it offers a fabulous case study of the dynamics of the emerging flow economy.

Inevitably, there is a fierce and multi-layered battle for standards. The lower layers of web services, including XML and some simple integration protocols, are by now clearly defined and effectively true standards. The really critical issue is whether web services developed using different types of software can work together. The Web Services Interoperability Organization was founded in early 2002 by Microsoft, IBM, Intel, and software provider BEA Systems. There will be many issues to iron out between the major players as the field of web services evolves and functionality increases, but it is in everyone's interest to see a system in which all computers can readily talk and integrate.

Where the true competition lies is in the platforms that are used to develop web services software. Microsoft's offering is its .NET platform, that allows developers to use almost any programming language, but the resulting software can only be run on Microsoft operating systems. Virtually all of its competitors, including IBM, Sun Microsystems, and BEA Systems, use an open standard framework for software development called Java 2 Enterprise Edition, or J2EE for short. This means that software developed on any of these platforms can—in theory—be readily moved across to run on other hardware or even operating systems. The key factor that will tip this standards battle is the software developers themselves. If developers prefer a particular software environment and become familiar with it, then it will be easier to hire people with those skills, projects will tend to use that platform, and more developers will acquire those skills. Microsoft in particular is expert at wooing the developer community, however the flexibility of J2EE is currently attracting many developers.

An oft-quoted illustration of the potential of web services is the stock ticker available on many websites. This discrete service can easily be provided by a third-party and integrated seamlessly into a website, as long as everyone agrees on the necessary standards. However once this is achieved, this also means that if another firm offers you the same stock ticker for a penny less, you can almost press a button to change suppliers, rather than having to go through any effort to integrate the new service. This shows how both content and services can quickly become commoditized through the widespread implementation of web services. When everything slots seamlessly into everything else, and the only things that make a difference are quality, brand, and price. Quality will always make a difference, however in many cases brand is becoming less visible. Increasingly price is coming to the fore in selected suppliers of modular services and content.

This shift will make relationships with end-customers more important than ever. If you control the customer relationship, then you are entirely at liberty to pull together whatever services and content are required from a vast community of potential suppliers. Their offerings are highly commoditized, and you can take the vast majority of the value created. This was exactly Microsoft's thinking when it initiated .NET My Services. This suite of personal services for consumers takes full advantage of web services to provide complete integration of almost every way in which an individual would want to tap the flow economy. The central concept is providing a secure database that allows consumers to store their personal information, and to choose exactly how they make that available to third-parties, either to enable them to receive better service or in exchange for value in some form. The information that can be stored includes people's personal details; contact files; where, when, and on what devices to contact them; financial transactions; and a wealth of other vital data. For example, you could book your travel arrangements with all your usual preferences automatically taken into account, pay for them, share your calendar with the people you're meeting, and get both you and your contacts immediately alerted if there are any changes to travel schedules.

Microsoft's initial objective was to offer this powerful system on a subscription basis to consumers. The software giant was positioning itself to effectively control consumers' access to the wealth of the flow economy, attempting to dominate the increasingly important flow element of relationships. However in early 2002 it had to stop and reconsider its initiative. The main problems were that other major corporations had no intention of letting control of customer information shift to Microsoft, and consumers were reluctant to entrust it with all of their personal information. Microsoft has recognized that the center of the information world is no longer PC platforms, but rather access to a whole world of integrated online services. However this enormously valuable positioning will not yield itself easily, and the battle for this space has but begun.

Easy connectivity and integration—epitomized by Web services—have given us a new modular world of business, in which processes can be broken down into software elements, and then recombined to result in powerful and flexible ways of doing business. However not all services can be embedded into software. Highly-skilled professionals play an important role in providing customized, knowledge-based services on demand. The worlds of digital services and professional services are now merging.

The evolution of professional services

Ten weeks after desktoplawyer.co.uk launched an online legal service for no-contest divorces, it captured six percent of the market for British separations.[9] Why contribute to your lawyer's new sports car fund when you can do it all for £59.99, including telephone support? Corporations are benefiting from the same trends. Clifford Chance, the world's largest law firm, established NextLaw in 1997 to provide online legal services to its corporate clients. Australian law firm Blake Dawson Waldron—among its many innovative online initiatives—implemented for one of its large retailing clients an Advertising Copy Advisor, which is an expert system that examines the text of proposed advertisements and asks a series of questions to the copywriters. It then provides initial recommendations to the company's in-house counsel on the degree of legal risk posed by the advertisement, and highlights any specific areas for concern.

Not just lawyers, but professionals of all stripes, including accountants, consultants, financial advisors, advertising executives, and engineers, are discovering that digital services and connectivity are beginning to transform their world. So far the impact has been minor in most quarters, but the pace is rapidly accelerating. Professionals can no longer rely on a steady flow of supplicants coming to their door and paying them handsomely for their time when in some cases technology can assist in providing comparable services at a fraction of the cost.

The rapid evolution of connectivity has led to the emergence of three distinct types of professional services, as illustrated in Figure 9-1. Digital execution covers services that are provided end-to-end by digital systems, with no human involvement. Britain's convoluted car tax legislation means that determining whether cars should be leased or bought is a complex calculation based on cost, marginal tax rates, planned usage and more. Deloitte & Touche has launched an online system that provides recommendations for car acquisition plans, and sells this not only to individuals, but also to companies managing their employee benefits, and even accountants who find it easier to use the service on behalf of their clients than do the calculations themselves. Digital interface refers to situations in which people are performing the services, but the interface and delivery of those services is entirely digital. PricewaterhouseCoopers' tax division has implemented Online Consulting Services, which gives online answers to specific tax questions within 48 hours, priced by the question. And of course the traditional approach of face-to-face professional services remains. Increasingly there must be a good reason for people to bear the cost of these highly interactive services, such as gaining knowledge and capabilities that would not be possible online.

Commoditization

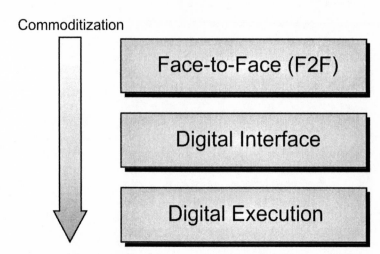

Figure 9-1: Three types of professional services in a digital world

In the middle ages, professional guilds punished their members with expulsion and sometimes worse if they revealed the secrets of the trade. The livelihoods and prestige of professionals were based on keeping information exclusive. Today, the transparency of our highly-connected world means that professionals usually no longer even attempt to keep most information from their clients. Almost all large professional firms have been publishing documents and newsletters for their clients since before the Internet era, and by now have largely shifted those information services online. In some cases they can charge for access to high-value content, however there is constant downward pressure on prices. Their competitors will frequently offer similar information for free in order to attract the attention of prospective clients, and hopefully win lucrative projects. The McKinsey Quarterly, the journal of prestigious consultancy McKinsey & Co, used to be distributed only to clients, but is now available for free online. At the same time, many less complex services are gradually shifting to lower cost alternatives, such as do-it-yourself kits for simple legal matters.

After giving access to information online, the next phase for professional services firms has been to implement digital interfaces to their services. This can be more efficient for both the service firm and its clients. However as soon as face-to-face contact disappears and services are accessed electronically, there is a tremendous degree of commoditization. Clients see only the interfaces and results, and these can begin to look very similar between competitive offerings. As a result, price—and in turn the ability to provide the service at the lowest cost—become the driving issues. In fact the best way to reduce costs is to take people out of the process as much as possible, shifting to digital execution service. Expert systems are not ready to supplant people in every field, but in some cases they can begin to provide low-level advice, or facilitate people in performing their tasks.

The translation industry handily illustrates these trends. Because texts used to have to be physically transported back and forth, clients had to use local translators, unless they were prepared for long delays. The advent of e-mail and the Internet made the process far swifter, and meant that it became easy to use the best or cheapest translators wherever they were in the world. Translation firms—which already almost always had their work performed by independent professionals— broadened their scope to work with translators worldwide, and focus more on the quality assurance function. Today, you can get a rudimentary machine translation for free on Altavista, Google. and other websites.

No firm can ignore that at least some elements of the services it provides can now be performed digitally, more effectively and at lower cost than by traditional methods.

What many translation services do now is use machine translation to get a first draft of a translation, then use cheaper professionals to edit the text into something readable, and sometimes to check the meaning of the original when in doubt.

One of the dominant trends in professional services today is implementing collaborative tools to interact with clients. This itself is blurring the boundaries between face-to-face services and digital interface services. Professionals can work closely with their peers, with clients in different locations, and if necessary professionals from other firms, in order to execute projects. For example New York law firm Davis Polk & Wardwell regularly uses online "deal rooms" to work with clients on large projects, inviting the investment banks, consultants, and accountants involved in the deals to participate, resulting in a far more efficient process. In addition, these collaborative systems result in far greater transparency to clients. They can see what goes on as it happens, significantly shifting the client-professional relationship.

These dramatic shifts in professional services are relevant to almost every company. Most firms today offer professional advice and consulting services in some form, either as a defined part of the business, or sometimes simply as an increasingly necessary element of the sales process. Firms like IBM and Hewlett-Packard, that used to be simply hardware vendors, are now major providers of professional services. Chemicals company Buckman Laboratories offers consulting on knowledge management as part of the services available to its largest clients. United Parcel Service provides logistics consulting. Every company must consider how professional services—in its new multi-tier form—fits into and enhances its complete range of offerings.

The new professional services strategy

Not long ago now professional services consisted of a single, clear business model. Provide highly-skilled professionals to clients, charge them out by the hour, and pick up the difference between the fees and the professionals' salaries. In the space of just a few years, the situation has become far more complex. No firm can ignore that at least some elements of the services it provides can now be performed digitally, more effectively and at lower cost than by traditional methods.

When Ernst & Young released its groundbreaking online service Ernie in 1996, it was the first major professional services firm to delve into this challenging territory. Ernie provided prompt e-mail answers to specific questions, and a number of online tools such as an IPO Advisor to help young firms through the process of raising capital. In the gradual evolution of its suite of online services, Ernst & Young Online now provides a complete interface to the firm's online services, including the same online answers to client questions, personalized news, interactive tools, and flexible team rooms that allow messaging and discussions both between executives in a client firm, and within engagement teams. Ernst & Young is now seeking new channels to distribute its online offerings, for example offering its Online Tax Advisor and other services as part of FinancialOxygen's capital markets trading hub.

Ernst & Young's initial strategy was to target its online services to medium-sized enterprises that were not yet large enough to merit a full-scale relationship with the firm, but could grow into substantial clients if they were developed early. Since then the primary focus has shifted to providing a spectrum of services to its large corporate clients, mainly to provide the benefits of digital services as a key part of its "full-service" offerings. As shown by its deal with FinancialOxygen, it also sees its online services suite as a business development tool, and to address markets it cannot effectively service face-to-face.

In this new world, professional service firms must take five key steps in developing powerful strategies for success, as shown in Table 9-2.

DEVELOPING PROFESSIONAL SERVICES STRATEGY

1.Develop complementary business models
2.Design for lock-in
3.Implement flexible processes, sourcing, and quality assurance
4.Create knowledge-based relationships
5.Actively migrate clients

Table 9-2: Action steps to developing professional services strategy

1. Develop complementary business models

Professional services began as a single core business model. It has now evolved to cover an entire spectrum of distinct business models. These businesses, ranging from traditional face-to-face consulting to websites, can each be treated as independent operations with their own profit responsibilities. However today one of the fundamental planks of professional services strategy is making these business models complementary.

Few professionals are sympathetic to the idea of their firms offering online versions of services that have up until now paid them well. However an increasing number of firms have recognized that if they don't commoditize their own offerings, someone else will, taking away part of the business, and in addition eroding their client relationships. You have a choice between demonstrating leadership, or being forced to respond to others' moves.

This first step is simply coming to terms with the fact that part of the services that they offer can be performed online. This can open up many possibilities. These digital services can be offered to a whole new class of clients such as smaller companies or those in other locations or countries. Be-Professional, a UK joint venture offering online compliance services for small companies, has become a free-standing business that has opened up an entirely new market for its founding firms, and Ernst & Young launched Ernie with the intention of building relationships with up-and-coming businesses that it could then sell its higher-value services into. Other firms have offered their online services to major clients for free, to consolidate the relationship and keep competitors out.

The way the three types of professional services complement each other depends not only on effective cross-selling from one to another, but also on a balanced application of available resources. The valuable knowledge, systems, and processes of professional firms can be packaged and sold in more than one way. The expert systems designed by Blake Dawson Waldron leverage existing knowledge to generate additional revenue. Ernst & Young Australia has developed a diverse suite of online consulting tools, including systems for companies to monitor corporate governance risk, evaluate tenders, and assess privacy legislation compliance.[10] These begin to shift the firm from the traditional fee-for-service model to one of licensing intellectual property, that provides ongoing revenue once it is developed. The firm is generating income not just by signing up clients directly, but also by making the systems available to its sister firms globally.

2. Design for lock-in

Strong personal relationships are enduring. However when interaction shifts to the digital, it becomes far easier for clients to switch to other providers, so new approaches are required to help them to stay. In Chapter

4 you saw how being more effective at customizing information and services can result in powerful lock-in, since clients will lose a valuable resource if they change relationships. JP Morgan Chase's Executive View service provides its clients with customized websites that include not just information, news, and research on the firm's industry and peers, but also current indicative pricing of the likely cost to the client of raising capital today through loans or commercial paper.[11] As with any website, in order to get people to use a site regularly and increase familiarity, some of the services should include time-sensitive information and analysis, and be designed to become part of users' daily work habits. The most powerful lock-in is to integrate clients' actual business processes into extranet offerings. This requires understanding their processes, and designing systems that can match them exactly.

Temporary staff firm Manpower builds websites for its major clients, using the same look and feel as their in-house systems so that these can fit neatly into their intranets. The websites provide detailed stories, information, and instructions on how to go about sourcing and hiring temporary staff. Real case studies of how people at the client firm have had to find staff, and how they've successfully found them through Manpower, are presented in a lively style aligned with the client's culture. Guidance on how to go through the firm's internal approval procedures are given, along with contact details for relevant staff both internally and at Manpower. In addition Manpower changes its own ways of working if necessary, so that they are aligned with their clients' key processes. All this makes it easy for the client to use Manpower, and a major effort to change to use any of its competitors.

3. Implement flexible processes, sourcing, and quality assurance
Every day over one billion words are published, with almost all going through a proofreading or editing process. Editor.com is an online editing and writing service based in Australia that taps this potentially huge market, using both in-house and external editors. With its larger clients, that include Cisco, Merrill Lynch, and Ericsson, it tends to have a fairly traditional service firm relationship, with regular meetings and interaction. Its international clients can interact with Editor.com entirely online, from estimates through to final work completion. Given the nature of its work, the firm's operations are centered on quality assurance. Currently all work done by external contractors is checked internally by senior editors, though managing director Grant Butler foresees being able to get some of the company's most experienced external editors to take on that role once there is sufficient mutual familiarity and trust. Online workflow systems mean that the jobs can be assigned, performed, and checked seamlessly using editors around the world. It's now easy to find writers and editors anywhere in the world, sometimes prepared to work for very low rates, but Editor.com chooses to develop strong relationships with a small pool of experienced professionals. Its business is driven by providing quality output

to clients, so it would be counter-productive to use cheap external talent, and as a result spend far more in managing them and correcting their work.

Professional services delivered through a digital interface can still sometimes attract premium prices. Editor.com charges standard rates for corporate editing work, and Ernst & Young and PricewaterhouseCoopers both charge literally thousands of dollars for a single e-mail response to a question. However the reality is that as soon as clients interact using only digital channels there are keen pressures on prices, and in turn on costs. Firms must be as efficient as possible. Clear, streamlined internal processes must be established if digital interface services are to succeed. If these are implemented in an existing professional services firm, one of the most important issues is allocating work to professionals. The workflow of the digital interface services must be integrated into the existing work practices, by identifying staff that have the expertise and time to respond to incoming work. It is also critically important to design remuneration systems so that staff are motivated to allocate their time appropriately between traditional projects and incoming digital work. Whether work is performed internally or externally, the quality assurance function is critical, both to ensure work is up to standard, but also to maintain consistency of style and approach. If work is performed externally, then the entire operation becomes one of designing effective workflow processes, managing external contractors, and providing quality assurance.

Interestingly, many advertising agencies effectively implement this highly-outsourced model. The advertising concept is usually developed internally, but much of the execution such as design and media production is done externally, with the agency co-ordinating the external contractors. The ability to manage the work and provide quality assurance is a large part of the value created for the client, who would rarely be interested or effective at doing this.

4. Create knowledge-based relationships
Raves are not only for teenagers. Cap Gemini Ernst & Young's in-house think-tank, the Center for Business Innovation (CBI), regularly organizes its own brand of raves: invitation-only events that bring together top thinkers in their field for free-ranging discussion on themes like connectivity, the future of software, and the implications of economic webs. Designers visually map the discussion as it happens, resulting in colorful structured charts of the proceedings. In one rave, participants were given mobile devices that enabled them to buy and sell ideas on an open market, with the agenda of the second day chosen by the closing market value of the ideas. These raves are primarily intended to explore ideas that can be later applied in the firm's consulting operations, and to establish thought leadership, but similar approaches are also used with clients. The CBI hosted Nokia's Insight & Foresight Group, which is charged with

investigating emerging trends and selecting those that the company should incorporate into its practices. In a two-day session, the firm demonstrated to the group how complexity science can be applied to organizations, using interactive models and dialogue to generate ideas... and insight.

The highest level of value in professional services is enhancing clients' own knowledge and capabilities. Digital services can only go so far in achieving this, and rich interaction with very bright people remains essential not only to create fantastic outcomes, but also to build deep, lasting relationships. While most firms will find they need to offer all three tiers of professional services, the low-end digital services are always being commoditized, and the only way to maintain premium prices is to create true knowledge-based relationships. This requires developing enabling structures, processes, and skills to complement technology-based strategies. Relationships with clients need to be structured so that professionals' specialist knowledge is integrated into the clients' operations and decision-making. Processes to ensure knowledge is transferred to the client in the course of engagements should become part of standard practice. And professionals need to develop new skills, including understanding how their clients think, and interacting so as to develop clients' knowledge and capabilities. My book *Developing Knowledge-Based Client Relationships: The Future of Professional Services* gives detailed advice on how to implement effective knowledge-based relationships with sophisticated clients. This is the only way to maintain differentiated, extremely high-value services in a world of driving commoditization.

5. Actively migrate clients

The whole culture of investment banking revolves around the payment of the annual bonus, which can be a time of joy, commiseration, and sometimes obscene profligacy. One global bank based in Europe has made the bonuses of its foreign exchange salespeople depend on how effectively they migrate their large clients to using electronic trading platforms. Traders' bonuses are primarily based on revenue generated, but will only be paid in full if a sufficient proportion of the business has been done online. One of the many challenges of migrating professional services clients to online channels is professionals' fear of losing the client relationship, revenue, or even their jobs. This bank is making it crystal-clear what it expects from its salespeople.

Professional services firms should have in place detailed, current strategies for each of their substantial clients. One of the most important issues today is the desired balance of channels for service delivery, based on the client's profitability, business potential, and strategic importance, and the steps required to migrate the client. Risks and opportunities for the client relationship need to be taken into account, and sometimes it can be an issue of how to move clients to greater face-to-face interaction rather than shifting them to digital channels. Just as for the overall firm strategy, these individual client strategies should be designed to make the different service delivery and communication channels complementary in developing deeper relationships.

The rise of professional networks

In Swedish, *ska* means "we shall". SKA is also the acronym for Sveiby Knowledge Associates, a global consulting network that counts around 30 members from 15 nations, representing every inhabited continent. Karl-Erik Sveiby, a leading light in knowledge management and intellectual capital, wanted to bring together a global network of independent consultants, to try to provide them some of the benefits of working within a larger organization, without sacrificing the freedom of choice and flexibility of self-employment.

One of the glues that holds SKA together is the use of common tools and consulting frameworks. All members are licensed to run Tango, a highly participative workshop that helps corporate executives understand the dynamics of managing intangible assets in their firms. Many other structured consulting processes are used by SKA members, often under license, with the SKA adminstrative hub handling payments from users to the holder of the intellectual property. At the outset of the group, many of the processes used had been created by Sveiby, however the structure of SKA actively encourages all members to develop licensable consulting processes, with the knowledge that there is already a sizeable group of successful and like-minded professionals ready to apply them with their clients globally.

Each member of SKA has his or her own clients, all of which are registered in a central database, including contact details. The owner of a particular client relationship will bring in other consultants from the group as necessary; several major projects have brought together members from multiple continents. Every proposal submitted to a client must be posted on the group's private website. Clearly this kind of openness can only happen in an environment of trust. The network has established a set of seven shared values, which provide a foundation for behavior by the members. It is a mandatory requirement for SKA members to attend the annual meeting, which so far has been held in Australia and South Africa, with the next one scheduled in Guangzhou in Southern China. Only by regularly meeting everyone else in the group can the necessary cohesiveness and trust develop.

Another professional network is also succeeding, using a quite different business model and approach. The founders of Axiom Legal saw that the clients of major law firms were paying extremely high fees which rarely reflected the cost of the lawyers doing the work. Salaried associates do virtually all the work, and clients fork out a hefty premium to pay for both the swanky offices in prime real-estate, and the partners who sit at the top of the pile. The million-dollar plus packages of top legal partners consist primarily of the difference between the salaries of their associates and what clients are billed for that work.

Corporate clients are increasingly happy to consider independent professionals as service providers, and in some cases actually prefer effective professional networks to expensive global firms with cookie-cutter approaches.

Axiom was set up to provide the same quality of advice as the top New York law firms, with a substantially lower cost to the client. Partly because it is a virtual organization, it finds it easier to gets its lawyers out to its clients' offices, which helps drive the hands-on way of working with its clients in-house counsel that is Axiom's trademark.

Clearly individual lawyers are not able to provide the same level of service as large firms, as they do not have access to the same resources and diversity of experience. Axiom established a similar infrastructure to that a large law firm would have, with complete libraries, support staff, and knowledge management systems to allow its lawyers to work closely together and tap each others' expertise. It then set out to recruit the best lawyers, going through a stringent selection process, but in return being able to offer work flexibility, higher income, and an escape from the intense office politics of partnerships. The enormous demand to join the network has allowed Axiom to be very selective in its recruitment. The firm's attorneys all gather for a monthly meeting, as the firm is still primarily based in the US North-East.

These two cases represent very different manifestations of the new brand of professional networks. In SKA, highly independent but like-minded consultants congregate because of the mutual value of sharing their practices, tools, and sometimes clients. Axiom Legal presents a centralized corporate face to the world, and implements innovative structures for performing legal work that can benefit both lawyers and clients.

Professional networks, although hardly a new phenomenon, are rapidly rising in importance. Their evolution is being driven by both the new ways of working enabled by connectivity, and the swift shift to professionals working as free agents. Corporate clients are increasingly happy to consider independent professionals as service providers, and in some cases actually prefer effective professional networks to expensive global firms with cookie-cutter approaches. The bottom-line is that for many types of business, professional networks are increasingly viable competitors to large, established firms. This is already apparent, but will become more obvious in coming years. We will cover some of these issues from the perspective of the individual in Chapter 10.

Success factors for professional networks

In many years as a keen observer and participant in nascent professional networks, I have seen considerably more failures than successes. Clearly there is no one successful model or formula—any number of extremely different approaches can work. However there are six common issues that all professional networks must address in order to result in real benefits to their members.

- **Structure and leadership**. The reality is that few professional networks are truly self-organizing—there needs to be a core team which leads the group and co-ordinates its functioning. Axiom Legal represents one of the more centralized professional network models. The capital required for the necessary infrastructure is raised by a company at the core, and a specific offer of labour for pay made to the participating lawyers. Swedish management consulting firm Consultus similarly provides a central administration facility for its affiliated consultants. At the other end of the spectrum some small groups of professionals informally agree to pay referral fees to each other. However this isn't sufficient to provide the fully integrated service that creates the real potential benefits to professionals and clients.

- **Coherence.** Most failed professional networks stumble because the individuals in the network do not have enough in common or anything to bind around. Trust is essential for a network to work, and for that network members need to share beliefs and values. Rob Pye, founder of the consulting network c-people, refers to the importance of "shared purpose". One of the most important decisions made by any network is its recruitment policies. If it is too easy to join, the risk is the network will become a database of contacts, however bringing complementary skills into the group can create value for everyone, as long as their attitudes and approaches are aligned. If the overly rapid expansion of a network results in insufficient trust between all members, its ability to function can suffer dramatically.

- **Clarity.** The basis for any network is a set of principles or working guidelines for how members work together. Their clarity is the foundation of success. Transparency is essential, so all members can see precisely where any money is flowing in the network. SKA has clear principles and guidelines in place, and its accounts are completely visible to all participants.

- **Identity.** One of the dilemmas for a professional is whether to promote his or her own brand, or that of the network. The solution for most professionals is to keep their own identity, and in addition show their network membership on their business cards and marketing material. The Delphi Consulting Network, based in Raleigh, North Carolina, consists of seven independent consultants who brand themselves individually, as well as with the network name. They have had enough experience working together to be able to manage the dual branding with their clients.

- **Relationship ownership.** Probably the most sensitive aspect of professional networks is sharing clients. The reality is that there are many professionals who are simply not suited to working in networks, because their attitude is to grab what they can. The level of trust within SKA enables them to post everyone's client lists for all other members to see. It is unambiguous who "owns" and manages the client relationship. While Axiom Legal effectively controls its client relationships, referral fees and incentives mean that its attorneys are actively interesting in helping to broaden relationships and introduce their peers to clients.

- **Sharing value.** Loose networks can be fairly straightforward in simply providing access to referrals and resources when required. However in order to compete effectively with larger institutions, professional networks require more complex ways of integrating their work so that they can present an common face. C-people has bid for and won substantial projects. Its revenue sharing model is for the network member that sold the project receives 10% of the first year's revenue, 20% of revenue goes to the network hub for administration and overheads, and 70% is allocated between the project participants, with the split among them agreed before the project is begun. The flows of money within SKA are primarily based on licensing the intellectual property of other members, with the individual consultants simply invoicing the relationship manager for their time on services in the case of larger team projects.

Vital Connections: Chapter 9

Connectivity and integration are allowing a large and increasing proportion of services to be performed online. Software is being delivered as a service, business processes can be easily outsourced, and web services are creating a world in which companies are becoming modular. Strategy for high-value professional services strategy must shift to allow face-to-face and digital services to be complementary rather than competitive. The same drivers that are shifting services firms are enabling the birth of professional services networks, that are taking an increasingly important role in the economy.

Today, we are all professionals. We need to develop strategies to participate fully in the networks, and extract value proportional to our contribution. Chapter 10 shows free agents how to develop and implement successful strategies for a networked world.

Network Strategy for Free Agents

As the rise of the connected economy blurs organizational boundaries, the individual is increasingly becoming the center of value creation. Workers—whether they are employed or free agents—must develop and implement effective career strategies. They need to position themselves effectively in the evolving networks, and ensure they extract value from the intellectual property they create.

Why is it that so many of the most savvy, connected people have at one time been journalists? Esther Dyson, one of the leading thinkers on emerging technologies, and a key participant in Internet policy, began her career as a fact-checker and then a reporter at Forbes magazine. After moving into technology research for investment banks, she bought a research company, renamed it EDventure, and reshaped it to suit her style.

As a researcher and writer, you get access to the top people in their fields, can learn immense amounts from them, and create lasting relationships, if you can impress people with your capabilities. Rather than building a large and complex empire, Dyson has focused her five-person company on three clearly-defined and deeply interrelated activities. She publishes a pricey monthly newsletter, Release 1.0, that provides commentary and analysis on emerging information technologies. Its influential role in the technology community helps to give her privileged access to the leading players. The company also runs the two annual must-attend conferences for the tech elite in the US and Europe respectively. This helps her extensive contacts to develop into a broad community, with herself at the center. Finally, she uses her unparalleled access to information and contacts—combined with her own insight—to invest in and help to manage start-up companies.

Your personal connections, and access to the flow of the best information and ideas, are at the heart of the value you can create. This is just as true whether you are employed, or work for yourself. Within organizations, your network both inside and outside the firm is the primary asset that enables you to work effectively. When companies collaborate, it comes about and is implemented through the connections between individuals. Free agents, that shape and forge their careers every day, depend entirely on their connections. In the networks, people are the most meaningful unit, not organizations. In this world, there are four drivers that are recreating how individuals build personal success.

- **Value is shifting to the knowledge worker.** When the hit TV program Friends was extended for a year, the six stars demanded—and received—a cool $1 million each per episode. The talent took the bulk of the immense value of the series, and the producers had to be content with the leftovers. Top professionals, researchers, and creatives can earn a small fortune annually, and their job moves sometimes influence stock prices. The viability and success of every company, from start-up to multinational, depends on its ability to attract the best staff. Those people that are good know it, and are able to demand an increasing share of the pie. At the same time, companies are actively seeking to hire the very best people they can find as contractors and consultants, and don't mind paying the steep prices required. They recognize that the top people in their fields are increasingly likely to work for themselves rather than for large firms, and they are more than happy to deal with independents and networks of professionals.

• **Technology gives the means of production to creative and knowledge workers.** Before desktop publishing, personal printers, and the Internet, people needed to pay for expensive designers and printing equipment to publish a professional-looking document. Now anyone can create high-quality material sitting at home with an inexpensive computer. The ability of people with a reasonable digital home studio to create CD-quality music is transforming the industry. Anyone can research the catalog of all US patents from home for free. Powerful computers and software, combined with connectivity, mean that almost any creative or knowledge-based work can be done with minimal capital. Collaborating with anyone worldwide is a breeze. No longer do the people who are creating the most value in the economy rely on other people's capital to do their work.

• **The role of the individual is far more fluid and flexible.** In his best-selling paean to the independent worker, Free Agent Nation, Daniel Pink estimates that one in four American workers is a free agent.[1] This conservative estimate includes those freelancing, contracting, and running tiny businesses. At the same time, many of those classed as employees frequently work from home, on flexible hours, or on productivity-related pay. Individuals now have a wide range of choices in how they create value and relate to corporations. In turn, companies that want to attract the best workers are offering great flexibility in working conditions. Together, these allow fantastic scope for individuals to negotiate all the details of their working terms as well as pay, and create a world in which many of the best professionals choose to work independently.

• **Work flows through connectivity and exchanges.** Aim Technologies, a small New York Internet marketing firm, uses the online exchange eLance.com to bid for potential work, as a result gaining international clients and increasing its profits. eLance.com is the largest of a host of sites that have sprung up to match clients with freelance workers in fields such as IT, design, and writing. The fact that a remarkable 40% of its transactions occur across national borders is stark proof that the markets for professional work are already global. Matching freelance professionals with clients is proving a natural for online exchanges. Connectivity and technologies like peer-to-peer have also made it straightforward to run projects that seamlessly integrate internal and external workers. On most projects, no one can tell—or cares—whether a team member is employed by the firm or not. Independent workers can easily collaborate with colleagues to bid for and perform work that they couldn't do on their own.

Many of the opportunities for individuals resulting from these four key drivers are evident. Skilled and talented people now have far greater negotiating power with corporations. Often they can dictate terms, going beyond the ability to share fully in the value they are creating, to encompass every aspect of their employment conditions. Anyone involved in creating and marketing intellectual property can distribute directly to customers, often at no cost. Independent professionals can do high-value work, and team with others to compete effectively with large corporations. Their potential market has expanded to anyone, anywhere in the world.

But there are very real downsides too. When everyone in the world can bid for the same jobs as you, the competition is suddenly a whole lot tougher. Mark Fertig, a freelancer graphic designer and professor at James Madison University in Virginia, reports he's had to cut his prices to get work online.[2] Other seasoned professionals say they are finding themselves competing with prices that are so ridiculously low that they've given up bidding for work through Internet exchanges. The danger is that many knowledge workers will find themselves becoming commodities, increasingly competing with low-cost offshore professionals on price. The impact of globalization is rapidly moving beyond manufacturing to encompass professional work.

It's been clear for a long time that value is shifting from capital to knowledge. Read Tom Stewart's fine book The Wealth of Knowledge if you still need to be convinced on that score.[3] At the same time, more of the value in the economy is being taken by individuals rather than companies. More people are working for themselves, or extracting more of the value they create from the companies they work for. But it's not evenly distributed. The connected world is providing enormous opportunities for some, and major challenges for many others. Free agents must think and act strategically. They need to position themselves effectively in the networks, and develop strategies for profiting from the intellectual property they create.

Positioning in the networks

The Emmy-award winning science fiction series Babylon 5 has some of the most loyal fans in television. The program's producer, J. Michael Straczinski, almost universally known by his online tag JMS, has for years spent hours daily interacting with his fans in online communities, discussing and answering questions about the series' complex storyline. This began even before he had gained funding for the initial run, so in selling the series he was able to point to the lively online buzz. The wide network of fans then pressured local television stations to buy the program.[4]

Free agents exist through their connections, their presence in the networks. They must be connected to clients and potential clients, and almost always have to collaborate with others to create value. It is vital to participate in the flow of information and ideas, just as JMS has done. Many who leave companies to work for themselves suddenly realize how dependent they were on the contacts and information flows that came about in their daily work. They have to develop new networks in order to remain switched in to what's happening. For independent workers, effective positioning in the networks is what makes the difference. In a world in which individuals will be either commodities, or able to attract extraordinary rewards, three key actions will make the difference.

POSITIONING IN THE NETWORKS

1.Create and evolve a unique identity.
2.Build wide and deep connections.
3.Add value to communities.

Table 10-1: Action steps to positioning in the networks.

1. Create and evolve a unique identity

In the late 1970s a young Englishman secured a position on the faculty of Harvard Business School. David Maister, in exploring suitable topics to research, soon found himself focusing on professional service firms, in industries such as law, accounting, advertising, and consulting. Not only did these firms have interesting and unique dynamics, but somehow this important sector of the economy had been almost completely neglected by both academics and consultants. Then Maister made a scary commitment. He promised to the editor of *The American Lawyer* magazine that he would write an article every month for the next three years. This not only gave him an excellent profile in the industry, but forced him to structure his ideas and be extremely productive.

This provided an ideal launch pad for him to establish his own consulting business targeting professional service firms, a field with almost no competition at the time. Maister pulled together many of his best magazine articles into his first general business book, *Managing the Professional Service Firm*, in 1993.[5] He had literally written the book on this massive field, and now held an undisputed claim as the doyen of a large and underaddressed market. More recently professional services have started to attract the attention such a large and rapidly growing business sector deserves, but Maister had staked his claim early, and by continuing to publish regularly remains the master of his domain. He still spends all of his consulting time on professional services, but his recent books, including *Practice What You Preach* and *First Among Equals*, have extended the scope of his work and recognition to a far broader audience.

Maister pulled off a masterly coup in spotting and successfully appropriating such a large and unserviced market. Most of us won't discover and mine such large opportunities, but it is essential to create a clear specialization and unique identity. You want to position yourself so that it's impossible for your customers to go to an online exchange, find dozens or hundreds of people around the world who can do what they want, and select the lowest bid. This takes both creating a skill set that is neatly positioned in a gap in the market, and building a reputation for your work. Starting from a clear specialization is critical, but increasingly, multi-disciplinary skills hit the sweet spot. British lawyer and academic John Angel shifted over to run a software company, then consolidated his multiple expertise by taking a degree in information technology. Global leading law firm Clifford Chance, after hiring Angel as a consultant, asked him to work full-time to lead the development of their online services, after which he again became an external consultant, as part of his diverse portfolio of activities.

Having a media presence is increasingly important for success as an independent, and this almost always comes from having a unique identity or angle to present to reporters. Why should they contact you or listen to you if you appear the same as dozens of others? If you can identify a clear niche that suits your expertise, that's great. Otherwise, perhaps you can create it yourself. But it is critical not to drive yourself into a dead-end. You must consider how you can later shift to other directions. Many architects have found that their skills are very difficult to transfer to other fields. When I worked in Japan, I met many foreign "Japan experts" in their respective fields that did well for themselves, but found it very hard to do anything different when they wanted to move back home, or the flagging Japanese economy made things tough for them.

Today, the greatest value is in being a connector. This requires both knowing a wide range of people, and actively bringing them together

2. Build wide and deep connections

Finding a book agent is like finding a life partner. It's a close and highly trusting relationship that can indeed last a lifetime. When I was at the point in my career of needing a good agent, I sent one e-mail to one person in my network, asking for his suggestions. Napier Collyns immediately responded by introducing me to Henning Gutman, who is now my agent, and was instrumental in bringing this book to reality. During Collyns' early career with Royal Dutch/ Shell, he was part of the initial team that developed scenario planning as a discipline, and subsequently worked in other parts of the oil industry, and as on the boards of many of the international chambers of commerce in New York. He was one of five founding members of Global Business Network (GBN), together with former colleagues like Peter Schwartz and Stewart Brand. GBN brings together a network of companies interested in using scenarios to explore their future and strategic directions, with a network of stimulating thinkers from science, business, art, and academia. Put together musician Peter Gabriel, biologist Lynn Margulis, science fiction writer William Gibson, economist David Hale and a few dozen of their peers, and some pretty good ideas are likely to emerge. Within the group, GBN is often jokingly referred to as "Global Buddies of Napier", in respect for Collyns' remarkable personal network.

In his bestseller *The Tipping Point*, Malcolm Gladwell identified three types of people who help the flow of ideas become epidemics: connectors, mavens, and salespeople.[6] Connectors connect people, mavens are sought for their expertise, and salespeople get people to buy their ideas. Each plays a vital role in the flow of information and ideas. Today, the greatest value is in being a connector. This requires both knowing a wide range of people, and actively bringing them together. In Chapter 1 you saw how a few people's diverse connections can vastly shrink the networks, by acting as the bridge for people to establish contact. You must create value for others as a connector in order to take some value for yourself. Endeavor to make yourself a valued connector, and at the same time, build strong ties with the best connectors you know.

When independent workers risk becoming commodities, what makes the most difference is their personal connections. This is both with their clients, and at least as importantly, with the people they work with. Collaboration is essential. If you participate in a professional network, your work as part of a team can be worth far more than if you only work alone. As you saw in Chapter 9, networks of professionals can only function with a high level of trust. You will only be invited to join a high-value professional network on the basis of people's direct experience of having worked with you. That is the only basis for the degree of trust that is required, when they are exposing their clients to others. One consultant I know is keen to create and participate in professional networks, but the people he works with soon realize he is only interested in getting more business for himself, and he ends up working alone. You need to create opportunities to demonstrate your trustworthiness. The guidelines in Chapter 4 for how to develop trust can be applied equally to companies and individuals.

3. Add value to communities

A book packager works for publishers, taking a basic idea and pulling together a ready-to-print manuscript. Michael Cader had worked independently in this role for twelve years, when in 2000 he wondered at the lack of good information for the New York publishing industry. He created a web page offering an insider's perspective on the industry, including news, deal reports, and personal commentary. This quickly shifted to become a daily e-mail newsletter, that Cader called PublishersLunch. With a circulation of over 10,000, the newsletter has attracted the attention of a large part of this tightly-knit community. Initially Cader used third-party sources to compile news of industry deals, but soon people started calling him directly with news. He then started running real lunch events with prominent industry speakers, providing opportunities for the trade to get together.

Cader kept experimenting, creating PublishersMarketplace, which allows industry participants to find each other and deals to get done, and a job board to post available positions to the community. Already getting paid advertising in the newsletter, at the 2002 BookExpo America convention Cader was sponsored by exhibitors to produce a daily report on happenings at the event. Next he wants to produce his own New York book fair. He has become at the center of information flow in the industry, and is still finding innovative ways both to add value to the publishing community, and benefit substantially himself through the network. Cader has chosen to focus on providing accessible, quality services rather than to maximize revenue, and not to use his newsletter to directly promote his core business of book packaging. However clearly his industry profile has increased immensely, it has opened up many new opportunities for him, and in the future his role in bringing greater transparency to the publishing industry could become his primary business.

One of the greatest boons of connectivity is the ability of communities of like-minded people to form and interact. However these communities rarely happen by themselves—they are created and remain vital from the energy of a few key people. If you create value for a community by bringing them together or actively contributing, you will also reap the rewards. In launching his newsletter and other initiatives, Cader has brought a community together, enabling the flow of information and connections, and creating opportunities for participants to interact and make deals. He has also made sure that he has gained significant tangible benefits from the venture, but even the early recognition from the daily effort and commitment of the newsletters made it worthwhile.

If there is a community that has not been provided with an opportunity to connect, create one. If there is already an existing group, you can contribute and add value in many ways. Bringing in new members is useful for them and everyone in the community. Sharing information and insights establishes you as someone with expertise, and who people are willing to help. In many communities, those who are valued the most are often the ones who contribute links to useful information, rather than weighing in with heavy-handed opinions. You may help to promote the group to the media, get sponsors, or create ties with other communities with related interests. All of this takes effort and time, but the value you put into communities is almost always returned many times over. However it is critical to be selective. The energy and commitment required to add value to communities means you can only participate effectively in those that are most worthwhile.

As you've seen, the heart of free agent strategy in the networks is effective positioning, in order to differentiate yourself. The set of your connections defines your identity in the networks. You need to decide what you want those connections to be, and how to build them. The other key dimension is the shift of value in the economy to intellectual property. Individuals need to place a greater emphasis on creating and leveraging intellectual property, and the networks are changing the rules of how this is done.

Intellectual property strategy for free agents

It's a pretty safe bet that you, my dear reader, participate in creating intellectual property. Or if not, you should, as this may well be where much of your future value lies. One aspect of this is creating content for publication. This content can be in the form of books, articles, reports, music, films, multimedia, software, processes, online learning packages, or any other of a multitude of ways to capture people's creativity and knowledge. The markets for all of these are opening up, as content embodies what is most valuable today, and in addition can now be readily distributed over the networks. Another key aspect of intellectual property is patents, those legally-protected inventions that are, in the end, the fruits of the imagination and research of individuals, not corporations.

The most important strategic issue for content creators is choosing when to distribute direct, and when to go through publishers or distributors

You have already seen that the relationship of the individual and the corporation is changing. This is absolutely the case in intellectual property. Ultimately it is people that generate ideas, yet often some of the resources required to generate protectable content and ideas come from corporations. In the past the vast bulk of the value went to corporations, but their dependence on the most talented people, and often on collaboration outside the firm, means that the landscape is shifting. Individuals—whether they are employees or independent—must make sure to appropriate their fair share of the value they create. There are three key elements to intellectual property strategy for free agents:

INTELLECTUAL PROPERTY STRATEGY FOR FREE AGENTS

1.Create career-long content distribution strategies.
2.Develop collaboration and protection policies.
3.Negotiate your share in value creation.

**Table 10-2: Action steps to intellectual property
strategy for free agents.**

1. Create career-long content distribution strategies
Upwardly mobile management guru Seth Godin, in his book Unleashing
the Ideavirus, proposed turning around the usual book publishing approach
of selling an expensive hardcover edition before releasing a paperback. The
traditional model means that fewer people read the book initially, which
means fewer tell their friends and contacts about it, and word spreads
slowly. Why not make it as cheap as possible initially to allow interest to
take off, and then sell more expensive versions for people that like
something hefty on their bookshelves?[7] Godin practiced what he preached,
making the entire book available for free download on his website, and at
the same time selling it in hardcover at a premium price of $40. The reality
is that many potential customers weren't interested in reading the book on
a screen or a print-out, and didn't care too much about the price, so word
spread like wildfire, the physical book actually sold fairly well, and Godin
could rake up most of the profits by bypassing the large publishing houses.
Not only that, but the major positive impact on his reputation through the
widespread distribution of his book and his radical approach meant he
could command a significantly better advance when he returned to work
with a traditional publisher for his following book.

Until recently, self-publishing was often rightly called vanity publishing—
it was about spending money to look good. Connectivity is rapidly changing
the situation. You can now distribute content directly online, and often
fairly easily access major distributors. As such, the most important strategic
issue for content creators is choosing when to distribute direct, and when
to go through publishers or distributors. This is largely an issue of
managing your creative lifecycle, using publishers for the specific value they
can offer, and distributing direct the rest of the time, either to gain
awareness or take a larger share of the rewards.

A publisher can offer three main things: credibility, broad distribution, and
risk transfer. Whether you're a writer, musician, or software coder, having
your work distributed by a major firm is an important seal of approval. It's
possible to do well working solo, but it's far easier when you're backed by

a recognized name. In addition, major firms can always access better distribution possibilities than an individual can. If you distribute direct, you may get all the profits, but at the same time you take all the risk. Any worthwhile publisher commits capital to creating and promoting its products, and often offers a non-refundable advance payment to the content creator. The major downside of working with a publisher is that in return for its credibility, distribution, and taking on the risk, it takes the majority of the rewards.

The most basic career strategy for content creators is quite simple. In the early stages, use the free flow of the networks to distribute direct, demonstrate that you can tap an attractive market, and attract the interest of a publisher. New York reggae and ska band The Pilfers sold 10,000 CDs at its concerts and on its website, using the leverage to secure a favorable record deal with Universal Music Group.[8] Many others have signed contracts with record labels on the basis of the success of their freely distributed MP3s. In the next stage, you work with the publishers for as long as it is worthwhile, getting them to take much of the risk, and commit capital to advances and promotion. Finally, hopefully with reputation well established, you can once again distribute direct, taking all the profits. Many rock stars later in their career, like David Bowie, Todd Rundgren, or the estate of Frank Zappa, sell directly to their fans. Scott Adams, the creator of the Dilbert cartoon, chose to publish his first non-Dilbert book, God's Debris, directly as an ebook, later also selling a hardcopy version.[9] He had full creative control, and could reap all the profits. This generic creative career strategy is illustrated in Figure 10-1.

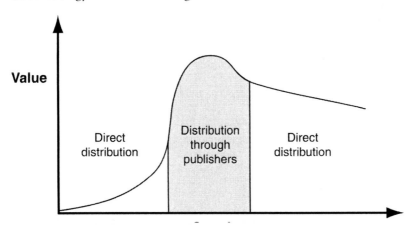

Figure 10-1: The basic creative career strategy in the networks

It's increasingly easy to self-publish, even when you have a physical product, and want to access major distributors rather than just selling through your own website. However it is essential to get a barcode on your product. It's not overly expensive to get an ISBN barcode in the case of a book, or a UPC (Universal Product Code) for CDs, videos, or other goods. Alternatively, companies sometimes offer to act as a bare-bones distributor, simply allocating a UPC and putting the product in their catalog for retailers. By offering this service, record label The Orchard has made it extremely easy for many bands to get wide distribution for their CDs, and broadened the range of music we all can access.

2. Develop collaboration and protection policies
Successful science fiction writer Eric Flint believes that tighter regulation of copyright piracy damages social and political freedom. He also believes that providing books for free online promotes rather than detracts from sales of physical books, and has collaborated in setting up the Free Library, which provides access to free ebooks. Flint has researched the trends in sales of his books, and correlated these to when he released the books online. His research has led him to the conclusion that providing books online never adversely impacts sales of physical books, and often increases sales.[10] His personal intellectual property policy—based on both his beliefs and self-interest—is to earn his income by publishing paper books, and at the same time provide them for free download.

Individuals have an increasingly broad array of options available in how they protect and share their intellectual property. Your personal beliefs about both how intellectual property should be protected, and how it can benefit you, will help to determine the policies you adopt. The open source software movement, as discussed in Chapter 5, opened up new ways of participating in developing intellectual property. No-one made revenue directly from their input, but many benefited in other ways, for example through gaining valued skills, enhancing their reputation, or providing services associated with the software.

We all now have far greater flexibility in how we choose to protect or make available our intellectual property. As you saw in Chapter 5, Creative Commons gives people free access to customizable intellectual property licenses. This means you can establish and implement specific policies on how you make your intellectual property available. The scheme may contribute to individuals working collaboratively becoming a far stronger economic force.

3. Negotiate your share in value creation
Shuji Nakamura developed the blue light emitting diode (LED) that is used in, among other common applications, CD players and computer displays. His employer, Nichia Corporation, reportedly paid him the standard fee of 20,000 yen (around $150) for his patent, and went on to reap well over $1 billion in sales for products based on his inventions. For some reason feeling hard done by, Nakamura left to become a professor at University of California at Santa Barbara, and is now suing Nichia for 2 billion yen, and 80% ownership of the key patent.[11]

If you are employed, I hope you read your employment contract closely before you signed it. Many contracts contain clauses assigning to the company the ownership of all intellectual property developed while employed, or even for a period after employment ends. Sometimes, for example for high-level research positions, the contract also specifies how the employee will be compensated if inventions are commercialized, and these days they are usually a little more generous than Nichia Corp.

One way to protect your intellectual property rights as an employee is, when starting, to provide a written list of ideas or inventions you have already developed. This will exclude these from the contract. Depending on the state or country that you work in, you may be able to claim rights to intellectual property that you've developed entirely with your own time and resources. This means no phone calls, no photocopies, no e-mails at work; any of these can jeopardize your rights to your ideas. You must be careful about your employer's potential claims to your ideas, unless they are the best ones to commercialize them and let you share in the benefits. In many cases, firms never develop the ideas they get from their employees.

Free agents working to develop intellectual property with others need to be very careful in negotiating their share of the value created. In some cases they will only be able to get a working salary; in others they may be able to get a share of any resulting licensing revenues. These terms must be established upfront. Maintaining flexibility is critical in negotiating contracts. One overseas software developer was pleased to secure a distribution agreement with a US company, but after the software package became a hit on its own merits, the developer discovered that the contract was essentially for life. The firm couldn't renegotiate terms, despite the distributor taking the bulk of profits and doing very little to earn it. In the music industry, multi-album contracts are standard practice, which means that if an artist does extremely well, he or she will still be rewarded in the same way as an aspiring novice. Avoid locking yourself into long-term, inflexible agreements. When you gain bargaining power, you want to be in a position to use it.

Intellectual property is just one aspect of how the networks are dramatically changing everyone's career outlook. The most important outcome of massive connectivity is that people are at the heart of the networks rather than corporations, and as a corollary, value is shifting to the individual. This doesn't necessarily mean that things will become easy for all. The global competition of a networked world may make things very tough for many, as we will explore further in the postscript to this book. However those that position their careers so they participate fully in the networks will not only create wealth for themselves, but also find the joy of collaborating and creating with the most talented people, all around the world.

Vital Connections: Chapter 10

In this chapter, we have seen that individuals as well as companies need to develop strategies for success in the networks. The connected economy has been largely responsible for the recent rapid rise of free agents, but it also creates challenges. Independent workers have to position themselves effectively, and create their own intellectual property strategies. In Chapter 5 you saw how intellectual property is changing, and in Chapter 9 you discovered the shift to professional networks. This chapter has described the other side of the picture, the perspective of the individual on these vital issues.

This brings to a conclusion our examination of the living networks today, how organizations and strategy are evolving, and what actions to take for success. We will conclude with a postscript, which offers 10 key insights into the future of the networks, and thus of all business.

PART 4: Future Networks

Having examined in turn *Evolving Networks*, *Evolving Organizations*, and *Evolving Strategy* in the first three parts of this book, it is time to turn our attention to the future of business in the networks.

We are now participating in the birth of the living networks. The networks that comprise almost our entire business environment will rapidly grow and evolve in the years and decades to come. Now that you understand the fundamentals of the living networks today, you will discover how the networks are likely to develop from here, and the implications for business.

The Evolution of Business

The networks have only just come to life, placing you at the beginning of an extraordinary adventure. The remarkable pace of change leading to this point is likely to accelerate further, so you need to gain insights into a promising yet highly uncertain future. Ten predictions for the future of business in the networks are offered to help you act more effectively in the present.

Cast your mind back to the deep, distant past. If you can, think back as far as the late 1980s. Individual workers in companies were barely touched by communication technologies other than the telephone on their desks. All internal communication in companies was by inter-office memos, picked up and shuffled around by mailroom people sauntering by with their trolleys. Typing pools—rooms of women with bob-cuts (or bouffant hairdos, depending on your vintage)—were the interfaces between executives and typed documents. The only way to get information about a company and their products was to call them and get them to send a salesperson or catalog. At conferences, you had to wait in long queues for the payphones during breaks, and if you were late to meet someone you often had no way to let them know.

Just for a moment, consider quite how much the world has changed over the last dozen years. Much of what we take for granted today was almost inconceivable just that long ago. Humans are incredibly adaptable, and as our environment evolves over the years, it can be very hard for us to realize how much has changed. Many senior citizens who a few years ago were daunted by the technologies are now happily chatting on cell phones and exchanging e-mails or even videoconferencing with their children and grandchildren. The benefits of digital connectivity now seem totally natural to us.

Through this book you have examined how to succeed in business as you participate in the birth of the living networks. The time has come to cast your mind forward, to how the networks and the world of business will evolve. The extent of the change in the next dozen in years is likely to dwarf that of the past dozen years. The most successful businesspeople will be those who are sensitive and responsive to change, who are able to anticipate the future, and be highly adaptable in continually evolving their strategies as the landscape unfolds.

The future is unknown. The one thing we can be sure of is that we will be surprised. But thinking about the future is still useful. The heart of understanding the future is to distinguish clearly between what it is that you do know, and what it is that you don't know. From this platform you can create powerful, robust business strategies.

For example, we know as a certainty that technology will continue to progress. In some domains that progress is actually quite readily foreseeable. Telecommunications pundit George Gilder forecasts that the communications bandwidth available to consumers and business will triple every year. It may accelerate faster or slower than that, but we know for sure that it will grow extremely quickly.

On the other hand, we cannot know how social attitudes and consumer behaviors will shift, especially in response to unforeseen shocks or new choices. SMS text messaging was provided almost as an afterthought by European mobile service providers, and totally surprised them by spreading like wildfire with virtually no promotion. SMS now accounts for a large proportion of revenue for many European telecom firms, while downloading ringtones for cell phones is another unanticipated billion-dollar industry. We must also keep in mind that legislation is a key foundation for much of the business environment. Because this emerges from immensely complex interactions within the triangle of business, government, and individuals, its evolution is next to impossible to forecast.

Given this, and taking all we have learned through this book, I will venture 10 predictions on the future of business in the living networks. I believe these all have a high likelihood of being correct, and some are in fact very safe bets. However the primary intent of these predictions is to provoke you to think for yourself about what is likely to happen, and how to shift your business and career to be massively successful in our rapidly changing world. My 10 predictions for the future of business in the networks are shown in Table 11-1.

THE FUTURE OF BUSINESS IN THE NETWORKS

1. We will soon be immersed in connectivity

2. Transparency will drive business and society

3. Collaborative filtering will be the heart of the networks

4. Information filtering will be an evolutionary battlefield

5. Open, accepted standards will predominate

6. Almost all value creation will stem from collaborative relationships

7. Collaborative intellectual property models will flourish

8. Highly virtualized organizations will be a dominant force

9. The rapidly increasing pool of free agents will be polarized

10. People and networks will merge

Table 11-1: Predictions for the future of business in the networks

1. We will soon be immersed in connectivity
How long will it be before the majority of the population in developed countries has access to mobile, always-on broadband communication?

Given the right sort of hand-held or wearable devices, this will allow people to access all the resources of the Internet, do video phone calls with friends, access music and video clips, participate in graphic multi-player online games, and far more, all while you're on the move. We know as a certainty that we will have easy, pervasive access to high-speed connectivity. What is open to debate—and in fact vociferous argument—is how long it will take for that to happen.

Certainly the roll-out of the much-vaunted "3G" third generation mobile telephone networks has progressed far more slowly than its proponents expected. The headiest peak of the turn-of-millenium technology boom was perhaps when wireless providers jointly paid $190 billion for the rights to 3G spectrum in Europe. That—combined with other telecom over-investment and slow demand—means that the sector must consolidate before it leaps forward again.

However, this pervasive access to connectivity could just as well emerge through entirely different means than the traditional telecom firms. Throughout America, people are setting up local wireless networks that allow anyone in the vicinity to tap into the Internet, using the 802.11b protocol (obviously not named by a brand consultancy!) that uses unlicensed radio spectrum. Many coffee shops, airport lounges, conference centers, and other venues are now using the technology to provide their visitors with high-speed Internet access. While many suppliers provide this access for a fee, there are an increasing number of enthusiasts that are intent on providing bandwidth for free.

The use of short-range wireless protocols can allow so-called "parasitic networks" to develop. In this system, wireless devices, rather than communicating with the nearest cell station, will transmit signals to the nearest wireless device, which in turn will pass the message on to others until it finds its destination. This can allow whole neighborhoods to be wired at minimal cost. Bill Wiecking has put together a free network that provides broadband coverage to over 300 square miles of Hawaii's Big Island.[1] Extending the principle, if enough people carry devices that use the same local wireless protocols, then in densely populated areas you will be able to make calls and send messages without paying a cent to your telecom provider.

We will soon reach a trigger point when demand for broadband—both from home and when roaming—will surge dramatically, probably primarily driven by access to entertainment. At that time a wealth of new applications, some of them based on providing people with the greater visibility described in the next section, will be launched to take advantage of the potential. Whether it is provided by telcos, community networks, or more likely a combination of these, sooner than many expect we will all live richly immersed in connectivity. Only those who choose to isolate themselves temporarily from the networks or stray too far from populated areas will be unconnected. Discovering specifically how people want to use that connectivity will be an evolving adventure.

2. Transparency will drive business and society

Before I go to the beach I check out the surf-cam, to see what the waves are like. When I receive a foreign currency payment through my bank, I can find out the spot interbank exchange rate and see exactly how much profit they are making on the trade. Vault.com gives me an insider's view of the latest internal politics at my professional services and investment banking clients. I can look at the Greedy Associates feature on FindLaw.com to find out my lawyer's likely paycheck, based on the firm, location, and his or her seniority.

Information flows freely. Everything is becoming visible. Trying to stop information from getting out is like trying to keep water from running down to the ocean during a rainstorm. As a direct result of surging connectivity, transparency is rapidly growing in every domain of business and society.

New business models will emerge to exploit this increasing transparency. I want to know the traffic conditions on all my possible routes, and exactly where someone has just vacated a parking spot near my destination. UK firm Applied Generics is using data from the movement of thousands of mobile phones as they register with the local cell station to generate an accurate and up-to-the-second picture of traffic delays.[2] When I'm in the initial negotiation stages with a potential overseas partner, reports and perspectives from all the people they have dealt with will help me decide how to deal with them. There will be entire new industries in gathering, aggregating, and analyzing the vast universes of data that will be available. This will require new ways of working, and new pricing models for both raw data and the high-value outputs.

Transparency also impacts traditional businesses. If they want, companies can now usually get a very good idea of their suppliers' profitability. As a result, many suppliers today are going with the trend rather than fighting it. Several investment banks give their clients the pricing models they use for complex derivatives, so their profit margins are known exactly. Many large firms have built sophisticated client profitability models, and some of these choose to show the results to selected clients, to help develop a more mutually beneficial relationship. Contract electronics manufacturers like Flextronics, Solectron, and Celestica usually provide their clients with minute details on their costings. Clients will increasingly expect to know their suppliers' business in detail, and will strongly favor those who provide greater transparency.

David Brin evokes two worlds in his book *The Transparent Society*.[3] In both, everything we do is visible. The difference between the two worlds is whether that transparency is one-way or two-way. We can take it for granted that government and big business will know almost everything about us. The question is whether individuals will be able look back, to make the institutions themselves visible and accountable. That will almost inevitably happen in time—the shift to transparency is unstoppable—however we all need to push hard so that it doesn't take longer than it should. In every aspect of our lives, transparency will be a reality, and we will need to change the way we think and act to make it an opportunity rather than a liability.

3. Collaborative filtering will be the heart of the networks
If you think we're living in a world of information overload, you ain't seen nothing yet. In addition to the established sources of information products, such as newspapers, newswires, publishers, and music labels, connectivity has opened the way for an entire universe of new sources and perspectives. Weblogs and independent media provide an immense amount of new, different, and often very high-quality reporting and analysis. Having expanded your choice in books from the 40,000 titles in your average bookstore to the 2 million or so available on Amazon.com, that figure is set to grow further as self-publishing becomes more common. MP3.com boasts 1.2 million tracks by 200,000 artists, and that's primarily non-mainstream material. In America alone, each and every day 360 hours of new television or film programming is created.[4]

Log onto MovieLens, and it will ask you for your personal ratings of a series of films. It then correlates this information with the opinions of its other members to provide you recommendations on what films you are likely to enjoy, and predictions of your ratings of any other film. This, together with some of the other instances we've looked at through the book, such as Slashdot.org, Open Ratings, and Media Unbound, illustrates how collaborative filtering is helping people to deal with the massive overload that is symptomatic of our times.

Formal collaborative systems such as these were first developed around 1995 by Pattie Maes and her colleagues at the MIT Media Labs. It is only now that the unbounded flow of immense amounts of information through the networks is bringing them into their own. In fact the entire structure of the Internet is already shifting to be based on collaborative filtering principles. As you saw in Chapter 1, the enormous success of Google is based on how it uses people's judgments to offer the best links, and weblogs inherently make visible the most useful and interesting information. In coming years, improved ways of tapping the power of collaborative filtering approaches will be at the heart of the networks. Those that implement them effectively will play a major role in bringing the networks to life, and will profit in the process.

4. Information filtering will be an evolutionary battlefield

Bats' use of echolocation to find their prey is one of the marvels of nature. Bats produce high-frequency sounds, and by picking up and distinguishing the immensely quieter echoes off insects in the air, can instantaneously calculate the location of their next meal. The evolution of this extraordinary capability has led to moths evolving in response. The soft outside of their wings and bodies absorbs the bats' ultrasound. Moths engage in evasive flying stunts when they hear bats squeaking. Some moths have even evolved the ability to produce ultrasound as well, possibly to startle and throw off bats. In turn, bats have developed complex flying behaviors to confuse moths, and occasionally turn off their echolocation to stop the moths jamming their signals.[5]

This is a case of what biologists call a "coevolutionary arms race". Each participant in a system evolves new capabilities and behaviors in response to others' development, in turn requiring them to evolve yet further in order to survive. There are many parallels in human society, not least the planet's very real arms races. One of the best examples in the years and decades ahead will be the coevolution of information dissemination and filtering, involving battles of words, legislation, and more than ever, technology.

AdSubtract is one of a wealth of programs available that remove advertisements from web pages. You can surf at will, and never see an ad. David Mann of the University of Toronto sees this kind of functionality going a lot further. He has designed spectacles that take into account your head and eye position, and replace anything you don't want to see with the images of your choice. His favorite example is a man standing at a urinal replacing a condom advertisement on the wall with a film of a soothing waterfall.[6] You could just as well replace every billboard on your route home with pictures of your spouse and children.

Jamie Kellner, chairman and CEO of Turner Broadcasting, was quoted in early 2002 saying that skipping commercials when watching television programs is theft. Fortunately, he did allow that there was some scope for taking bathroom breaks.[7] Phew. Several commentators recalled the scene from the book and film A Clockwork Orange, in which Alex has his eyelids forcibly held open as he is shown videos for his reeducation.[8] Hopefully our legislators will stop before we get to that point.

We know as a certainty that we will be swamped as marketers endeavor to reach us with their messages everywhere we look, everywhere we go. Companies are going to ever-greater lengths to get through to their target audiences. In response, individuals are trying to escape, using devices that make call center systems think their telephones are disconnected, setting up e-mail spam filters, and returning junk mail. As communication becomes increasingly digital, the nature of this will change. Agent technology, which we discussed in Chapter 4, will increasingly be charged with selecting and presenting to us only what we want to see from the onslaught of information. Indeed, this is the domain of some of the most promising— and useful—current developments in artificial intelligence. In response, marketers will develop technologies to attempt to fool and bypass those filters.

The battle is engaged. As people find ways of filtering advertisements and messages effectively, marketers will find ways around them, leading to yet further advances. Technologies will be pitted against other technologies in a coevolutionary dance. At some stage, we will become onlookers as our agents engage in information warfare on our behalf.

5. Open, accepted standards will predominate
Without open, accepted standards, the Internet would not exist. We would be struggling to communicate between different domains of technology. Indeed, we often still are. As you saw in Chapter 2, there are strong vested interests in developing and holding on to proprietary networks. Microsoft is not likely to open up Windows to its competitors any time soon. However, as discussed in Chapter 5, its Office suite of software is competing with OpenOffice, which uses the same file formats.

The forecast that open, accepted standards will dominate is perhaps the most contentious in this list. The powerful interests of some of the world's largest firms will at times be pitched to keep open standards from being adopted. It is possible that as new technologies succeed old ones, large companies or alliances will be able to establish and effectively own new standards. Standards bodies are notoriously slow and unwieldy beasts, and can often lag real-world technology developments in their work.

Despite these challenges, over time it will become increasingly difficult to set standards that are not open. Customers will not tolerate them, and companies that attempt to establish proprietary positions will find all their competitors very happy to collaborate in order to break entrenched market positions. Many of the top players in their industries, such as IBM and Nokia, have recently become powerful advocates of open standards. In addition, the enforcement of anti-trust legislation in the US and Europe has arguably never been more stringent than it has been over the last decade. The result will be that significant portions of many industries— and certainly the flows of information within industries—will be based on jointly agreed and controlled standards.

Even given this powerful trend, there will still be profitable business opportunities based on trying to lock-in customers over the medium-term. There are degrees of openness, and many companies will pretend to be fully open but weave in various proprietary approaches. However the only truly sustainable business models will be based on open standards, and those that make that push early will be the best poised to profit from the evolving landscape.

6. Almost all value creation will stem from collaborative relationships

The pace of commoditization is accelerating. In a connected world, any new and better offerings can be easily copied by competitors, sometimes almost literally overnight. It is becoming ever-easier for competitors to replicate your offerings, and then steal your customers by undercutting your prices. In addition, the shift to open, accepted standards dramatically levels the competitive field, and makes it far easier for customers to switch to new suppliers.

Virtually everything that will enable companies to escape the powerful gravitational force of commoditization is based on collaborative relationships. Those companies that can create value with their customers rather than for them, will have relationships that are both far more valuable to their customers, and immensely difficult for others to reproduce. They will lock-in their customers simply by how much value they can create, while others will struggle as they reluctantly discover they are nothing more than commoditized vendors. The practice of collaborative customer relationships is illustrated by many of the examples given in Chapters 3, 4, and 6, such as Convergys' integration into its customers' operations, FMC Corporation's technology alignment with customers, and how Lucas Arts gets its customers to help develop its games.

In addition to customer relationships, the other key factor that will continue to provide differentiation is excellence at innovation. If you can consistently create new and better products, services, processes, and business models, you can exploit the market space before competitors copy you, even though that time advantage is ever-more fleeting. In addition, intellectual property gives legal protection to innovative ideas, and can often generate licensing revenue. As in the case of customer relationships, innovation is increasingly a collaborative endeavor. As you saw in Chapter 5, in order to innovate in a world of accelerating technological development, you must create the conditions and structures for effective collaboration both inside and outside the firm.

The most successful companies—those that achieve a better than marginal return on their investment—will be the ones that are outstanding at collaborative relationships with their customers and partners. This requires implementing enabling technologies, but far more importantly organizations must shift to cultures and behaviors that support this new business mentality.

7. Collaborative intellectual property models will flourish

We are at the beginning of a new phase in intellectual property, based on collaborative models for working and sharing value. The emergence of open source software as a serious market participant has paved the way for this shift, and the lessons learned are proving invaluable as a foundation for a new generation of business models. Some models will not be primarily commercial, for example the more liberal approaches to open source, but as you saw in Chapter 5, it is possible for similar principles to be applied to profit-making businesses. These approaches range from providing customers with products that are under development, as implemented by IBM alphaWorks, to the patent pooling approaches used to license MPEG-4 and Firewire.

The key driver for these new models to proliferate is that they allow companies to be better at creating valuable intellectual property, which is increasingly where the most value lies. Traditional approaches to intellectual property are rigid. This can severely limit innovation in an economy based on the swift flow and interaction of ideas. Those that can be more flexible in developing intellectual property will do better. It's that simple.

Many of the initiatives and approaches described in Chapter 5, notably Creative Commons, provide examples of the new approaches and initiatives that are charting the domain of collaborative intellectual property models. There is much further exploration and experimentation to be done. Some models will do well, others will founder. What we can be sure of is that new, collaborative business models for intellectual property and innovation will flourish. Companies and innovators will have far more choices in how they create new value with others, and extract their fair share of that value.

8. Highly virtualized organizations will be a dominant force

In 1992, the year the web browser was invented, Davidow and Malone published *The Virtual Corporation*.[9] The book put the topic squarely on the management agenda, however the reality was that the technologies were not yet available to implement the vision, and the concept was still treated primarily as an internal management issue. Since then the idea has become a reality, with companies like Visa, Cisco, Dreamworks SKG, and many of the companies mentioned in this book leveraging connectivity to create virtual organizations within a broad web of alliances.

It is only now, however, that the emerging technologies described in Chapter 2 and through this book are allowing an almost unlimited degree of choice over what is done inside and outside the company—if indeed those boundaries still have any meaning. We know that the economy will not be reduced to a set of individuals interacting. The need for significant capital in many industries, the realities of economies of scale, the value of a consistent workforce, and many people's desire for a highly social work environment and the stability of employment contracts mean that large companies will endure. Many of these will not be true virtual organizations, in the sense of having no solid core, but most will have virtualized many aspects of their operations. They will use technology to implement to varying degrees the modular organization described in Chapter 9.

Many companies will on the surface look similar to contemporary firms, but their underlying processes will be distributed across many customers, suppliers, and partners. An increasing number will be more obviously virtual, with a small nucleus responsible for massive yet far-flung value-creation.

The simple fact is that those firms that do not take full advantage of the possibilities of reshaping their boundaries will not be competitive. Managers who insist on maintaining monolothic organizations will see their companies left behind. One particular instance of virtual organizations, professional networks, will become a significant force in the economy. It is only recently that groups of independent professionals working collaboratively have the tools to compete with large firms. As you saw in Chapter 9, new models for professional networks are now being explored. The most effective of these networks will form a vibrant new sector of the economy that many traditional firms will have to treat as a major competitive threat.

9. The rapidly increasing pool of free agents will be polarized

In truth, we are all free agents, working for ourselves. Sometimes we choose to indenture ourselves to a company to gain access to resources and a more regular income. However, increasingly, people are working independently. For many, it is a choice—they gain flexibility, often earn more, and very importantly, don't have to deal with office politics and deadbeat bosses! Others are pushed, making the transition to life as a free agent in the wake of being made redundant. Over time, the boundaries between employment, contracting, and running a successful micro-business will blur, for these to look increasingly similar.

In the global connected economy, it is not just companies that are subject to the powerful forces of commoditization. Individuals too are finding new competitors springing up on all sides, offering the same services at lower prices. As you saw in Chapter 10, unless you clearly differentiate yourself, you will have to sell your services on the basis of price. For free agents, connectivity can be both a blessing and a curse. Some will benefit enormously by being able to tap into global markets, and collaborate with the best in the world. Others will find that there is relentless downwards pressure on the fees they can charge. The result will be a polarization of knowledge workers, with on the one hand many reaping massive rewards, and on the other many more who struggle to do well.

The differences between the workers at each end of this spectrum will be those we discovered in Chapter 10. A precisely chosen specialization, the inclination and skills to collaborate with others, and a diverse network of trusting relationships will be the foundation to spectacular rewards. This polarization of workers could have significant social impact, both within nations, and across the globe. We need to ensure not only the broadest possible access to connectivity, but also that people have the skills and attitudes to work effectively in a networked world.

10. People and networks will merge

In the 1957 film *The Invisible Boy*, a supercomputer plots to take over the world and destroy all organic life—an early contribution to what is now a long tradition in the theme. Since computers were conceived, mankind has feared being enslaved by machines with superior intelligence. Despite the very disappointing progress in artificial intelligence over the last two decades, the trend is clear: computers are getting smarter. The debate rages over whether computers will ever become more intelligent than people, with esteemed scientists ranged against each other. No one argues over the inevitable continuing improvement of computers' capabilities. Ray Kurzweil estimates that computers will exceed the ability of the human mind sometime between 2020 and 2050. Others suggest that there is something ineffable about the human mind that can never be replicated by a machine.

However the real issue is not whether humans will be replaced by machines, because at the same time as computing technology is progressing, people are merging with machines. If machines take over the world, we will be those machines. As you saw in Chapter 2, the interfaces between systems and people are still very limited, primarily based on clunky technology like keyboards, but things are swiftly changing.

Scientists at Duke University in Durham, NC, implanted electrodes in a monkey's brain, and were able to program a robot arm to replicate and even anticipate its movements as the monkey reached for food. They then hooked the signals up to the Internet so that the monkey's thoughts controlled a robot arm at MIT in Boston, almost 1000 kilometers away.[10] In a similar experiment, monkeys were able to control the movement of a cursor on a computer screen, earning orange juice as a reward.[11]

Others are working on ways to integrate computers into our brains. It will certainly be useful if I can get a massive database plugged directly into my brain—no more forgetting people's names! But it doesn't need to go that far. David Mann envisions that his intelligent spectacles will use face recognition software to attach nametags only we can see to the people we encounter.

The key issue is that as the interfaces between people and digital technology improve, people can be better connected. We can share our experiences, our ideas, and our thoughts with whoever we choose. The micro-messages that are currently conveyed by brief text messages will be as broad in scope as we wish. The boundaries between the individual and the networks will have dissolved.

Connected to the future

Whatever the future holds for business and humanity, there is one thing we know for sure. The networks that link us, that make us one, will be at the heart of our destiny. We are living at a critical juncture in the history of our species. While we will all continue as individuals, in control of our own destinies, at the same time we are participating in the birth of a higher-order lifeform. Just as a living human brain is ultimately a set of neural impulses, the living networks consist of the flow of information and ideas. Together, human minds and technology form the substrate for that flow.

The implications of the networks' birth encompass every aspect of society, politics, and business. This book has examined how business is changing, focusing on the present, and what actions businesspeople need to take today in order to be successful in this emerging world. Business is in fact central to the vast majority of these flows. Those who are actively engaged in the issues covered in this book will play a fundamental role in how the networks develop, impacting our entire future as a society. As you finish reading this book, consider your personal role in our shared evolution. It is an important one. You have the choice of leadership, of helping to bring the living networks to reality, and in the process achieving success for yourself and those around you. Please grasp that opportunity fully—your energy and vision will help to accelerate us into the most exciting time in human history.

Thank you for accompanying me on this journey into the living networks. I wish you every success as you participate in the growth and evolution of this exhilarating new world.

Notes

Chapter 1
1 Farhad Manjoo, "Flash: Blogging Goes Corporate", Wired News, May 9, 2002, at www.wired.com/news/culture/0,1284,52380,00.html

2 Tony Kontzer, "Instant Messaging Takes Off in Bond Market", Wall Street & Technology, at www.wallstreetandtech.com/story/topNews/WST20020418S0009

3 Manjoo

4 Keith Oliver, Anne Chung, and Nick Samanich, "Beyond Utopia: The Realist's Guide to Internet-enabled Supply Chain Management", Strategy + Business, Issue 23.

5 Jim Welte, "Capitol Records' IM Marketing Plan", Business 2.0, April 25, 2001, at www.business2.com/articles/web/0,,16001,FF.html

6 Duncan Watts, Small World Theory, Princeton, NJ: Princeton University Press, 2000

7 Tom Standage, "A survey of the mobile Internet", in The Economist, October 13, 2001, p13.

8 Herbert G Wells, World Brain, London, Ayer, 1938.

9 Pierre Teilhard de Chardin, The Phenomenon of Man, New York, Harperperernnial Library, 1976.

10 Susan Blackmore, The Meme Machine, Oxford: Oxford University Press, 1999.

11 See www.slashdot.org

12 See blogdex.media.mit.edu. A similar service is provided by www.daypop.com.

13 Tetiana C. Anderson, "Egypt's Cyber Cafes for the Poor", United Nations Development Programme, at sdnhq.undp.org/it4dev/stories/egypt.html

14 Robert Guest, "Getting Better All the Time: A survey of technology and development", The Economist, Special Supplement, November 10, 2001.

Chapter 2
1 Beth Schultz, "Assembling a top-of-the-line Web services model", Network World, February 18, 2002.

2 Napster in fact is not a true peer-to-peer system, as it uses a central directory to identify where files are located and link users. The functionality is essentially the same as systems without a central directory, except that it makes it easier for legal challenges to shut down the system.

3 David Anderson, "SETI@home", in Peer-to-Peer: Harnessing the Power of Disruptive Technologies, edited by Andy Oram, Sebastopol, CA: O'Reilly & Associates, 2001, p67-76.

4 Olga Kharif and Alex Salkever, "A Chat with the Master of P2P", Business Week Online, August 1, 2001.

5 Ed Scannell and Heather Harreld, "Groove breathes life into p-to-p", InfoWorld, April 16, 2001.

6 Alorie Gilbert, "Peer-to-peer makes for speedy design", Informationweek, January 29, 2001.

7 Carl Shapiro and Hal R. Varian, Information Rules: A Strategic Guide to the Network Economy, Boston: Harvard Business School Press, 1999.

8 Jim Hu, "New battle plans alter IM wars", ZDNet News, at zdnet.com.com/2100-1105-911844.html

9 John Rice, "Tensions and Dynamics in Standards Based Networks in Periods of Industry Contraction", Proceedings of DRUID Academy Winter 2002 PhD Conference, Aalborg, Denmark

10 Richard Shim, "Microsoft Plays For Keeps", News.com, at news.com.com/2009-1040-275793.html

Chapter 3
1 SEI Center for Advanced Studies in Management, Information Technology and the Changing Boundaries of the Firm, The Wharton School, January 26-27, 1995.

2 Larry Downes and Chunka Mui, Unleashing the Killer App, Boston, Harvard Business School Press, 1999.

3 C.K. Prahalad and Gary Hamel, "The Core Competence of the Corporation", Harvard Business Review, May-June 1990

4 Faith Keenan and Spencer E. Ante, "The New Teamwork", BusinessWeek E.Biz, February 18, 2002.

5 Anonymous, "Poachers Are Out to Steal Your Intellectual Property – Can You Do Anything?", Knowledge@Wharton, at knowledge.wharton.upenn.edu/articles.cfm?catid=13&articleid=404

6 Derek Slater, "Portal Potential", CIO Magazine, September 15, 2000.

7 Ibid.

8 John M. Covaleski, "XBRL Spurs Great Expectations", Bank Technology News, Vol. 15, No. 2, February 8, 2002.

9 David Welch, "Can Covisint Climb Out of a Ditch?", BusinessWeek, May 21, 2001.

10 Keenan and Ante.

11 Ibid.

12 Ed Scannell and Heather Harreld, "Groove breathes real life into p-to-p", Infoworld, April 16, 2002.

13 Voluntary Interindustry Commerce Standards Association, "Procter & Gamble Pilot", Roadmap to CPFR, 1999.

14 RosettaNet, "RosettaNet Background Information", RosettaNet, 2001. 15 Haimes.

16 Patrick Porter, "Deciphering RosettaNet", CIO Insight, July 1, 2001, at www.cioinsight.com/article/0,3658,s=306&a=9610,00.asp

Chapter 4

1 "Broader" and "deeper" are similar to, but not the same as, Evans' and Wurster's concepts of "reach" and "richness". See Philip Evans and Thomas S. Wurster, Blown to Bits: How the New Economics of Information Transforms Strategy, Boston: Harvard Business School Press, 2000.

2 Association of Strategic Alliance Professionals, Alliance Summit 2002 Agenda.

3 Charles J. Corbett, Joseph D. Blackburn, and Luk N. Van Wassenhove, "Case Study: Partnerships to Improve Supply Chains", Sloan Management Review, Summer 1999, p.71-82.

4 PricewaterhouseCoopers, "High-Performing Strategic Alliances in the Pharmaceutical, Biotechnology and Medical Device and Diagnostics Industries", 1999.

5 Gwendoline Davies, "Put it in Writing – A Supplier is Not Always a Supplier!", April 2001, at www.walkermorris.co.uk/whatsnew/press96.htm

6 Edward Flynn and Jim Sabogal, "Advanced ERP Integration Gets Results", Chemical Engineering, August 2000.

Chapter 5

1 Ephraim Schwartz, "IBM demos car of the future", InfoWorld, August 14, 2001.

2 US Patent and Trademark Office, at www.uspto.gov/web/offices/ac/ido/oeip/taf/us_stat.pdf

3 Brunelleschi's Il Badalone, see www.stanford.edu/~broich/tamingnature/brunelleschi.htm

4 Matt Loney, "BT suffers blow in hyperlink patent case", ZDNet (UK), at zdnet.com.com/2100-1106-860214.html

5 Seth Shulman, "The Morphing Patent Problem", Technology Review, November 2001, p.33.

6 Jeanne Clark, Joe Piccolo, Brian Stanton, and Karin Tyson, Patent Pools: A Solution to the Problem of Accces in Biotechnology Patents?, United States Patent and Trademark Office, December 2000.

7 Ibid

8 Nicholas Dimarino, "Making the Most of Your Corporate Intellectual Assets: Understanding and Initiating Technology Licensing", at http://www.yet2.com/app/insight/insight/20010805_dimarino

9 Anonymous, "The Place to Make Connections is the Marketplace", at yet2.com/industry_insights/2000_amsterdam/marketplace.html

10 Neal Stephenson, In the Beginning was the Command Line, New York: Avon Books, 1999.

11 Eric Raymond, "The Cathedral and the Bazaar", First Monday, Vol 3. Issue 3, at www.firstmonday.org/issues/issue3_3/raymond/index.html

12 Ibid.

13 Rob Pegoraro, "The Office Suite That Lets You See Past Redmond", Washington Post, May 12, 2002, p. H07.

14 Matthew Broersma, "Free OpenOffice picks up from StarOffice", ZDNet (UK), at zdnet.com.com/2001-11-0

15 Renee Wijnen, "Unlocking the Code", Waters, July 2001. 16 See www.creativecommons.org

17 Linda Tischler, "He Struck Gold on the Net (Really)", Fast Company, Issue 59, June 2002, p.40.

18 Nitin Sawhney, Saul Griffith, Yael Maguire, and Timothy Prestero, "ThinkCycle at M.I.T.", TechKnowLogia, January-March 2002, p.49-53.

19 Howard Rheingold, The Virtual Community: Homesteading on the Electronic Frontier, Revised Edition, Cambridge, Massachusetts: MIT Press, 2000.

20 Steve Lakin, "BT's Approach to Ideas Management", Knowledge Management Review, March/April 2001, p.24-28.

21 Bill Breen, "Lilly's R&D Prescription", Fast Company, Issue 57, April 2002, p.44

22 Ibid.

23 Lew Irwin, "Reeves gives part of his salary to cast, crew", Hollywood.com, September 7, 2001, at www.hollywood.com/news/detail/article/1091512

24 Mark Weinstein, "Profit-Sharing Contracts in Hollywood: Evolution and Analysis", Journal of Legal Studies, Vol XXVII, January 1998, p67-112.

25 Ibid.

26 Ibid.

27 Ibid.

28 Gary Susman, "We Call It Martian Accounting", Guardian Unlimited, August 31, 2001, at www.guardian.co.uk/friday_review/story/0,3605,544319,00.html

Chapter 6
1 Marc Weingarten, "Get Your Buzz to Breed Like Hobbits", Business 2.0, January 2002.

2 John Hagel III and Arthur Armstrong, Net Gain: Expanding Markets Through Virtual Communities, Boston: Harvard Business School Press, 1997.

3 Michael Parsons, "A Flytxt in the digital soup", Red Herring, January 2002.

4 Anonymous, "Berry sly strategy gets desired result", Australian Financial Review, June 28, 2001.

5 Renee Dye, "The Buzz on Buzz", Harvard Business Review, November-December 2000.

6 Scott Kirsner, "Your Good Name", Darwin Magazine, at www.darwinmag.com/read/120100/ecosystem_content.html

7 John Gaffney, "How Do You Feel About a $44 Tooth-Bleaching Kit?", Business 2.0, September 2001.

8 Kurt Squire, "Star Wars Galaxies: A Case Study in Participatory Design", at www.joystick101.org/?op=displaystory&sid=2001/7/14/18208/3248

9 Charmaine Jones, "Rainbow Factory", Appliance Manufacturer, December 27, 2000, at www.ammagazine.com/CDA/ArticleInformation/features/BNP__Features__Item/0,2606,17 344,00.html

10 Shell International Exploration and Production, Story-Telling in Shell: Managing Knowledge Through New Ways of Working, November 2001.

11 Ibid.

12 Morten T. Hansen, Nitin Nohria, and Thomas Tierney, "What's Your Strategy For Managing Knowledge?", Harvard Business Review, March-April 1999.

13 Morten T. Hansen and Bolko von Oetinger, "Introducing T-Shaped Managers: Knowledge Management's Next Generation", Harvard Business Review, March 2001, p.107-116.

14 Henry Edmundson, "Technical Communities of Practice at Schlumberger", Knowledge Management Review, May/June 2001.

15 William Fulmer, Case Study: Buckman Laboratories, Harvard Business School, 1999.

16 Don Cohen and Laurence Prusak, In Good Company: How Social Capital Makes Organizations Work, Boston: Harvard Business School Press, 2001, p66.

Chapter 7

1 Frank Rose, "Pocket Monster", Wired, September 2001, p127-135.

2 Stewart Alsop, "A Handful of Convergence", Fortune, November 2001.

3 David Lascelles, Europe's New Banks: The "Non-Bank" Phenomenon, London: Centre for the Study of Financial Innovation, June 2000.

4 David Lieberman, "Sony Exec Sees Wired Future", USA Today, January 8, 2001.

5 Jim Hu, "Real catches baseball deal – at a price", CNET, March 27, 2001, at news.com.com/2100-1023-254825.html.

6 Dan Briody, "Brand Power: Mobile Virtual Network Operators", Red Herring, December 2001.

7 The five forces model was originally proposed in Michael Porter, "How Competitive Forces Shape Strategy", Harvard Business Review, March-April 1979.

8 The seminal paper was C.K. Prahalad and Gary Hamel, "The Core Competence of the Corporation", Harvard Business Review, May-June 1990.

9 See www.vernaallee.com

10 Steve Lohr, "Clash of the Titans: Microsoft Does Its Bit to Undermine AOL", International Herald Tribune, December 21, 2001.

11 Ron Ashkenas, Dave Ulrich, Todd Jich, and Steve Kerr, The Boundaryless Organization: Breaking the Chains of Organizational Structure, San Francisco: Jossey Bass, 1995, p.94-97 and 233.

12 Gary Hamel, Leading the Revolution, Boston: Harvard Business School Press, p.260-262.

Chapter 8

1 Emma Duncan, "Survey: e-Entertainment", The Economist, October 7, 2000.

2 Stephen H. Wildstrom, "This Video Recoder Has Some Enemies", BusinessWeek, January 15, 2002.

3 Brett May and Marc Singer, "Unchained Melody", The McKinsey Quarterly, Number 1, 2001.

4 Neil Blackley, Brett Hucker, Paul Sullivan, Jessica Reif Cohen, and Andrew Slabin, Music Industry: Can Majors Control Online Growth?, Merrill Lynch Research, November 9, 2001.

5 Janelle Brown, "Personalize me, baby", Salon.com, April 6, 2001, at

6 May and Singer.

7 See for example Lawrence Lessig, Code and Other Laws of Cyberspace, Basic Books, 1999./

8 Jim Welte, "Capitol Records' IM Marketing Plan", Business 2.0, April 25, 2001, at www.business2.com/articles/web/0,,16001,FF.html

9 Jonathan Weber, "The Ever-Expanding, Profit-Maximizing, Cultural-Imperialist, Wonderful World of Disney", Wired, February 2002.

10 M.J. Rose, "Stephen King's 'Plant' Uprooted", Wired News, November 28, 2000, at www.wired.com/news/print/0,1294,40356,00.html

11 Gwendolyn Mariano, "MPEG-4 plan shakes video industry", ZDNet News, February 8, 2002, at zdnet.com.com/2100-1104-833400.html

12 John Morrish, "Getty's New Digital Empire", Business 2.0 UK Edition, April 2001.

13 The History of Comic Art in America, at www.comic-art.com/history/history1.htm

14 Noam Shachtman, "Content Sites Test Their Strength", InternetWeek.com, March 14, 2001, at www.internetweek.com/indepth01/indepth031401.htm

Chapter 9

1 Jim Kerstetter, "The Web at Your Service", BusinessWeek e.Biz, March 18, 2002.

2 John Hagel III and John Seely Brown, "Your Next IT Strategy", Harvard Business Review, October 2001.

3 Cynthia Murphy Doyle and Samantha Ker, PwC Strengthens Ties with BP Amoco: Wins Large BPO and Application Support Contract, IDC, November 1999.

4 Kerstetter.

5 Hagel and Brown.

6 Beth Schultz, "Assembling a top-of-the-line Web services model", Network World, February 18, 2002.

7 Allen Bernard, "IT Departments Turn ASPs", ASPnews.com, at www.aspnews.com/trends/print/0,,10571_978151,00.html

8 Kerstetter.

9 Casey O'Brien Blondes, "First, Get Rid of the Lawyers", The Industry Standard, May 8, 2000, at www.thestandard.com/article/0,1902,14535,00.html

10 See www.eyware.com

11 Internet Awards 2001: Fixed Income, Euromoney, November 2001.

Chapter 10

1 Daniel H. Pink, Free Agent Nation, New York: Warner Books, 2001, p. 44.

2 Michelle Conlin, "And Now, the Just-in-Time Employee," BusinessWeek Online, August 28, 2000, at www.businessweek.com:/2000/00_35?b3696044.htm.

3 Thomas A. Stewart, The Wealth of Knowledge: Intellectual Capital and the Twenty-First Century Organization, New York: Doubleday, 2001.

4 Henry Jenkins, "Interactive Audiences? The 'Collective Intelligence' of Media Fans," at web.mit.edu/21fms/www/faculty/henry3/collective%20intelligence.html.

5 David Maister, Managing the Professional Service Firm, New York: Free Press, 1997.

6 Malcolm Gladwell, The Tipping Point: How Little Things Can Make a Big Difference, New York: Little, Brown, 2000.

7 Seth Godin, Unleashing the Ideavirus, Dobbs Ferry, NY: Do You Zoom, 2000.

8 Alex Salkever, "Upbeat at Napster – and the Growing New-Media Music Crowd," BusinessWeek Online, June 23, 2000 at http://www.businessweek.com/bwdaily/dnflash/june2000/nf00623f.htm.

9 Scott Adams, God's Debris: A Thought Experiment, Kansas City, MO: Andrew McMeel, 2001.

10 See www.baen.com/library/palaver6.htm.

11 Irene Kunii, "An Inventor Takes on Japan Inc.," BusinessWeek Online, December 10, 2001, at www.businessweek.com/magazine/content/01_50/b3761138.htm.

Chapter 11

1 Erick Schonfeld, "The Island of the Wireless Guerrillas", Business 2.0, April 2002.

2 Anonymous, "Jambusters eye cellphones", BBC News Online, June 12, 2002, at news.bbc.co.uk/low/english/sci/tech/newsid_20400000/2040519.stm

3 David Brin, The Transparent Society: Will Technology Force Us To Choose Between Privacy and Freedom?, Reading, MA: Perseus, 1999.

4 Stewart Alsop, "I Want My File-Served TV!", Fortune, June 24, 2002.

5 Gary William Flake, The Computational Beauty of Nature: Computer Explorations of Fractals, Chaos, Complex Systems, and Adaptation, Boston: MIT Press, 1998, Section 20.1.

6 Bruce Schechter, "Real-Life Cyborg Challenges Reality With Technology", New York Times, September 25, 2001, Late Edition - Final, Section F, Page 4, Column 2.

7 Peter Lewis, "Turning Replay TV into Spy TV", The Fortune Weblog, at www.fortune.com/ontech/20020506.html

8 See for example www.kuro5hin.org/story/2002/5/2/22720/40202

9 William H. Davidow and Michael S. Malone, The Virtual Corporation: Structuring and Revitalizing the Corporation for the 21st Century, New York: HarperBusiness, 1993 (Reprint).

10 Anonymous, "Monkey brain operates machine", BBC News, November 15, 2000, at news.bbc.co.uk/hi/english/sci/tech/newsid_1025000/1025471.stm

11 Associated Press, "Monkey think, monkey do", Wired News, March 13, 2002, at www.wired.com/news/medtech/0,1286,51039,00.html